Kitchen Remodeling FOR DUMMIES®

by Donald R. Prestly

WILEY

Wiley Publishing, Inc.

Kitchen Remodeling For Dummies®

Published by
Wiley Publishing, Inc.
111 River Street
Hoboken, NJ 07030
www.wiley.com

Copyright © 2003 by Wiley Publishing, Inc., Indianapolis, Indiana

Published by Wiley Publishing, Inc., Indianapolis, Indiana

Published simultaneously in Canada

For general information on our other products and services or to obtain technical support, please contact our Customer Care Department within the U.S. at 800-762-2974, outside the U.S. at 317-572-3993, or fax 317-572-4002.

Wiley also publishes its books in a variety of electronic formats. Some content that appears in print may not be available in electronic books.

Library of Congress Cataloging-in-Publication Data:

Library of Congress Control Number: 2003105851

ISBN: 0-7645-2553-0

Manufactured in the United States of America

10 9 8 7 6 5 4 3 2 1

1B/QY/QZ/QT/IN

About the Author

Don R. Prestly is a former Senior Editor for *HANDY Magazine* for The Handyman Club of America, as well as a former Associate Editor for *The Family Handyman Magazine*. In addition to his nearly 20 years of writing and doing home improvement projects, he spent several years as a manager for one of the Midwest's largest home centers. Throw in the everyday upkeep needs of being a homeowner, dealing with the same problems and repairs as other homeowners, and it's obvious that he has the background and experience to help you make your kitchen dreams come true.

Dedication

I dedicate this book to the tens of thousands of homeowners who have all said the same thing: "This old kitchen has got to go!" Whether your project involves changing the wall color, upgrading with new appliances, or tearing everything out down to the bare wall studs, just remember that you're not alone. You may even be surprised to find out that your neighbors, whom you haven't seen since last year, really aren't being unfriendly. They're just so darn anxious to complete their kitchen remodel and can't wait to show you! For all of you, your neighbors, and you kitchen dreamers, this book's for you.

Acknowledgments

Where do I begin? Some 20 years ago I left the world of home improvement sales and management and got started in the industry known as DIY. And who would have known that I'd end up writing a home improvement book for the great team at Wiley Publishing? All of their books make information interesting, understandable, and, for the most part, fun. Certainly enlightening! From my first dealings with the gang in acquisitions to my day-to-day working with my wonderful Senior Project Editor Alissa Schwipps, the subject of kitchen remodeling has been met with enthusiasm and excitement.

I'm also grateful to my agent, LaVonne Carlson. Without her, I wouldn't be writing these words of thanks. Thank you, LaVonne, for staying on me when needed, and for backing off, too. You're the best.

Making sure that the information I'm giving you is accurate is a crucial step to the success of any publication. And without a fantastic technical expert, I'd be lost. A big thank you to Dwayne Ganzel, carpenter/craftsman by trade and an English major to boot! How often do you find that combination? I've watched and worked alongside Dwayne on a number of home improvement projects and I come away every time admiring his skill and care in everything he does. His critical eye on the jobsite, as well as his keen and discerning eye for correct information, has made my final product one to be proud of. Thanks, Dwayne.

Finally, I wouldn't be expressing myself in this book today if it weren't for my first boss in the home improvement magazine industry, Mark Thompson. Mark has been a wonderful mentor, as well as a good friend. His skill at writing and editing, his quick wit, and his sharp eye for distilling information down to what you need to know without sounding pretentious have been keys to my success. Thanks for getting me started in this crazy business!

Publisher's Acknowledgments

We're proud of this book; please send us your comments through our Dummies online registration form located at www.dummies.com/register/.

Some of the people who helped bring this book to market include the following:

Acquisitions, Editorial, and Media Development

Senior Project Editor: Alissa D. Schwipps

Acquisitions Editor: Tracy Boggier

Copy Editor: Jennifer Bingham

Editorial Program Assistant: Holly Grimes

Technical Editor: Dwayne Ganzel

Editorial Manager: Jennifer Ehrlich

Editorial Assistant: Elizabeth Rea

Cover Photos: ©David W. Hamilton/Getty Images/The Image Bank

Cartoons: Rich Tennant, www.the5thwave.com

Production

Project Coordinator: Erin Smith

Layout and Graphics: LeAndra Hosier, Lynsey Osborn, Shae Wilson, Melanee Wolven

Special Art: Lisa Reed

Proofreaders: Andy Hollandbeck, Carl William Pierce, TECHBOOKS Production Services

Indexer: TECHBOOKS Production Services

Publishing and Editorial for Consumer Dummies

Diane Graves Steele, Vice President and Publisher, Consumer Dummies

Joyce Pepple, Acquisitions Director, Consumer Dummies

Kristin A. Cocks, Product Development Director, Consumer Dummies

Michael Spring, Vice President and Publisher, Travel

Brice Gosnell, Associate Publisher, Travel

Kelly Regan, Editorial Director, Travel

Publishing for Technology Dummies

Andy Cummings, Vice President and Publisher, Dummies Technology/General User

Composition Services

Gerry Fahey, Vice President of Production Services

Debbie Stailey, Director of Composition Services

Contents at a Glance

Introduction 1

Part 1: Zoning In on the Scope of the Project 7

Chapter 1: Envisioning the Big Picture 9

Chapter 2: Planning Your Kitchen 21

Chapter 3: Establishing a Budget and Sticking to It! 33

Chapter 4: Bringin' In the Big Guns or Doin' It Solo 45

Part 11: Gettin' Down and Dirty: Preparing Your Kitchen for Greatness 57

Chapter 5: You Can't Have Tool Much of a Good Thing 59

Chapter 6: Getting Your Kitchen Ready for Construction 79

Chapter 7: Evaluating Your Plumbing, Electrical, and Ventilation Systems 85

Part 111: Selecting and Installing Cabinets and Countertops 101

Chapter 8: Your Old Cabinets: Spruce 'em Up or Scrap 'em? 103

Chapter 9: Making Old Mother Hubbard Proud: Putting New Cabinets Up 121

Chapter 10: Considering Creative Countertop Options 137

Chapter 11: Making Sure Your Countertops Are Level 145

Part 1V: Selecting and Installing Sinks, Faucets, Appliances, and More 161

Chapter 12: "Pouring" Over the Choices for Sinks and Faucets 163

Chapter 13: No Runs, Drips, or Leaks: The Right Way to Install Your New Sink and Faucet 177

Chapter 14: Appliance Appreciation: Choosing the Right Ones 189

Chapter 15: Fridges, Ranges, Disposers, and More: Installing Appliances 203

Part V: Adding the Final Touches: Walls, Windows, Floors, and More 219

Chapter 16: Illuminating Your Kitchen Lighting Options 221

Chapter 17: Lighting the Way: Installing Lights and Windows 237

Chapter 18: Walls That Wow: Selecting Elements for Your Walls ...253

Chapter 19: Preparation for Wall Transformation 263
Chapter 20: Floors: Stepping Out with Style 279
Chapter 21: Installing Your New Kitchen Floor 289

Part VI: The Part of Tens 309

Chapter 22: Ten Critical Design Issues 311
Chapter 23: Ten Hot Trends in Kitchen Design 315
Chapter 24: Ten Easy Kitchen Upgrades 319

Index 323

Table of Contents

Introduction 1

About This Book 1
Conventions Used in This Book 2
Foolish Assumptions 2
How This Book Is Organized 3
    Part I: Zoning In on the Scope of the Project 3
    Part II: Gettin' Down and Dirty: Preparing Your
        Kitchen for Greatness 3
    Part III: Selecting and Installing Cabinets and Countertops 3
    Part IV: Selecting and Installing Sinks, Faucets,
        Appliances, and More 4
    Part V: Adding the Final Touches: Walls, Windows,
        Floors, and More 4
    Part VI: The Part of Tens 4
Icons Used in This Book 4
Where to Go from Here 5

Part 1: Zoning In on the Scope of the Project 7

Chapter 1: Envisioning the Big Picture 9

Establishing a Plan: Builders Do It, So Should You! 9
    Assessing your kitchen's potential 10
    Deciding how much you can afford to change 11
    Getting your city's blessing 12
    Putting yourself into a remodeling state of mind 14
    Let the games begin! Tearing out and putting in 15
    Heading down the home stretch: Adding the final touches 17
What's Your Forte? Determining Your Skill and Comfort Level 18
    Determining your skill level 18
    Determining your comfort level 18
Shopping Tips before You Even Spend a Dime! 19
    Choosing cabinets and countertops 19
    Selecting sinks, faucets, and appliances 19
    Finishing touches: Lights, flooring, and wall treatments 20

Chapter 2: Planning Your Kitchen 21

Working with Your Kitchen's Shape 22
    L-shaped kitchens 22
    U-shaped kitchens 23

G-shaped kitchens 24
I-shaped or single wall kitchens 24
Corridor/Galley/Parallel wall kitchen 25
Working efficiently: The work triangle 25
Exploring a Few of Your Design Options 26
Considering new counter space: A dream come true 27
Adding eat-in dining space 27
Installing an island oasis in your kitchen 28
Mulling over multiple workstations 29
Constructing containment areas for recycling 30
Dealing with paperwork 30
Putting Your Plans on Paper 30
Measuring your kitchen 31
Playing with your plan 32

Chapter 3: Establishing a Budget and Sticking to It! **33**
Crunching the Numbers 33
Step 1: Determining the scope of the project 34
Step 2: Pricing products and gathering estimates 35
Step 3: Budgeting for breakfast, lunch, and dinner 37
Step 4: Refiguring until it fits 38
How Am I Going to Pay for This? Financing Your Project 38
Refinancing your home 39
Applying for a home improvement loan 40
Charging on a low- or no-interest credit card 40
Considering cold, hard cash! 40
A Little Overspending Adds Up to a Lot of Going Over Budget 41
Track and review your expenses regularly 41
Keep an eye open for sales 41
Swanky shops or practical places 42
Delivery's on you 42
Time Equals Money — Budgeting Your Time Wisely 42

Chapter 4: Bringin' In the Big Guns or Doin' It Solo **45**
Introducing the Pinch Hitters 45
Dreaming up your kitchen with a designer 46
Asking an architect for assistance 46
Letting a general contractor make your project easier 47
Contracting a Professional 47
Putting out an APB 48
Interviewing the prospects 48
Getting three bids 50
Getting It All on Paper: Drawing Up a Contract 52
Dealing with the Day-to-Day during Construction 54
Nearing the Finish Line 55
Developing a punch list 55
Final sign-offs 55

Part II: Gettin' Down and Dirty: Preparing Your Kitchen for Greatness 57

Chapter 5: You Can't Have Tool Much of a Good Thing 59
Safety First 59
    Eye protection 60
    Gloves 60
    Masks 61
You Get What You Pay for 62
Ripping Your Kitchen Apart with Demolition Tools 62
    Smashing and tearing tools 62
    Hauling and holding equipment 63
Power Shopping for Tools 64
    Hammers 64
    Handsaws 65
    Circular saw 66
    Screwdrivers 68
    Pliers 69
    Measuring and marking tools 69
    Levels 70
    Clamps 71
    Power drills 72
    A couple more things to have on hand 72
    Plumbing tools the pro's use 72
    Getting wired: Electrical tools 73
Renting Your Way to Tool Heaven 74
    A cut above: Saws 74
    Power nailers 75
    Tile tools 76
    A few more good rentals 77

Chapter 6: Getting Your Kitchen Ready for Construction 79
Packing Up the Kitchen 79
Removing Everything Including the Kitchen Sink 80
    Taking out the cabinets 81
    Getting rid of countertops and sinks 82
    Tearing up the old floor 83
    Disposing of your old cabinets, countertops, and appliances 83
Opening Up the Walls and Seeing What's Inside 84

Chapter 7: Evaluating Your Plumbing, Electrical, and Ventilation Systems 85
Preparing Your Plumbing 85
    Repositioning drain lines 86
    Installing new water lines (and moving old ones, too) 87

Vetting Ventilation Needs 92
    Locating existing ductwork 93
    Fitting the old ductwork to the new appliances 93
    Adding ductwork 94
Keeping Current: Electricity Concerns 95
    Conforming to code 95
    Upgrading with additional circuits and outlets 97
    Running electrical cable 98

Part III: Selecting and Installing Cabinets and Countertops 101

Chapter 8: Your Old Cabinets: Spruce 'em Up or Scrap 'em? 103

Renovating Your Cabinets 103
    Handles and hinges make a huge difference 104
    Refinishing existing cabinets 105
    Refacing your existing cabinets 107
    Replacing the old cabinets with new 107
Checking Out New Cabinet Choices 108
    Comparing stock versus custom-made 108
    Shopping sites 109
    Considering cabinet construction 110
    Taking note of cabinet types and sizes 112
    Mulling over material choices 113
    Dealing with doors and drawers 115
    Finishing options 116
    Making the "hard" ware choices 117
Storage Design Options 118
    Efficient interior designs 118
    Avoiding dead corner spaces 119

Chapter 9: Making Old Mother Hubbard Proud: Putting New Cabinets Up 121

Gathering the Right Tools 122
Marking Reference Lines and Mounting Locations 123
    Checking your floor for level 123
    Measuring cabinet heights 124
    Locating the wall studs for mounting 125
    Checking your walls for plumb 127
    Noting cabinet position 127
Hanging Wall Cabinets First 128
    Installing the first cabinet 129
    Finishing the cabinet run 131
Adding The Lower Level — Base Cabinets 132
    Installing the first cabinet 132
    Finishing the cabinet run 133

Chapter 10: Considering Creative Countertop Options 137

Considering Your Countertop Options 137
    Countertops you can install yourself 138
    Countertops that require a professional's touch 141
Where to Shop for Countertops 144

Chapter 11: Making Sure Your Countertops Are Level 145

Gathering the Right Tools 145
Installing a Pre-formed Countertop 147
    Ensuring a perfect fit: Scribing and trimming 147
    Installing a mitered corner 149
    Attaching countertops other than corners 150
    Cutting the hole for the sink 152
    Sizing and finishing your countertop 154
Installing a Ceramic Tile Countertop 156
    Gathering additional tools for tile 156
    Constructing your ceramic countertop 157

Part IV: Selecting and Installing Sinks, Faucets, Appliances, and More 161

Chapter 12: "Pouring" Over the Choices for Sinks and Faucets . . .163

Selecting the Best Sink Material for Your Needs 163
    Metal: Affordable and easy to clean 164
    Enameled: The power of cast iron and steel 164
    Solid surface: So sleek and smooth! 165
    Composite: Making it fancy with faux marble 165
Choosing the Right Sink Design for Your Space 166
    Looking into sink bowls 166
    Lefty or righty? Choosing the multiple-bowl setup that
       works best for you 168
Recognizing the Many Facets of Faucets 169
    Considering the faucet and sprayer setup 169
    Is two better than one? Deciding on a faucet handle design 170
    What's new in faucet colors and finishes 171
    Filtering faucets 172
    A separate drinking water faucet 172
    Spouting off 174
Adding Extras 174
    Soap dispenser, anyone? 175
    Hot water NOW! A point-of-use hot-water dispenser 175
    Is a garbage disposer in your future? 175
Checking Out Those Warranties! 176

**Chapter 13: No Runs, Drips, or Leaks: The Right Way to
Install Your New Sink and Faucet** **177**

Gathering the Right Tools 177
Setting the Stage: Preparing to Install Your Sink 178
Taking the measurements 178
Making sure to attach the faucet before installing the sink 179
Attaching water supply lines to the faucet 181
Putting Things in Position: Finishing Your Installation 183
Setting in your sink 183
Installing the sink baskets 184
Connecting the supply lines 185
Hooking up the drain line 185
Checking for leaks (Put on your raincoat first) 187

Chapter 14: Appliance Appreciation: Choosing the Right Ones . . .**189**

Making Money-Related Decisions First 190
Considering a fuel source change 190
Deciding between commercial-grade and
residential appliances 191
Analyzing your exterior options 191
Chillin' Out: Exploring Refrigerator Options 192
Selecting a setup 193
Sizing up your choices: Freestanding or built-in 194
Paying a little more for the extras 194
Warming Up to Cooktops, Ranges, and Ovens 196
Keeping with tradition: Slide-in, drop-in, and
freestanding ranges 196
Getting creative with additional cooking surfaces 197
Ogling your oven options 198
Sizing up your range hood 199
Moving in on microwave ovens 200
Getting the Dish on Dishwashers 200
Taking Out the Garbage: Disposers and Compactors 201
Working with Warranties 202

**Chapter 15: Fridges, Ranges, Disposers, and
More: Installing Appliances** **203**

Installing Ranges, Ovens, and Cooktops 204
Changing the power/fuel source 204
Wranglin' with a range 208
Installing a cooktop 209
Built-in baking — Installing a built-in oven 209
Installing a New Fridge Complete with Dispenser Unit 210
Installing Other Popular Appliances 212
Doin' the dishes — Automatic style 212
Takin' out the trash — Sink style 215
Mashin' the trash 217

Part V: Adding the Final Touches: Walls,
Windows, Floors, and More 219

Chapter 16: Illuminating Your Kitchen Lighting Options 221

Making Thomas Edison Proud: Getting the
  Most Out of Interior Lighting 221
    Determining your needs 221
    Matching your lights to your task 222
    Fancy's fine, but function is foremost:
      Shedding light on fixture options 225
    Deciding whether you need major changes 228
    What you can do if you can't make major changes 229
Letting the Light Shine In: Natural Lighting Options 229
    Boldly going where no window has gone before:
      Adding new windows 230
    Replacing existing windows 232
    Sprucing up the windows you have 233

Chapter 17: Lighting the Way: Installing Lights and Windows 237

Gathering the Right Tools 237
Installing a Bright New Ceiling Fixture 238
    Removing the old fixture 238
    Hanging the new fixture 240
Circulating in Style: Adding a Ceiling Fan 241
    Supporting a fan 242
    Wiring a fan 242
Getting on Track with Track Lighting 243
    Attaching the mounting plate 243
    Positioning the lights 244
Can It! Installing Recessed Lighting 245
Lots of Light Levels at Your Fingertips: Installing a Dimmer Switch 245
Ambiance and Function: Installing Under Cabinet Lighting 246
    Looking at two kinds of under cabinet lighting 246
    Installing a hard-wired system 247
Drawing In Natural Light: Upgrading Your Windows 249
    Measuring and sketching your plan 249
    Installing your new windows 250

Chapter 18: Walls That Wow: Selecting
Elements for Your Walls 253

Picking Paint for Your Kitchen 253
    Considering color: A rainbow of choices 254
    Paint prototypes: What's best for the kitchen? 255
    Paint quality: Getting what you pay for 256

Calculating your paint quantity needs 257
Finishing options for that extra-special look 258
Working with Wallpaper 260
Picking the right paper 260
Knowing where wallpaper won't work 261
Breaking up a flat surface 261
Wallpaper math: Deciding how much to buy 262
Adding Final Touches 262

Chapter 19: Preparation for Wall Transformation **263**

The Importance of Preparation 263
Repairing Drywall 264
Fixing holes 264
Dealing with cracks 268
Repairing bad tape joints 270
Fixin' to Paint 271
Smoothing the rough spots 272
Dulling shiny surfaces 272
Cleaning the surface 272
Getting Ready for Wallpaper 273
Removing wallpaper 273
Prepping the surface for new wallpaper 276

Chapter 20: Floors: Stepping Out with Style **279**

Keeping Your Needs in Mind 279
Perusing the Possibilities 280
Staying resilient: Sheet flooring versus vinyl squares ...280
Choosing tile — Ceramic versus stone 282
Keeping it real with wood — Or going synthetic 283
Staying away from carpet 286
Choosing to Remove the Old Flooring — Or Not 287

Chapter 21: Installing Your New Kitchen Floor **289**

Preparing to Be Floored 289
Gathering the right tools 290
Taking the measurements 291
Prepping your subfloor 291
Laying down underlayment 293
Installing Your Floor 296
Installing sheet flooring 296
Installing vinyl tile squares 299
Installing ceramic tile 301
Installing a wood floor 305
Dealing with not-so-perfect edges 307
Securing an Island Unit 307

Part VI: The Part of Tens 309

Chapter 22: Ten Critical Design Issues 311

The Work Triangle Formula 311
Making Sure Your Workspace Is Separate 311
Installing Adequate Doors 312
Avoid Knocking Knuckles When Opening Doors 312
Easy Dish Loading 312
Situating One Sink 312
Considering Countertops at Different Heights 313
Storing Those Dirty Dishes 313
Grocery Resting Area 313
Microwave Oven Safety 313
Plenty of Floor Space 314

Chapter 23: Ten Hot Trends in Kitchen Design 315

Adding an Extra Sink 315
Spreading Out the Work: Multiple Workstations 315
Visiting the Islands — Mon! 315
Entertaining in the Kitchen 316
Eating-In Areas: Casual Style 316
Gathering the Family 316
Creating Kid Friendly Kitchens 316
Merging Kitchens with the Rest of the House 316
Adding Decorative Touches 317
Visiting Europe without Leaving Home 317
Toning for Elegance 317

Chapter 24: Ten Easy Kitchen Upgrades 319

Brightening Up the Room with a Fresh Coat of Paint 319
Working with Wallpaper That Wows 319
Venturing Beyond the Border 320
Treating Your Windows to a New Dress 320
Replacing Handles and Knobs 320
Giving Your Faucet a Facelift 320
Lightening Up 320
Trimmin' Time 321
Racking Up Your Pots and Pan 321
Throwing In the Towel 321

Index 323

Introduction

This book shows you how to take your kitchen — no matter what shape it's in now — and remodel it so that it not only fits your wants and needs but also becomes a room you can be proud to use and show off. You can find information here on everything from cabinets and flooring to appliances and decorating. I even throw in information about the kitchen sink.

The kitchen in today's home has become a focal point for the family as well as for entertaining. And for that reason, you want it to be as functional as possible, without breaking your bankbook. To do that, you need to think through design ideas and plans and recognize the materials and equipment that your kitchen must have to meet your needs. Obtaining all of your wants is another story, but don't be afraid to include a few dream ideas in your design, too.

This book gives you information on what materials, appliances, and so on go into making your kitchen function well. This information helps you understand the kitchen remodeling process, and makes you a smarter consumer. Along with tips for understanding what makes up a kitchen, I include hands-on, how-to-do-it info that shows you how you can tackle many parts of the project, saving you money and giving you the satisfaction of doing it yourself. And if you decide that tackling the project yourself isn't your cup of tea, the how-to information will make you more informed and give you a better understanding when talking and dealing with contractors.

About This Book

I hope you find this book not only full of information but also fun. My years of working with customers every day in one of the country's major home centers, along with my decade and a half of researching and writing about — and doing! — home improvement projects gives me the real-life insights into what you can expect to find in your kitchen-remodeling project. The information in this book is organized into six parts, and the chapters within each part cover specific topics in detail. You can read every chapter or pick and choose the ones that are of interest to you. Either way, you come away with a clearer understanding of what to expect when it's time to remodel your kitchen.

One additional way to get your remodeling juices flowing is to use the color insert in this book for inspiration and ideas. It features new items that are being integrated into today's kitchens, as well as photos of kitchen designs, styles, products, and equipment that you may not have seen or even been aware of. Dream your dreams and wish your wishes — and use this section as your springboard!

Conventions Used in This Book

The following conventions are used throughout the text to make things consistent and easy to understand:

- ✔ DIY refers to the do-it-yourselfer, that's you!

- ✔ All Web addresses appear in `monofont`.

- ✔ New terms appear in *italic* and are closely followed by an easy-to-understand definition.

- ✔ **Bold** is used to highlight the action parts of numbered steps.

- ✔ Sidebars, which look like text enclosed in a shaded gray box, consist of information that's interesting to know but not necessarily critical to your understanding of the chapter or section's topic.

Foolish Assumptions

Remodeling a kitchen is a big job. But it's not so big that anyone, with the right guidance and understanding, couldn't feel comfortable tackling at least some parts of the job. As I wrote this book, I made the following assumptions about you:

- ✔ You're interested in remodeling your kitchen for any number of reasons: you want to use the space more efficiently, there are new appliances and gadgets that you'd love to have, or maybe you're just sick of looking at the avocado green appliances that remind you of life in the 70s!

- ✔ You've at least attempted a home repair project or two.

- ✔ You're comfortable using both power and hand tools and probably own a few of each.

- ✔ Or maybe you want to know about how a project should be done and then hire someone to it. This book is perfect for you, as well.

How This Book Is Organized

Kitchen Remodeling For Dummies is divided into six parts. Each part explores an area or item in a kitchen that could be upgraded or remodeled.

Part I: Zoning In on the Scope of the Project

This part answers your questions about what's the difference between a bunch of upgrades versus a complete redo. It also looks at what's involved with planning, establishing, and sticking to a budget — key factors in any successful kitchen remodel. And it includes information about finding and hiring professionals to help you complete part of or the entire remodel.

Part II: Gettin' Down and Dirty: Preparing Your Kitchen for Greatness

Gaining a better understanding of the tools, equipment, and materials that are involved in a kitchen remodel makes all aspects of the job less intimidating and more fun! Some of the tools are probably on your workbench already.

Beyond tools, this section discusses demolishing your old kitchen (doesn't that sound like fun?) as well as evaluating your existing plumbing, electrical, and ventilation systems before you start putting your kitchen back together.

Part III: Selecting and Installing Cabinets and Countertops

Cabinets and countertops are the two most commonly upgraded items in a kitchen remodel — and two of the biggest budget eaters! Before you start shopping for either one, you should understand what makes one brand or style better than another. You might also like to know why you may not want to use a certain material or product in your kitchen. No name-bashing here, just solid information to make your new kitchen work its best for you.

After you make your choices, you need to know how to install your new items. Here's the clear scoop on what's involved with the most common types of installations — and a few tips and pointers to help out when things get a bit dicey.

Part IV: Selecting and Installing Sinks, Faucets, Appliances, and More

Every kitchen needs appliances, a sink, and a faucet. But with all the choices out there, how do you decide what's best for you? In this section, I guide you through the shopping and selecting processes and explain all the features to help you buy the best products to meet your needs. After you buy your new stuff, it's time to put it in place. And guess what? I provide pointers for that, too!

Part V: Adding the Final Touches: Walls, Windows, Floors, and More

What turns an average kitchen into an extraordinary showplace? The final touches. From color choices to light fixtures, from skylights overhead to the floor beneath your feet, exploring all your options and looking at what's new and exciting in the world of kitchens is the icing on the cake of your beautiful new kitchen. You'll be so proud of it you may not ever entertain in another room of your house again!

Part VI: The Part of Tens

No *For Dummies* book would be complete without the Part of Tens. In this part, you find ways to deal with issues of space, the scoop on current kitchen design trends, and a list of ten easy upgrades. These chapters can help you get your creative juices flowing.

Icons Used in This Book

This book is loaded with helpful icons that point out key information. Check out the following list of icons and what the accompanying text provides:

Make a note that when you see this icon you find time-saving, money-saving, and keep-you-from-pulling-out-your-hair advice.

Tuck these key bits of information away in your brain because you need to recall them throughout the kitchen remodeling process.

Think of these as the flashing lights and sirens alerting you to things that have the potential to cause you and your helpers physical harm.

It's okay to admit that you can't do it all and it's time to hire a professional who can help. I attach this icon to information about tasks better left to a pro.

Where to Go from Here

I recommend that you begin with Part I, especially if you're unsure about your level of expertise or how large (or small) you want your kitchen-remodeling project to be. Or, if you know exactly what you want for your new kitchen, feel free to skip around to glean the wisdom and insights I share that I've gained over the years.

But remember, it doesn't matter where you start, just as long as you get going. I think you'll find that once you start your remodeling project, you'll want to keep charging ahead until you get the kitchen you've only ever dreamed about.

Part I

Zoning In on the Scope of the Project

The 5th Wave   By Rich Tennant

We did a lot of the renovations ourselves. For instance, Jerry installed the pot rack.

In this part . . .

Is your current kitchen really that bad? If you answer with a resounding *"Yes"* and you want to change things, you need a clear understanding of what's involved with a kitchen remodel. In this part, I give you an overview of the whole process, help you initiate planning, and assist you in figuring out how you're going to pay for it all.

I also go over what to do if you find that you can't do everything on your own. Knowing where to go for help can be tricky, but I give you some pointers on how to find trustworthy professionals so you won't get taken to the cleaners.

Chapter 1

Envisioning the Big Picture

In This Chapter

▶ Planning the job

▶ Figuring out how much you can handle

▶ Evaluating your kitchen needs and wants

*L*et me start by asking you a question: What's the busiest room in your house? You guessed it: the kitchen! This room is fast becoming the number one place for family, friends, and neighbors to gather to talk, grab a cool beverage in a casual setting, and even entertain larger dinner parties without dragging out the fine china and crowding into the formal dining room. Maybe all this activity explains why the kitchen is the room that seems to be in constant need of upgrading.

Take heart: According to real estate, building, and remodeling surveys, the one project that is likely to give you a 100 percent return on the dollars invested is a kitchen remodel. And whether the project is as involved as gutting things back to the wall studs or as simple as applying a fresh coat of paint, each freshening up or upgrade is an investment in your home's value. And ultimately in your enjoyment of using the space.

In this chapter, I introduce you to all aspects of a kitchen remodel. I guide you in establishing your budget and through the various levels and types of work that are included in most kitchen remodels.

Establishing a Plan: Builders Do It, So Should You!

If you've ever visited an area where new homes are being built, you probably saw houses in various states of construction. Some have only the foundation walls or slab in place, others have the bare wood wall studs and maybe the roof trusses in place, whereas others appear to be fairly far along on the outside. The same is true for the interiors, too. Some have ductwork in place, others have the electrical wiring and plumbing roughed in, and the ones in a

Taking the pro's kitchen quiz

If you want to dig into just about every area of your kitchen to see whether its current design works or if things really need to change, then contact The National Kitchen and Bath Association (NKBA) and request a copy of their *Kitchen and Bath Workbook*. Find the section "Rate-Your-Present-Kitchen," which is a one-page quiz that asks all the right questions to find out just how well your existing kitchen functions (or doesn't function). This quiz is a great companion to have when you begin your quest for the perfect kitchen design. You can contact the NKBA by phone at 1-877-NKBA-PRO (1-877-652-2776) or on the Web at `www.nkba.org`.

more completed state have drywall installed over the wall studs and maybe even some flooring and paint. Remember that none of this progress happens by chance. A plan is in place to keep all of the tradespeople busy at the right time, and to keep them from working and tripping over each other.

Assessing your kitchen's potential

You're probably considering remodeling your kitchen for a few reasons. Remember to note and write down what those reasons are, so that you can correct the things that you don't like. You also need to evaluate your current kitchen, and to evaluate it honestly.

Ask yourself the following questions:

- ✔ How do you use your kitchen? Start by evaluating your lifestyle and what part the kitchen plays in it. For example, do you only cook small meals, or do you cook large meals for a large family or lots of friends on a regular basis? Does your family have more than one cook? If so, how many? Who is the primary cook, and how tall is he, does he have any special physical needs, does he like certain types of cooking such as baking or grilling? If you entertain often, do you want family and guests to be able to socialize and eat in the kitchen? What other activities (such as homework or bill paying) do you or your family members do in the kitchen? Do you need space for a desk or a computer?

- ✔ How does your existing kitchen meet your needs and how does it fall short?

  - • Size: Is the size of the kitchen acceptable, or do you need more floor space, more counter space, more storage space, or more anything?

- Layout. What about the current layout works and doesn't work? (See Chapter 2 for more information about kitchen layouts.) For example, if several family members enjoy cooking, do you need additional work areas? Do you need a new layout for better traffic flow? Do you want the sink in a better location?

- Major appliances: Take note of the items you have in your existing kitchen that you really want (and need) in your new kitchen. I know, for example, that I would definitely include a dishwasher and an over-the-stove microwave oven in a new kitchen. Why? I'm so accustomed to using these two appliances on a regular basis that if they weren't in my new kitchen, I'd think the kitchen was incomplete in the design and function. And don't stop with the appliances: If you're used to having dimmer switches on the light fixtures, then you're probably going to want them in the new kitchen.

- Storage needs: If you buy food in large quantities, like from one of the club type warehouse stores, make sure your new kitchen has adequate storage capacity.

✔ What extras do you want to add to your new kitchen? Now you can have some fun and make an ultimate wish list for your new kitchen. Also take some time to find out what's new in kitchen trends such as design, material, and equipment (see Chapter 23). Some of your wants may include things as simple as better-quality hardware or rotating shelves in the cabinets. Other nice perks include commercial-grade appliances, glass-front cabinets, an in-house recycling center, pot racks, a second microwave oven, a pull-out faucet/sprayer, an extra deep sink, and even some of the new technology or "smart" appliances.

Lots of ideas to consider, I know. Of course, the level of remodel you undertake depends on the time and money you can devote to the project. Now that you've assessed your current kitchen and how you want to upgrade it in the near future, you're better prepared to decide whether your kitchen simply needs a fresh coat of paint, a complete makeover, or something in between to improve appearance and functionality. The following section helps you evaluate just how much of a remodeling project you're prepared to undertake.

Deciding how much you can afford to change

Kitchen remodels come in four different levels and each level comes with different and wide-ranging price tags. You can spend a few hundred dollars or thousands to simply freshen things up, or you can spend tens of thousands to move walls and put in new cabinets and appliances. Take a look at each price group to see what's included. Note, too, that each increased level of upgrade includes what's involved in the previous categories.

- ✔ Makeover: Most folks spring for a makeover every few years, just to keep things looking nice and stay current with colors and design trends. Some might simply refer to this task as a freshening up; it usually doesn't cost a lot, often only a couple hundred dollars (or less). But the refreshed look is often just what a kitchen needs to perk it back up! A makeover that includes upgrades such as painting or wallpapering walls, refurbishing cabinets, and replacing old cabinet and drawer hardware (knobs and hinges) can be accomplished for less than $1,000.

- ✔ Upgrade: If you plan to paint and refurbish cabinets, install a new floor and countertops, replace light fixtures, and buy new appliances, be prepared to pay anywhere from $1,000 to $6,000 in upgrading expenses.

- ✔ Minor remodel: A minor remodel will set you back roughly $5,000 to $15,000, and this price often includes the upgrade items plus replacing a sink and faucet, repositioning drain and supply lines, adding or replacing cabinets, and making at least one structural change such as closing or opening up a wall or doorway. A portion of the cost of a minor remodel is for hiring professionals to help with major parts of the remodel that you feel more comfortable leaving in a pro's hands. Some of you are probably wondering how spending $10,000, $12,000, or even $15,000 on your kitchen could be considered a minor remodel. You'll see how when you start to price appliances, cabinets, and countertops. Start adding these items together and you'll reach a five-figure price tag pretty quickly.

- ✔ Major remodel: You'll spend a lot of money ($15,000 and up) for a major kitchen remodel, but you won't recognize the place when you're finished. The layout is often changed, the size of the room is larger, you get new electrical circuits throughout the kitchen, and maybe even more windows or even a skylight (in addition to new cabinets, flooring, and so on). Talk about major changes!

All these numbers can seem a bit mind boggling right now. But don't worry. I go into more detail in several later chapters, covering everything from establishing a budget to looking at the prices ranges for all levels of kitchen remodeling to what you can expect to get for your dollars.

Getting your city's blessing

Your city building department has to like what you're doing or else you're in for a boatload of headaches. I've had people tell me that inspections are only good for two things: slowing down the pace of a project, and keeping city

---

Working with Mother Nature's schedule

Ask most homeowners and they'll tell you that there's no good time for remodeling. It takes time and disrupts your home life. However, if you plan to do a little, some, or a lot of the project yourself, then you need to decide what is the best time of year for your project. Here are some guidelines to remember:

✔ If you're going to paint walls or refinish cabinets, you need to do it in the spring or summer when warm temperatures allow for open windows and good ventilation. If you live in a cold winter region, starting such projects just before the winter snows begin flying probably isn't a wise decision. On the downside of summer painting, however, is higher humidity, which means you need to allow a few extras days of drying time between coats of paint, stain, and varnish.

✔ If new windows are in the picture, choose the time of year in your area where you can leave the hole from the old window open for a while. In some areas, rain and cold could be a problem, and extreme heat could be an issue in the southern or southwest states. And don't forget about bugs!

✔ If you live in a northern tier state where winter temps can be well below freezing, allow enough time for materials to warm up and acclimate to the interior environment. You don't want to try to install sheet flooring that's just been delivered in an unheated truck in the middle of January without giving the flooring time to soften up. If you rush it, you could crack the flooring and ruin it!

✔ On the plus side of doing major projects in winter, most folks have more free time especially on weekends. There's less opportunity for weekend distractions, such as going to the lake or cabin or having a weekend barbeque or party.

employees busy. Well, these comments couldn't be further from the truth. Inspections ensure that projects are constructed properly and that products are installed correctly to make your home as safe as possible. Believe me, I'm happy to have the inspectors check out my work. Their job is to understand and be current on the building and mechanical codes. All I can say is that I want an inspector to catch a problem that might damage my house or injure my family.

Take your plan to City Hall and have it reviewed *and* approved by your city inspectors before you begin. Getting approval will take several days to three weeks, depending on how much building is going on in your area. After your plan is approved, you need to purchase the necessary permits for the various parts of the project. Most cities base their permit fees on a percentage of the total estimated cost of the project. Don't try to fool the inspectors or permit officials, either. They know, for example, that a complete kitchen remodel is not going to cost only $3,000. And maybe most importantly, treat the inspectors with respect. It will make your life a whole lot easier. Remember: Inspectors are your friends, looking out for your best interest.

After your plans are approved, you still have a lot of red tape to go through, and the number of inspections required for a kitchen remodeling project may seem a bit over the top, but remember they're for your safety. After you apply for your permit, you'll receive an actual written (typed) permit, sometimes called a *permit card*. This card lists what inspections are needed as well as when they should be done. Most permits are good for one year. If your project falls behind, call the inspector and tell her as soon as you know that the project won't be completed before the permit expires. Most cities will give you an extension.

Call the inspectors well in advance (usually a week to ten days is sufficient) to set up inspection times and be prepared for multiple inspections at various stages of the project. The construction portion, for example, may require a *rough-in* inspection (the wood wall framing and other structural changes, left visible without other materials installed — the rough stage of construction), an insulation inspection, and a finished inspection. The plumbing phase usually requires a rough in and a finished inspection, as do most electrical installations. (I list each permit you may need on the handy Cheat Sheet at the front of this book.)

You probably won't get an approved finished inspection if a rough-in inspection is required and wasn't completed, so make sure you get all of the inspections completed. I have an acquaintance that forgot to call and schedule a rough-in electrical inspection and boy was he sorry! The inspector who came out to do the final inspection noticed that the rough-in inspection hadn't been completed. My friend had to open up sections of the finished walls so that the inspector could see how the installation was done before he approved the installation. A lot of extra work, frustration, and anger? You bet! Will my friend ever forget a to call for a rough-in inspection again? I doubt it.

The best way to know what you need to do is to check with the appropriate inspector before the project is started. Get their input about your design, and ask them what's new and current in your area. They can also give you an abridged, yet accurate, version of what must be done in a kitchen remodel to meet codes.

Putting yourself into a remodeling state of mind

Now that you've had your plan approved, you need to start thinking "remodeling." And believe me, you do need to put yourself in a remodeling mindset. For most folks it will be easy because you're excited about the project and can't wait to begin using your new kitchen. But for a small few, it's still easy to let other things come first. When this happens, and the kitchen remains torn up for longer than expected periods, don't get upset. Just get your priorities back in line and get at the remodeling!

Okay, my lecture on attitude is over. Here are some tips on what to do to make getting started more orderly:

✔ Get firm delivery dates on all custom and special-order items. You can't plan your construction schedule if you don't know when to expect special materials.

✔ Start packing up the kitchen. Packing always takes longer than you think, plus you want to take your time so that you know what's in each box. Remember, even if your kitchen isn't working, you still need to eat.

✔ Begin acclimating to living out of boxes. Sounds simple, huh? Be prepared to be frustrated when the utensils you used to grab without thinking are nowhere to be found.

✔ Practice patience! Tolerate change and unexpected surprises. If you're having a bad day, just remember to envision the beautiful kitchen you'll have after you work through this mess!

Let the games begin! Tearing out and putting in

Get out your safety glasses and gloves 'cause it's time to get down and dirty. The demolition process is one area that many homeowners can handle, and you save some money if you tackle this process yourself. If you plan to do some or much of the installation yourself, you'll also see significant savings. Here's a list of what to expect, both on the removal and installation-side of things:

1. Go ahead and make some dust! Tear out all of the old stuff and get rid of whatever is not going to be reused (Chapter 6 provides advice on the demolition process).

2. After the demolition is complete, start doing the rough-in work, which includes any framing, plumbing, or electrical changes (see Chapter 7).

   Don't be in a rush to get beyond the rough-in stage until you've had the first inspection, called the *rough-in* inspection.

3. Have all of the work inspected.

   If you've followed your codes, you should pass the inspection. If not, or if you didn't understand the code clearly (believe me, many people make errors!), make the necessary changes and have the work reinspected and approved.

4. After you're approved, start by finishing the walls.

   In most cases, you'll be hanging, taping, and finishing drywall. Don't forget you need to prime the drywall, too; now's a good time to prime it even though you won't be painting for a while. (Priming drywall involves applying a coat of primer paint, which is like a thinned version of white paint. The primer seals the drywall's facing paper.)

5. Install the doors and windows.

   You need these items installed and have the trim installed, too, so that you'll work with "finished" dimensions from the edge of the door and window trim and not from the rough opening in the walls when installing the cabinets.

6. Next install the cabinets (see Chapters 8 and 9).

   Hang the wall cabinets first and then install the base cabinets. You can hang the wall cabinets more easily when you're not reaching over the base cabinets.

7. Install the countertops (see Chapters 10 and 11), sink, and faucet (discussed in Chapters 12 and 13).

8. Install the new appliances (see Chapters 14 and 15).

9. Now it's time to shed some light on the subject and install new light fixtures, if they're part of the plan (see Chapters 16 and 17).

10. Finally, you can put down the new floor (see Chapters 20 and 21).

    Don't install the floor, no matter what material you're using, before you install the cabinets.

Living with dust, rubble, and constant change

Dealing with all the disruption around you may be a test for your sanity. Just go in remembering that dust, dirt, and debris will end up being moved or tracked well beyond the kitchen. Your heating and cooling ductwork will also distribute dust throughout your house. Plan on doing a top-to-bottom cleaning of your house after the project is finished, or you'll find dust and dirt for months. (Sort of like when you find pine needles from last year's Christmas tree around the house the following July!)

Here are a couple more hints to help you keep a grip on your project and your peace of mind:

✔ Allot enough time at the end of each workday for cleaning up. Don't just set down your tools and knock off for the night. Be sure to get the debris and other trash collected and put in the appropriate place (a dumpster or garbage can).

✔ Always restack or organize the materials you didn't use that day; this not only keeps the jobsite neater, but also lets you see exactly what you have left and what you may need to purchase before continuing the job.

Levels of work

You'll find various types and levels of work throughout a kitchen remodel. Each one is critical. Here's a quick overview of the types or levels of work you're likely to encounter:

✔ **Electrical:** Changes in the electrical design of your kitchen could be as simple as upgrading all old receptacles, or as involved as removing old wire and cable and installing new wire and cable throughout the kitchen. New circuits are also a strong possibility, especially if you're adding appliances. Don't forget about changes or upgrades to lighting, too.

✔ **Plumbing:** Adding a second sink or relocating an existing sink requires that you move or install new drain lines. Either way, plumbing must be completed during the rough-in stage of the project, then inspected and approved before you can close up walls and begin finishing things off. Early on is

also a good time to check any changes made to water supply lines, especially if you had some soldering to do. Repairing a leaky solder joint is much cheaper and easier to do while the wall is still open. (I explain how to solder a joint in Chapter 7.)

✔ **Carpentry:** If you're moving doorways, adding windows, or simply changing an existing window's location, then carpentry comes early in the process. You want to be sure that all new framing is in place before you pull new electrical cables or install plumbing pipes.

✔ **Finish work:** Finishing includes installing all of the new stuff in your kitchen including cabinets, flooring, and appliances. Don't start finishing until all of the rough-in work has been completed, inspected, and approved.

Heading down the home stretch: Adding the final touches

Your kitchen may still seem far from being finished, but you should actually be seeing that old light at the end of the tunnel. A few final touchups and the all-important final inspection and sign-off, and you're ready to enjoy your new kitchen.

1. Make the final hookups and connections for the appliances.

   Or have the subcontractors come back and finish the job if you've hired out (see Chapter 4 for advice on hiring a professional).

2. Add the finishing touches to bring everything together.

   Touch up the paint, take care of any little nicks or scratches, and so on (more on finishing up in Chapters 18 and 19).

3. Schedule the final inspection.

   This baby verifies that your new kitchen is ready for everyday use. If you've followed this schedule and obeyed the codes, you should be cookin' now! (Literally.)

What's Your Forte? Determining Your Skill and Comfort Level

So, how much of the project do you plan or want to do? When answering this question, you must be truly honest. If you try to take on more than you're qualified to do, be prepared for problems.

Determining your skill level

We all want to think we're the next Al Borland from *Home Improvement:* The person who can take on any problem or task and fix it the first time. In reality, however, we're more likely to be like Tim "the Toolman" Taylor — in over our heads but too proud to admit it. If you're uncomfortable handling certain parts or maybe even all of this type of project, admit it up front. You'll save time, money, and possibly your marriage!

If you've already mastered projects such as installing a prehung door or window (one that's already on a frame and you simply install it into a framed opening), then a kitchen remodel may be a project you could handle. But even if you have installed a door, that doesn't mean you'll be comfortable working with electricity or installing plumbing lines and fittings. On the other hand, if you have trouble just driving screws, you'd better plan on hiring someone to do just about everything for your kitchen remodel. (I help you get in touch with remodeling professionals in Chapter 4.)

Determining your comfort level

Most folks fall somewhere in the middle of a DIY (do-it-yourself) skills level rating or grading. However, if you're uncomfortable operating certain types of power tools or working on a specific area of your home, hire someone to do that part of the work. I, for example, usually hire an electrician when it's time to get into the main service panel. I know I could do the work, but I'm just not comfortable working around high voltage. I'd rather let a professional handle it. (Yes, seasoned DIY professionals know when to call in the pros!)

And speaking of calling in the pros, recognize when you need to ask for help. A good resource in this process is working with your city inspectors. Their job is to make sure things are built following the current building codes and they're usually happy to answer your questions. Just don't abuse them by phoning every other hour. If you find you're running to their aid more than once or twice a day, consider bringing in a professional — you're probably in over your head, at least on this part of the project.

If you decide to call a pro, be sure to get bids (three is the recommended minimum for price comparison) before you hire someone. Chapter 4 gives you more advice on finding and hiring professionals.

Shopping Tips before You Even Spend a Dime!

Whether you're shopping for cabinets and countertops or sinks, faucets, and appliances, prices are going to range widely. You need to understand that different manufacturers make different models and one company's top-of-the-line product may be equivalent to a mid-priced version from another company. Remember to compare apples to apples to get a clear and even comparison between like category products.

If you want a good, honest and unbiased evaluation of many of the items you need, check out *Consumer Reports* magazine. You can visit their Web site (www.consumerreports.org) and pay a fee to search for advice, or you probably can find back issues of the magazine at your local library

Choosing cabinets and countertops

New cabinets and countertops are among the most expensive items in any kitchen remodel. However, they're also very visible and you'll probably only replace them once while you own your home. Cabinets vary widely in quality and the amount of work you have to put into them. You can purchase ready-to-assemble cabinets with all the components disassembled and flat in individual boxes. Cabinets can also be site-built, although this is very expensive and generally only seen on high-end remodels. The most popular type of cabinets is custom made to fit your kitchen layout but consists of the standard sized cabinets used in today's housing industry. This type of cabinet is sold at home centers and even some cabinet stores.

Countertops also vary in quality and price, ranging from preformed plastic laminate to custom-made ceramic tile, granite, and composite materials. I discuss cabinets and countertops in Chapters 8 and 10 respectively.

Selecting sinks, faucets, and appliances

Most homeowners can find an attractive and functional sink and faucet fairly easily. Just take a trip to your local home center; sometimes referred to as a big-box store. You can find several major brands of sinks and dozens of faucets. And if you don't find exactly what you want, you can look through the manufacturer's catalog and special order just about anything to fit your needs. Chapter 12 helps you explore your options.

As for appliances, home centers know they need to provide everything a homeowner needs. You can find all of the traditional major appliances for the kitchen, as well as some that aren't in every kitchen; for example, a trash compactor or maybe a wine refrigerator (see Chapter 14). However, if you plan to upgrade to commercial- or restaurant-grade appliances, plan to look beyond the home centers. High-end appliances are sold through a limited number of outlets around the country that typically sell to contractors. In many cases, however, you can purchase the high-end appliances even if you're not a contractor.

Finishing touches: Lights, flooring, and wall treatments

A complete kitchen remodel includes new equipment and fixtures from top to bottom. You get new lights (see Chapter 16), wall treatments (see Chapter 18), and flooring (see Chapter 20). Once again, you can find all of these products at home centers. I'd recommend, however, that you try to find a lighting showroom when shopping for light fixtures. These showrooms are designed to show off lights in their best form, often in actual room settings. Surprisingly, lighting showroom prices are not that much more than the home center prices. And if you do pay more, you're generally getting a better quality fixture.

If you're coordinating wall treatments and window treatments, then find a good paint and wallpaper store. These professionals are in the color and design business and know exactly who to talk to and where to go to find you the designs that you desire. They also often work with or know whom you can contact regarding fabrics and furniture coverings, if you're trying to match and coordinate pieces of furniture as well. Check out more than one of these stores, too. Visiting multiple stores and locations allows you to get the expertise and advice from more than one design person. Remember, you're looking for all the ideas you can get to help you focus in on and realize your dream kitchen.

You can't beat a home center's price and selection when it comes to flooring, however. Most home centers offer a wide selection of brands, styles, and designs, and the store's large purchasing volume really helps keep prices down, which means less money spent on flooring and more money available for other parts of the project. And you can find just about any type of flooring you desire. They offer wood (both real and man-made), sheet vinyl, vinyl tiles, and ceramic tile; some carry slate and even granite.

Chapter 2

Planning Your Kitchen

In This Chapter

▶ Deciding what you want

▶ Exploring your kitchen shape

▶ Looking at remodeling options

▶ Getting your plans on paper

*W*hether your kitchen-remodeling project is large or small, you need a plan. Not something sketched on a napkin or jotted down on a few scraps of paper. You need a solid, realistic, accurate plan of what you want, need, and can afford. And by a plan I mean spending time thinking through what you want your new kitchen to be, drawing it to scale with accurate measurements, and then having the entire project reviewed and approved by your city inspectors.

Designing your kitchen takes more effort than merely measuring the existing space, deciding where to place the needed fixtures, and then ordering the materials. You need to know, for example, how choosing a darker wall color will affect the overall brightness of the kitchen. Or how a lighter wood color on the cabinets will brighten up the whole room, without even adding a light!

You may need help in some of the decision-making steps. Bringing in professionals at the right time can make planning, designing, and executing the job easier for you and can save you money in the long run. Paying the professionals for their years of experience in design or installation can be a great investment. Notice that I said "invest" and not "spend." Upgrading your kitchen is one of the best investments you can make in your home and you want to do it right in order to reap the benefits and the highest return on the dollars spent.

Professionals also help you meet the current building codes. Meeting codes in all steps of the remodel is critical for completing the project on schedule and within your budget. An error in complying with any of the parts of any of the codes — such as building, electrical, plumbing, or heating, ventilating, and air conditioning (HVAC) — will cost you time and money.

Working with Your Kitchen's Shape

Before you even think about how many cabinets you need and where you want specific items and appliances to go, you need to choose the basic kitchen shape that fits your needs and your home's design and flow.

If your budget is tight, you may decide to stay with a kitchen shape or layout similar to what's currently in your home. But if you've saved extra money for this project and are unhappy with your current kitchen layout, now is the time to make improvements.

Most homeowners usually only do one major kitchen remodel in the time they live in a home. And if you plan to be in the same home 10 to 20 years from now, you need to like the way the kitchen's designed, because you'll probably be working with it until you move.

With that said, take a look at the current choices in kitchen shapes.

L-shaped kitchens

According to a recent survey conducted for the National Kitchen and Bath Association (NKBA), the leading association of kitchen and bath designers, almost two-thirds of their customers who had their kitchen designed professionally rated the L-shaped kitchen as a popular kitchen shape. An L-shaped kitchen has two of the three major kitchen appliances on one wall. The existing plumbing and electrical setups dictate where you place things, unless you're planning some major repositioning of supply lines and wiring.

An L-shaped kitchen can also accommodate a center island or a peninsula, depending on the size of the kitchen space. Just make sure you have at least 42 inches of clearance between the island and any cabinets, and make that distance 48 inches if you have two cooks in the family. We'll look into recommended clearances in the section "Consulting the NKBA" later in this chapter. Figure 2-1 shows a typical L-shaped kitchen layout with an island.

The L-shaped kitchen is a popular design choice for folks purchasing their cabinets and countertops at larger home improvement centers because these stores carry a wide variety in the most popular and standard size cabinets and countertops. Plus, the installation steps are very straightforward with only one corner to deal with. Pricing is also fairly competitive. In fact, many home centers have package pricing for cabinets and countertops for L-shaped kitchens.

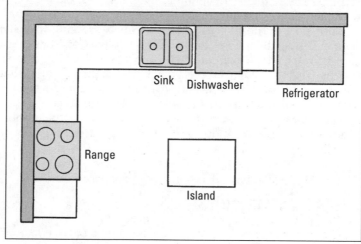

Figure 2-1:
An L-shaped kitchen.

U-shaped kitchens

A U-shaped kitchen is similar to an L-shaped kitchen, but with three wall surfaces instead of just two. In a U-shaped design, you typically have the sink on one wall, the range and oven on another, and the refrigerator on the third wall. The sink is usually in the middle wall section, with the range and oven opposite the refrigerator. Figure 2-2 shows you how many U-shaped kitchens are laid out.

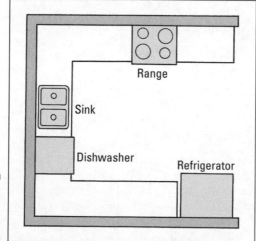

Figure 2-2:
A U-shaped kitchen.

This layout makes good use of counter space because usually it has more counter space per square foot than any other design. You have counter area on both sides of the sink, as well as adequate working space next to the range. A U-shaped kitchen also usually has plenty of counter space next to the refrigerator, which is great when you want a place to set those full bags of groceries. This layout makes everyday life a bit easier. The U-shape kitchen does have a couple of drawbacks, however. The two corners can turn into huge wasters of space. You can maximize the storage capabilities, though, by using an appropriate type of storage assembly inside the corner cabinets. More on that in Chapter 8. Another problem is that the work areas are sometimes too far apart for convenience.

G-shaped kitchens

This style is relatively new in kitchen designs and is becoming quite popular, but only when the kitchen boasts enough floor and area space to allow for a fourth wall. The short fourth wall is what changes the shape from a U to a G. Figure 2-3 shows a typical G-shaped layout. The G section is usually devoted to added counter and storage space.

I-shaped or single wall kitchens

If you're limited on space and you don't plan to knock out walls and really blow the space wide open, the I-shaped kitchen (see Figure 2-4) places all the appliances on one wall, and it doesn't provide a very efficient work area. However, in some cases the I-shaped kitchen is your only option.

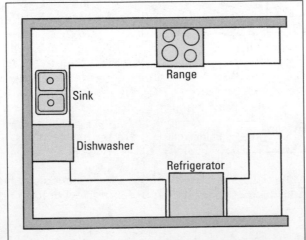

Range

Sink

Dishwasher

Refrigerator

Figure 2-3:
A G-shaped
kitchen.

If you do need to go with this layout, place the sink between the refrigerator and the stove. Make sure, too, that the refrigerator door hinges are on the side that's away from the sink. This way, the door will open away from the sink and not block you from moving food from the refrigerator onto the counter work area.

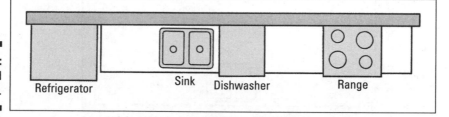

Figure 2-4:
An I-shaped
kitchen.

Refrigerator   Sink   Dishwasher   Range

Corridor/Galley/Parallel wall kitchen

Three names, same kitchen design. The galley kitchen is your best option when space is limited because you can at least place the appliances on opposite sides, which helps the workflow. The layout of items is a bit like the L-shaped kitchen (refer back to Figure 2-1 for a visual), two on one wall and one on the other. Typically, you'll find the range and oven and refrigerator on one wall and the sink on the other. Placing the sink by itself, you maximize the amount of counter space. This layout also lets you create a modified version of the "work triangle," which is what all kitchen designers use to establish placement, spacing, and traffic flow. Creating your kitchen's work triangle is discussed in the following section.

Working efficiently: The work triangle

The whole concept of the work triangle was created in 1949 by the Small Home Council of the University of Illinois to connect the three main areas of the kitchen — the cooking (cooktop or stove), refrigeration storage (refrigerator), and clean up centers (sink) — in an efficient manner. The addition of appliances such as a microwave oven, the emergence of multiple cooks in one household, and the inclusion of computers and entertainment items in the kitchen have led to some modifications, but the basic rules for an efficient work triangle still apply. For a visual, take a look at Figure 2-5.

According to NKBA guidelines, a work triangle's three sides should total 26 feet or less. No single leg should be shorter than 4 feet or longer than 9 feet.

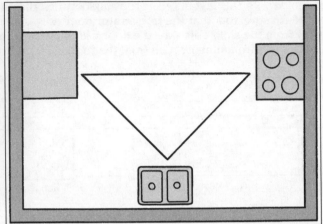

Figure 2-5:
A work triangle connects the sink, stove, and refrigerator into a smooth flowing work area.

The triangle should be located so that no traffic pattern will cross through it. Never interrupt any primary work area (preparation, cooking, or clean up) with a floor-to-ceiling cabinet, pantry, or refrigerator.

The true work triangle is designed for use in a U-shaped kitchen where the sink, range, and refrigerator are all on separate walls. An L-shaped kitchen or a straight or I-shaped kitchen will have a modified triangle or no triangle at all. But no matter what kitchen shape you have, do your best to arrange the appliances in a logical use order.

You may be able to achieve a real work triangle by moving plumbing lines from one wall to another. Or you may be able to make the legs of the triangle fall within the NKBA guidelines by repositioning a drain line along its existing wall. True, moving plumbing lines can be quite complicated and a project that you may want to leave to a plumber. But, getting a kitchen with a true work triangle is an incredible convenience that may be worth the sacrifice.

Exploring a Few of Your Design Options

Don't think that every kitchen remodel involves tearing out cabinets or ripping things back to the bare wall studs. Attractive and affordable kitchen makeovers can be accomplished with as little effort as painting walls or splashing in some new colors with wallpaper or window treatments. I'll go into greater detail on these less involved options in Chapters 18 and 19.

Before you settle on a kitchen shape or get too disappointed because you think you're limited to only one design, do some more homework and investigating. One option is to ask a kitchen designer to come to your house and assess the current kitchen and then go over what options are available to you. Most designers are happy to act as a consultant, even just for a few hours. You generally only pay an hourly rate. Just remember that you're the one in charge and make sure the designer knows when you want him to stop. Set some firm parameters about how many hours you want him to put into the project.

However you do need to have a good notion of what you want before talking with a designer.

Considering new counter space: A dream come true

One of the biggest complaints most folks have about their kitchens is lack of counter space to prepare food and store things. Unfortunately, finding extra room for more counter space can be a real challenge because it usually means altering the size and shape of the kitchen. Generally, the only way to find space is to open up or move existing walls. If you're set on gaining counter space, be ready for some major construction.

One other option for gaining space is reworking your layout. Your existing kitchen may be an L-shape that just doesn't seem to work for you, but a reconfigured L-design (moving the current location of appliances) may be all it takes to give you more space. If you seem to be hitting roadblocks, contact a kitchen designer.

Adding eat-in dining space

Just because your old kitchen had a small, cramped eating space, that doesn't mean your new kitchen has to have a similar setup. Take a look at this list for a few hints:

✔ **Smaller table and chairs:** If you can't gain floor space from anywhere, consider different furniture as part of your remodeling plan. For example, our first house had a very small kitchen with an eat-in kitchen area. The kitchen table was the typical size that fit four chairs, but had the option of adding a leaf and two more chairs. By its design, it also took up the same amount of room whether it was in use or not. We remedied that by purchasing a drop-leaf dining set. This gave us seating for six when fully extended, but a nice compact footprint of approximately 24 inches wide by 48 inches long when the drop-leafs were down.

✔ **Breakfast bar:** Making part of the counter top into a breakfast bar is a popular way to gain space. Extend an oversized area of counter top either into the kitchen or the adjoining area, often an informal dining area. The counter top extends out from the base cabinets by about 12 to 18 inches, which allows diners to slide a chair or stool up to the counter and sit comfortably. See the color insert for an example of a breakfast bar.

✔ **Booth:** Our current home had the usual eat-in space, large enough for a table and four chairs. It also looked like all the other eat-in kitchen areas I've ever seen. We changed the look of our kitchen and gave ourselves more storage by installing a booth. The table is a traditional-looking rectangle secured to the wall and supported with a single front leg. It has two bench seats, like you see in the old malt shops or restaurants. But what really makes this design appealing is the storage drawers under both benches. You can also build a kitchen booth in a U-shape and install a pedestal table, or mount the benches along each wall, forming a short L, and install a pedestal table.

Installing an island oasis in your kitchen

Some of you may be wondering why your large kitchen seems to be so inefficient. The fact is, many larger kitchens are designed with work areas too far apart, which makes them inefficient. A good remedy for cutting down traffic flow problems and making your kitchen easier to use is to add an island near the center of the kitchen. By adding the island, you can move a cooktop or even a sink into the island, thus creating a more compact work triangle. The island provides additional storage space, plus many island designs have eating space incorporated (as shown in the color insert). The island not only acts as a prep or cooking station, depending on its design, but also is often used for setting out the food, especially when entertaining large groups. This setup provides a nice setting and creates a sort of formal informality as you and your guest take a trip around the island filling up your plate.

Adding an island that will house cooking or food prep equipment will involve some mechanical changes such as adding plumbing, wiring, ventilation, or any combination of the three. If you install a sink, it needs hot and cold water lines and a drain line. If you install a cooktop, you'll need 240-volt electrical service to the island, plus at least one 120-volt outlet for small appliances. If your new cooktop is gas-fired, you'll need to run the gas line to the island. Island cooktops also need proper ventilation. Many cooktops have a grill for cooking, for example steaks and shish kabobs. If your cooktop has a grill, you'll need to install downdraft ventilation that pulls the smoke and odors down into ductwork that runs through the island, into the floor, and then exhausts it outdoors.

Most of these additions or changes are considered major projects. And unless you're a very experienced do-it-yourselfer, I recommend calling in the professionals for the changes.

The main question you need to answer is whether your kitchen is large enough to accommodate an island. You need to allow for sufficient clearance (42 inches) between the island, the other base cabinets, and appliances. Chapter 21 shows how to install an island, if there's one in your kitchen's future.

Mulling over multiple workstations

With the work, school, and travel schedules most families juggle these days, more and more households have multiple cooks. And quite often, two or more of the cooks work in the kitchen at the same time. In this situation, multiple workstations can be a blessing.

What type of workstations you add depends on what type of cooking you enjoy doing. If both of you enjoy baking and do a fair amount, be sure you have plenty of counter space for dough preparation and so on. A second oven may be a good choice, too. If you both like to cook on the stove, consider having a second range or adding a cooktop surface. Here are some other areas you may want to add, change, or improve:

✔ **Preparation:** Lots of counter space is essential when you have two or more cooks. Even if both of you are preparing the same foods, you'll want separate work spaces. Both preparation areas should be close to the refrigerator (for easy access to stored foods) and near or adjacent to the sink or sinks. Multiple-cook kitchens are more fun to use and more efficient with two sinks.

If adding new plumbing for a second sink is too much of an undertaking, plan to expand your preparation and cleanup areas by adding one large sink with two or three bowls, as described in Chapter 13.

✔ **Cleanup:** People sometimes forget that after all the preparation and presentation comes the cleanup. If you install a second sink, position it near the dishwasher and outfit it with a garbage disposer. The disposer is handy when you clean off dirty dishes before putting them in the dishwasher. Read more about buying and installing a garbage disposer in Chapters 14 and 15.

Consulting the NKBA

Okay, so just what is the National Kitchen and Bath Association and why should you contact this organization? The NKBA is a non-profit trade association that's designed to help you locate leading kitchen design professionals.

The NKBA can also help you find products and services available in your area. The NKBA Web site (www.nkba.org) includes planning guidelines that, although they aren't part of the building codes, have become the yardstick for how to design and build a functional, friendly kitchen. Besides finding out what's in and what's out in kitchens, you'll also gain general knowledge on construction and building trends. The Web site allows you to request NKBA's free kitchen and bath workbook, inquire about retailers and designers in your area, and get answers to many of the most commonly asked questions.

Constructing containment areas for recycling

One of the more popular features of today's kitchens is a separate area for holding recyclable materials. These areas can be as simple as a pullout bin area divided into sections for collecting plastics, glass, and metal or you can create a completely separate closet area. Chapter 9 talks about cabinet interiors and options, including rollout shelves, which are great for accessing recycling baskets housed inside a cabinet.

Dealing with paperwork

Today's kitchens have become such a central gathering place and work area that many kitchen designers include a designated area for doing paperwork, such as paying the bills or working on your home computer. Once again, finding this extra space may be a challenge, but after you have it you'll wonder how you ever did without it.

Putting Your Plans on Paper

Now is the time to take your wishes, wants, and needs and get them written or drawn out. So where should you start? How about figuring out how big your kitchen is.

Measuring your kitchen

If you want your kitchen remodel to be a success, then be meticulous in your measurements. Being off by even as little as an inch can cause real problems and frustration. Don't be offended, either, if your designer, cabinetmaker, or retailer asks you whether your measurements are accurate. They want to make sure the items they order for you fit where they're supposed to — inaccurate measurements are the best way to make sure stuff doesn't fit! Check out the Cheat Sheet at the front of this book, too, for tips on taking measurements the right way so things are correct the first time.

Using graph paper with corresponding squares equaling one foot of real space will aid in making the sketch accurate and to scale.

Measuring walls

Make a roadmap of all the walls in your kitchen. Start by facing the wall that has the sink on it and label the wall as follows: Wall #1 is the wall to your left, wall #2 is the wall with the sink, wall #3 is the wall to your right and wall #4 is the wall that's behind you. If your kitchen only has three walls (some will, you know), adjust the wall labeling to fit your kitchen layout.

Begin by measuring along the floor to get the exact length of each wall. Next measure the same direction about halfway up the wall. Then, measure the same direction a third time at the ceiling. Walls are rarely square and can often be off by as much as an inch or two. You need to know the exact size of each wall, so measure each one at these three points. Order your cabinets using the widest of the three measurements. If you don't, you'll have a gap between the wall and the end cabinet. And don't worry about fitting the extra width into the smaller opening. You'll trim the cabinet to-fit using a technique discussed in Chapter 11.

If your kitchen has a *soffit* (a boxed area located between the top of the old cabinets and the ceiling), measure distance from the floor to the bottom of the soffit. Also measure the soffit's depth and height. Take these measurements at the same time you measure the walls and record all of the measurements.

Measuring doorways

When measuring doorways, you want to measure both the location of the doorway on the wall and the size of the doorway, including the trim. Starting in the left-hand corner for each measurement ensures accuracy; it's too easy to make a mistake on the location of the door in the wall. Start in the left-hand corner of any wall that has a doorway in it. Start at a spot halfway up the wall in the left-hand corner and measure from there to the edge of the door trim. Next, measure the width of the door including the trim on both sides. This dimension will be greater than the size of the door. For example, a 32-inch wide door will have a measurement of 37 inches when measured from outside trim edge to outside trim edge. If the wall happens to have more than one door, measure each door location separately starting at the left-hand corner. Don't measure from the edge of one door's trim to the edge of the next door. Don't forget to measure the height of the door (including trim), too. Note the location and dimensions on your paper.

Positioning windows

Make sure you measure the position of the window on the wall, as well as the size of the window. Start in the left-hand corner of the wall with a window and measure the distance from the wall corner to the edge of the window trim. Measure the window's width and height including all sides of trim. Finally, measure the distance from the floor to lower edge of the bottom piece of trim. Use these measurements to draw the correct size window and transfer these measurements onto your paper.

Noting pipes, vents, outlets and switches

You also need to accurately note the location of all other openings in the wall. These include receptacles, electrical switches, drainpipes, and venting ductwork. Once again, start in the left-hand corner of the wall with each specific item in it. This time, however, measure to the center of the items including the outlets, drainpipes, or ductwork. Again, transfer these dimensions and positions onto your drawing.

Playing with your plan

Now that you have all of the dimensions you need, you can actually draw — or at least sketch — your new kitchen layout. Start by playing around with different locations for the appliances, but always keep in mind where the power sources are located, unless you're planning on moving them to accommodate an appliance's new spot. Don't be afraid to change the location of a specific size cabinet within a specific run, either. Let me explain what this means. Cabinet widths vary, usually by 3-inch increments, which gives you flexibility in positioning different size cabinets in the cabinet run. This works for both wall and base cabinet runs.

If all of this sounds a bit much, take your dimensions and sketch (if you have one) to your designer or local home center and ask for some design assistance. Most places are glad to help because if they come up with a great design, chances are good that you'll order the cabinets through their store.

Chapter 3

Establishing a Budget and Sticking to It!

In This Chapter

▶ Creating a budget

▶ Financing options

▶ Counting your pennies to avoid overspending

▶ Planning your time

*E*very home improvement project requires a budget. Even if you're simply painting the walls, you need to look at your current finances and make sure that you have enough money to pay for the materials. The same is true and critical for kitchen remodeling, which can cost anywhere from just a couple of hundred dollars to tens of thousands, depending on how much of your old kitchen you tear out and replace. This chapter shows you how to establish a budget that allows you to have a good shot at getting everything you want — within your budget.

Crunching the Numbers

Go over your budget and get down to the dollars-and-cents decisions and determine just how much you can spend on this project. Unfortunately, you might not get everything you want after you've done your homework. On the other hand, you might save some money in one area that allows you to keep and maybe even add a couple of extras — I tell you how in the following sections.

Expect the unexpected! I can't stress enough how important that concept is. No matter how sound your budget seems, the project can take an unexpected twist that adds unforeseen charges to your tab. So expect everything from prices being higher than originally expected to repairs being necessary before new appliances or flooring can be installed. Keep your cool as you work through these slowdowns and glitches. Don't let them ruin your project!

Step 1: Determining the scope of the project

Where and how do you begin? First you need to decide what about your existing kitchen you like and what you want to improve (as explained in Chapter 1). Then prioritize the projects from most important to least important, keeping the following facts in mind:

- ✔ **Cabinets and countertops:** Cabinets account for about half of the total cost of the project and will have the greatest impact on your budget. The price range is determined by quality, material, and whether you use stock or custom cabinets. Plan to spend anywhere from $100 to $250 and up per linear foot on quality cabinets.

- ✔ **Sinks:** The type of material the sink is made of is the biggest factor in the price, however, expect to pay at least $200 and don't be surprised when you find sinks costing over $600 and some over $1,000, depending on the material, size, and configuration.

- ✔ **Appliances:** Appliance prices are wide-ranging, so shopping for new appliances is sort of like trying to zero in on the price of a new car. You have a lot of options to choose from, as well as sizes and configurations. Major appliance (stove, refrigerator, dishwasher, and so on) prices start around $400 for dishwashers and go well into several thousand dollars for a professional- or restaurant-grade range, oven, or refrigerator.

- ✔ **Lighting:** Spending several hundred dollars on a single kitchen light fixture probably seems ridiculous to most folks. However, quality light fixtures aren't cheap, and you won't be disappointed if you do pay a bit more than originally anticipated. Under-cabinet lighting can also be expensive, depending on the type of lighting you choose, plus there's the labor cost of installation if you have it done professionally. Shop around to find fixtures within your budget.

- ✔ **Flooring:** Pricing in this category is always figured by the square foot so it's easy to compare costs. Ceramic tile generally costs between $1 and $3 per square foot for materials. Labor varies but is usually between $2 and $3 per square foot. Wood flooring ranges from just over $2 to almost

$5 per square foot for materials. Labor varies depending on the type of wood flooring, however, expect to pay between $3 and $7 per square foot for installation, with the type of material dictating the square foot costs.

✔ **Decorations:** A high-quality interior paint will sell for around $25 per gallon. Wallpaper can cost anywhere from $5 to as much as you want to spend for a single roll. As for window treatments, plan to spend between $75 to $100 per window, which includes material and sewing if you don't do it yourself.

After you determine what types of changes you want to make, list all of the materials and equipment (cabinets, countertops, appliances, and so on) that you want in your new kitchen. Without a complete list, you won't be able to determine the entire scope of the project. A complete materials list also helps you bargain to get the best prices on materials (for more on this see "Pricing products and gathering estimates" later in this chapter). You may need to look ahead to future chapters to determine what materials you'll need to complete each project.

One more important factor to consider is how long you plan to stay in the home. If you're only planning on staying for three or four years, for example, you may want to scale back the project somewhat. However, if this is the house where you plan to entertain your grandchildren and great-grandchildren, then I say shoot for the fence! Or at least go for whatever your budget allows.

Step 2: Pricing products and gathering estimates

A visit to your local home center is a great place to begin. Don't be afraid to visit a couple of different stores. Competition is fierce and you may be surprised by what a particular retailer will do (for example, a retailer may give you upcoming or previous sale prices on items or even throw in an item or two at no charge), especially if the store feels it can get your entire order.

This is where your complete material list is invaluable. Providing a store with a complete list allows them to do a *take-off* (an estimate of materials needed and their total cost). Give this list to each of the retailers and see which one gives you the best prices. Don't be afraid to ask one store to match a competitor's price, either. Most retailers will be willing to drop a few dollars (sometimes just pennies per item!) to get your business.

Try to work with one person at each store. I know that's not always possible, but give it a shot. You don't want to explain your project to a half-dozen people in the same store. Dealing with one person also helps resolve any problems that may arise if there's a problem with your order.

After you have a couple of estimates, do your homework. Don't pick the product or appliance that's simply the least expensive. Make sure that the prices are for the same products — brand, model, size, and so on. If the product brands are different, at least be sure that they're of similar or identical quality. You need to compare apples to apples and not apples to oranges. Check with your salesperson if you're not sure if two products are comparable, or you can check online at company Web sites for product evaluations. Also consider checking with *Consumer Reports* magazine either online at www.consumerreports.org (for a fee) or find back issues at your local library to see if they've tested the type of product(s) you're looking at. Their reports are very fair at evaluating and rating all types of products, especially appliances.

If you're not familiar with a specific brand that's listed on the estimate, ask to see the product and have all the features explained. Listen to how your salesperson talks about the product, too. If they're not behind it 100 percent, consider a different brand or model. I've always gone with my gut feeling when dealing with salespeople and product knowledge. If they sound like they're not familiar with the product, ask to speak to someone else about the product. I can't tell you how many times I've spoken to at least two people just to raise my comfort level about a product I'm not familiar with. Besides, any good salesperson won't be afraid to ask an associate for product information if they're not familiar with it.

If you're planning a complicated remodeling project — one that involves moving drain lines or knocking down walls, for example — you're going to need to hire help, so remember to factor in labor costs. A good way to get an estimate on labor costs is to visit your local home center. Many of them offer installation service, usually subcontracted out to local contractors, and have a do-it-yourself price versus an installed price. The difference between the two prices is the cost of labor. You can usually add this labor-cost figure to the price of materials to get a rough idea of how much the project is going to cost. Skip ahead to Chapter 4 for more advice on finding and hiring professional help.

Getting prices and construction cost estimates is only half of the financial picture. You need to set up a filing and/or tracking system so that you'll be able to check what you're spending versus what you've budgeted to spend. You'll find a number of budget/record keeping computer programs available. If you're computer-challenged or you don't have a home computer, you'll find home record keeping plans at most bookstores.

Give yourself a getaway

If you're planning a lengthy or involved kitchen remodel, plan a weekend away from everything somewhere near the middle of the project. Go to a hotel or motel for a couple of nights and relax. Take in a movie, see a play; do something other than remodeling! This short break may be the best gift you can give yourself during the project. Yes, you'll spend some money, but this hiatus will bring you back rested and energized, ready to finish up the project. If you do build in a mid-project getaway, try to schedule around parts of the projects that may have fumes or odors to deal with, for example, when the cabinet or floor finish is being applied and needs to dry. If you can't find the time for a mid-project getaway, you may want to reward yourself with a weekend getaway when the project's completed.

Step 3: Budgeting for breakfast, lunch, and dinner

After your kitchen's out of commission, you'll have a better appreciation of just how much time you spend in your kitchen and how much you miss having it. Besides the inconvenience, you'll also find that a sizeable chunk of money will be spent on eating meals out. Don't forget to build this expense into the budget. A family of four can easily spend $20 to $30 on an evening meal, even at a fast-food restaurant. Add in the cost of breakfast and lunch for the same size family and you're looking at between $75 and $100 a day for meals, so budget accordingly.

Here are a few ideas that will help you make it through mealtimes without breaking the bank:

- **Move appliances into other rooms:** Just because your cooktop and oven aren't available, doesn't mean you can't cook at home at least some of the time. The microwave oven and refrigerator can be moved to temporary homes and still be used. Move the microwave into another room to cook foods or heat up leftovers. Although frozen foods may not be five-star cuisine, they're cheaper than eating out. Just remember not to overload circuits and don't put both of these appliances on the same circuit — even for the short period of remodeling.

- **Alter your normal eating habits to save money:** For example, breakfasts don't have to include bacon and eggs every morning. Try eating fresh fruit and muffins instead. And when it comes to lunches and snacks, buy things that can be stored without refrigeration or don't need to be reheated or cooked. I'm not trying to change your diet or the way you eat. I'm simply suggesting that you be open to alternatives and willing to adjust your eating habits during the remodeling process. Besides, after your new kitchen's done, you'll be able to fix all of your old favorites in the new digs!

✔ **Ask for help:** If family or friends ask what they can do to help, tell them to invite your family over for dinner or to bring in lunch on a couple of days. Feeding the troops is just as important as swinging a hammer or hanging drywall!

Step 4: Refiguring until it fits

Establishing a workable and affordable budget usually means making some compromises on a few things. Here are just a few ways to make your budget numbers add up to what you can afford to spend.

✔ If new appliances are part of the remodel, consider getting ones with only the features you need. Wood grain panels and inserts are nice, but not essential to completing the project.

✔ Rethink moving a sink if your budget is tight. Although the new location may be nice, the old position probably works, too. You'll save a ton of money by not moving plumbing lines.

✔ Try to do as much of the work yourself as you can, especially the demolition work and painting. Why pay someone else to do things you know you can handle?

✔ But if you're set on having materials in your kitchen that are unfamiliar to you or you're uncomfortable installing, plan on paying for the installation by a professional rather than starting the project and calling someone in midstream. Besides paying prime dollar because you need their help immediately, you may also have to pay to have them correct your mistakes.

✔ Don't forget to figure in your time constraints, too. Too many people sell themselves short when estimating the value of their time and try to save money doing things themselves when they really knew right away that they wouldn't have enough time to do the project. Pay for someone to do the work if you know you won't have the time!

How Am I Going to Pay for This? Financing Your Project

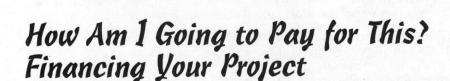

Now that you've determined how much money you need to remodel your kitchen, you need to find the funds.

Finding the money to pay for a kitchen-remodeling project may be the most important step in your project. After all, getting good prices on materials and labor doesn't do any good if you can't pay for things. You can choose from several financing methods, depending on the scope of the project, but what makes one better than another? Let's look at the options that work for most folks and should work for you, too.

The following information is not intended to be used as financial or investment advice. I'm providing it as a starting point to help you find the best way to pay for your kitchen-remodeling project. As with any financial matter, consult with your personal banker, investment banking counselor, or tax advisor. It's also important not to start the remodel project before getting your financing in order. Most lenders require that the house be appraised before they'll loan you money and the house must be in salable condition when it's appraised. It can't be in the middle of a tear-out when the appraiser comes to do her job.

Refinancing your home

Quite a few homeowners pay for a new kitchen by refinancing their home. Most have built up a considerable amount of equity in their home. *Equity* is your home's current assessed value versus the total amount of mortgages or loans against that value. *Refinancing* is the process of paying off the existing mortgage (or mortgages) based on the current value of your home.

The best thing about a refinanced mortgage is that the interest on the loan is still tax deductible. You not only generally lower your monthly mortgage payment, but quite often you can actually put cash in your pocket because many homeowners have considerable equity in their home. This means there's more value in the house than dollars owed on loans, so the difference can be money back to the homeowner.

Finding a lender for refinancing isn't difficult, especially in today's competitive lending market. Your bank or your personal banker are both good places to start looking. If you want to look elsewhere (and I recommend that you talk to at least two different lenders), contact a local real estate office. The real estate agents are in constant touch with mortgage officers who will give you a competitive current interest rate on a home mortgage.

Keep in mind that refinancing a home is almost the same as purchasing one, so you'll need all the closing documents from the current loan, employment information, and so on. Most mortgage officers are real professionals and will work with you through this seemingly daunting process.

Applying for a home improvement loan

Many homeowners have enough equity in their home that a *home improvement loan* or second mortgage is a viable option. The security for the loan is the assessed value of your home versus the amount you wish to borrow. Second mortgage rates are generally a few percentage points higher than first mortgages; however, they're still very affordable, and the interest on most second mortgages is also tax deductible. You'll find most first mortgage lenders also have second mortgage options available. Make sure you consult with a competent mortgage officer or your tax advisor before entering into a second mortgage.

Some lenders offer a second mortgage that can be as high as 125% of your home's current value. I don't recommend borrowing more than the value of the property. If you do borrow more than your home's value and the value suddenly drops, you could be in big trouble owing more than the house is worth.

Charging on a low- or no-interest credit card

Currently, interest rates are at a 40-year low. And with that, many credit card companies offer low-interest lines of credit and, in some cases, no-interest credit cards. If you're disciplined and can stay on track and pay off the balance of your credit card every month, then one of these low- or no-interest cards might be a good way to pay for your remodel. Credit cards allow you to purchase what you need when you need it, without dipping into your savings. Plus, the monthly statements help you keep track of what you've spent.

Considering cold, hard cash!

Okay, most of us don't have thousands of dollars just lying around waiting to be used. But if you do have enough ready cash available, consider using it to pay for the project. You'll have the satisfaction of paying for the project completely, plus you may just get some discounts on materials if you don't need to charge things. Some retailers will offer discounts to customers who pay cash. The retailer gets their money immediately and doesn't have to hassle with financing forms or credit cards.

If you do plan to pay cash, consider opening a separate checking account for the project. A separate account really helps you track your spending because only the project expenses are recorded in the account.

A Little Overspending Adds Up to a Lot of Going Over Budget

The number one problem with remodeling projects is going over budget. Most people don't consciously or intentionally overspend, and most folks do their best to adhere to the budget they've created. Unfortunately, a little overspending here and there usually adds up to going over budget. Here are some suggestions to keep your spending in check.

Track and review your expenses regularly

No matter what record-keeping method you choose (and you really do need to choose and use one), use it — regularly! Update the records as purchases are made, rather than saying, "I'll take care of things on a weekly basis." Continued purchasing without recording and checking things against your budget is a quick and easy way to go over or completely blow your budget.

And review your records weekly, even if you didn't spend any money that week. Besides seeing an up-to-date total of the bottom line, you're more likely to catch mistakes or remember an item that may not have made it in the records. Think about tracking your project purchases the same way you think about keeping your checkbook ledger and balance current. If you're like me, you hate finding one, two, or even several items that didn't get entered into the checkbook ledger. Boy, can that make your cash balance look bad, fast!

Keep an eye open for sales

Shopping for remodeling fixtures and materials should be no different than shopping for everyday items and household things. In other words, keep your eyes open for sale prices! For example, if you know you're going to get new countertop appliances and they're on sale now, grab 'em! The same is true for building materials and appliances. If you know you're going to need lumber, plywood, or other building materials, contact the retailer you plan to use and make sure you can get those sales prices when it's time to order. You may need to pay for the material now, but at least you'll get the sale price. Remember, buying big-ticket items doesn't mean you can't or won't find a good price on them, so be vigilant and watch for sales.

Swanky shops or practical places

If you find the product or material you like at one of the big-box stores, don't be afraid to buy it there. Being able to say you purchased your new kitchen at some fancy, high-end retailer may make you feel better, but could cost you money. Shop around for the best prices on comparable items and, in most cases, buy them where you'll pay less.

Delivery's on you

One other area where you can usually save a few dollars is on delivery charges. If you're ordering your entire kitchen from one store, see if they'll waive the delivery charge or at least only charge you the minimum. In my home center days, the company I worked for would sometimes only charge one delivery charge even if two trips were needed. Don't be afraid to wheel and deal or at least ask — the worse they can say is "no".

Another way to save the delivery charge is to haul home whatever you can in your own vehicle or maybe borrow a van, truck, or SUV from friend, even if it means making a couple of trips.

Time Equals Money — Budgeting Your Time Wisely

No matter how large or small your project is, it will take time to complete. In an ideal world, every remodeling project would have an absolute, dead-on timetable. But in the real world, things get delayed for a variety of reasons: Maybe items are backordered or they simply don't show up when promised. Or changes in your everyday life force you to rearrange your priorities and schedules. I've seen several kitchen remodels that lasted many, many months. One, in fact, took just short of a year to get to the final, everything-is-really-done finish. I've even seen small makeovers take several months. Don't forget to look ahead on your calendar, too. If you're planning on hosting Christmas dinner, for example, it probably isn't wise to start a major kitchen remodel in November.

How much time you can allot to the project along with the number of upgrades you plan to make are key factors in a kitchen remodel timetable. But the greatest time factor for most DIY projects is how much time you're able to commit to the project. If you've just spent 10 to 12 hours working hard at your "real" job, chances are good that you won't feel like doing too much after you get home. Especially if you have to head back to work within a few hours. The key to a successful and levelheaded remodeling project is allowing time. Don't be over-ambitious and try to do the same things a professional would do in the same amount of time. Remember, these skilled craftspeople do this stuff everyday and know exactly what to do to make the job go as smoothly as possible.

I've found that even an experienced DIYer should take the amount of time a professional would allot for a job and increase the time requirements by 50 percent. And, if your project is going to take several weekends in a row to finish, allow some extra time for getting back up to speed each weekend when you get restarted. You want to be sure that you didn't skip anything from when you stopped last weekend, so you may have to backtrack or even redo part of the project.

If you have a solid game plan for what needs to be done and when, you should be able to weather most delays without too much trouble. Do try to always have the next step ready to go, or at least have an alternate part of the project to complete. What could be more frustrating than having the entire project come to a halt just because one or two items (or people!) didn't show up. Even if you don't get as much accomplished as you intended, any progress is a plus. Do remember that if things look like they need to temporarily stop, then stop!

Remember, too, that unexpected situations are usually out of your control, so just do your best to keep things on track. I don't like surprises on a job any more than the next person does. But instead of getting mad, I try to accept the fact that things happen, correct the situation as soon as possible, and step back, take a deep breath, and just carry on. Unexpected situations aren't the end of the world (let alone this project!) and the job will get done.

Chapter 4

Bringin' In the Big Guns or Doin' It Solo

In This Chapter

▶ Looking at who can help

▶ Finding the right people to help you

▶ Making sure to have a contract

▶ Giving the final okay

In a perfect DIY world, every homeowner would successfully tackle and complete every step of her kitchen-remodeling project all on her own. But unfortunately, many remodeling projects include steps that most folks can't or don't want to handle. And if you want your new kitchen to look like a page out of *Architectural Digest* and not out of *Bob and Al's Pretty Good Ways to Tear Things Apart,* you may need to call in professionals along the way.

Evaluating your skill level and recognizing that you need to bring in the big guns are both key steps. Knowing what to ask these folks and what to expect from them are just as critical. This chapter examines the many steps you'll need to take if you decide you need to hire a contractor. I also overview the documents you'll need to protect yourself and the people you hire.

Introducing the Pinch Hitters

Many people don't like to admit that they need to hire someone to do certain parts of the remodel. Well, at least the guys usually don't (or won't!). If, however, you want the job done as quickly as possible and done right, then don't be ashamed to hire a professional.

You need to know about three types of professionals who could get involved in a kitchen remodel: designers, architects, and contractors (including plumbers, carpenters, and electricians). Any of these folks could be involved at the outset or on an as-needed basis throughout your project. The next sections go over the role of each one so you can see which (if any) you want to use.

Dreaming up your kitchen with a designer

Kitchen designers are a great resource if you can't zero in on what you want your new kitchen to look like or if you don't know what your design options are. Deciding to remodel your kitchen is easy, but finding the right combination of materials, appliances, colors, and designs can be overwhelming. Thankfully that's what a certified kitchen designer is qualified to do.

Most designers are willing to do as much or as little as you choose. You hire them as consultants and advisors, so you're the one who determines just how much they'll do. I've known people who hired designers for just a couple of hours, simply to help them find a direction for their remodeling project. I also know of couples that had a kitchen designer do everything from designing the kitchen to shopping for and purchasing all of the new items. Paying for all those services wasn't cheap (designers charge from around $25 an hour and up, depending on their level of experience), but you should see the kitchens!

So, how do you find a good designer? Word of mouth is a good starting point, especially if you know someone who just had his kitchen redesigned and remodeled by a designer and you like the finished product. Another way to find a local designer is to check the National Kitchen and Bath Association (NKBA) Web site at www.nkba.org.

Look for a designer who is a Certified member of the NKBA. This is the top professional organization for kitchen and bath designers. That way, you're more likely to be working with a designer who understands the real concerns and problems that plague poorly designed kitchens.

Asking an architect for assistance

If your kitchen remodel involves structural changes — like if you want to move a wall or install a new doorway or skylight (as shown in the color insert) — consult an architect or a qualified contractor who knows how to determine if beams and load-bearing walls are designed properly. They can also provide drawings and materials specifications so that your city's building inspector will approve your proposed plan.

When searching for an architect, look for one who is certified by the American Institute of Architects (AIA) — the top professional organization for architects. Consider the architect's years of experience, too. Most contractors I know use architects who have at least five years of experience. That number isn't set in stone, but my contacts seem to agree on it.

Letting a general contractor make your project easier

A *general contractor* is the person who makes sure that qualified tradespeople (subcontractors or *subs*) are hired, that all the materials are ordered and scheduled for delivery at the right time during the construction process, and that oversees the day-to-day work on the project. The general contractor also sees that the subs (electricians, plumbers, carpenters, and so on) get paid. Find yourself a good general contractor and what you won't notice are problems, delays, and headaches. She'll handle all the details for you.

If you have a lead on a general contractor but can't get to see or talk with her for a week or two, don't be discouraged. In fact, you should be encouraged. Good contractors are busy and should have people (and jobs) waiting to bid for their services. However, be wary of any contractor who doesn't show up for a scheduled appointment. If the contractor has a good reason for missing one appointment, okay. But if she misses a second one, especially for the same or a similar reason, consider hiring someone else. If you put up with unprofessional behavior from the start, you're only asking for continued troubles.

Many DIYers act as their own general contractors, but doing so takes a lot of time and can be a real nightmare. Consider this decision carefully before choosing to be your own general contractor.

Contracting a Professional

You may find yourself having to contract a professional (or *contractor*) for all or part of the kitchen remodeling. Hiring someone may seem like a daunting task — especially if you've never hired anyone before — but in the following sections, I give you some pointers to help you find an experienced and legitimate contractor.

The earlier you recognize that you need professional help the better. You can always call in a pro if you run into trouble on a project, but if you do bring someone into the project after the start, you may have to pay a little extra for his services, because he'll have to work you into an already busy schedule. But if you're willing to wait or be flexible with scheduling, you may find that you really won't have to pay too much extra.

Also, if you need to call a pro to fix a mistake you've made, be ready to pay for it! Mistakes often mean removing work or even demolishing back to square one (although hopefully not). Besides the added price of the additional new materials, you'll have to pay labor costs for both the removal of the old and installation of the new.

Putting out an APB

So, where do you start? Word-of-mouth recommendations and referrals are good places to begin. If a neighbor, friend, or relative hired a pro and they were pleased with the results, you should feel confident in at least talking with that contractor. Another good resource is your local home center — look into the contractors who subcontract for the store-offered installation services. You can also check with your bank when you're looking into financing. Bank officers shouldn't recommend any one contractor, but they usually can provide you with a list of names. Also, many contractors place ads in the newspaper, but be sure to ask for and check their references.

Interviewing the prospects

After you've narrowed the field, you need to ask your candidates some hard questions. Don't be afraid to really push them (in a civilized way!) for the answers to your questions. Remember the old adage, "There's no such thing as a dumb question." Well, that statement really holds true here. So, what questions should you ask? Here's a list to get you started:

✔ **How long have you been in the business?** Look for a contractor who has been around for at least five years. These folks should have an established business history, plus they've weathered both the good and the bad economic times. That says a lot in today's tough remodeling climate.

✔ **How many kitchen-remodeling jobs have you done in the last year?** Just because a person is a remodeling contractor doesn't mean she's experienced in remodeling kitchens. Hiring a contractor who's familiar with kitchen remodeling means he's more likely to be up on current trends, designs, colors, and so on.

✔ **Do you get a lot of repeat business or referral clients?** Good contractors often get a sizeable amount of their work from past clients. Speaking of past clients, ask whether you can have a list of names of some of their past clients. If the contractor hesitates or the "list" has only one or two names, be a bit wary. A reputable contractor should offer at least a half dozen or so names to choose from.

✔ **Can I visit one of your current job sites?** This provides you with a first-hand look at how they operate. You'll see things, such as how neat they are and how much space they take up versus what you think they actually need. Keep in mind, however, that no two jobsites are the same as you come to your conclusions.

✔ **Are you a member of a professional organization or association?** Contractors who are members of reputable associations and professional organizations usually do a good job. After all, none of the big-name associations want their reputation damaged by fly-by-night operations.

TIP

The National Association of Home Builders (NAHB) and the National Association of the Remodeling Industry (NARI) are two of the largest professional associations for the home construction and remodeling industries. Both have Web sites (and www.nari.org) and have local or regional offices where you can find help in your contractor search.

✔ **How long do you think the job will take?** You may not get a firm answer, but the contractor should be able to provide a reasonable estimate. If the time frame seems too short, check with a past client or two on the quality of work. Did they work so fast that quality suffered? On the other hand, if the estimate seems too long you may want to find out what their daily schedule is like. Find out what time they start in the morning and finish up in the afternoon. Late starts and early quitting times will extend the end-date of the project, which inconveniences you for a longer period. Find out whether they work weekends and, if so, whether it costs you more money. If you want the job done more quickly and want them to work six days a week rather than five, you should be ready to pay more for hourly labor.

✔ **Do you carry worker's compensation and liability insurance?** I can't stress enough how important it is that you ask this question and receive a "Yes" answer. If they answer "Yes," then ask for copies of both insurance policies to verify coverage. If the answer is "No," the interview should be over. If they don't have insurance and you hire them, they might get injured on the job, and guess who pays? You! Plus, you could end up in a courtroom battling over who's going to pay for the lost wages of the contractor injured on your property. Very simply put, if the contractor answers "No" to this question, you need to say "Good-bye" to the contractor.

Now that you know what to ask the contractors to find out about their history and work, it's time to start getting the numbers pulled together. The next section discusses costs for the projects and gives you some more specific questions to ask the potential contractors.

Getting three bids

Just as most people shop around for the best price on big-ticket items and even everyday stuff, so you also should shop around for your remodeling project's overall price. Get three bids on the project. Why three? Three bids help you identify potential problems, as well as get a good feel for what you're in for over the next several weeks, maybe months.

Be wary of the lowest bid. If, for example, two of the three bids are fairly close in price, say only a couple hundred dollars different, but the third bid is $3,000 or $4,000 lower, look out. Perhaps the low bidder's work standards are not very high, or he may be using cheap materials and products. Both of these possibilities will leave you very unhappy with the results.

Be sure that all three contractors work from the same materials and labor list. You want to compare apples to apples on the three bids. If you're only able to get two bids, spend some extra time examining and comparing them. Make sure that both bids cover the same work and materials. If you find some large or interesting differences, don't be afraid to question the contractors on how they came up with their estimate. They may have a different, yet legitimate way of doing something. Or, they could be completely off base. Either way, getting your questions answered will help you decide which contractor you want to hire.

Make sure that the contractor states in writing exactly what he will (and will *not*) do as part of the bid price. Everything from cleaning up at the end of the day to helping unload materials have been points of contention in remodeling projects that I'm familiar with. If something isn't in the written contract (which I discuss in the section "Getting It All on Paper: Drawing Up a Contract" later in this chapter), don't expect the contractor to do it just because you *think* that's part of their job.

Just ask my friend, Steve. After two days of accumulating debris from his home's new room addition and the contractor not throwing anything away, Steve asked when the garbage was going to be picked up. The contractor's response was that because that wasn't spelled out in the contract, the homeowner was responsible for getting a dumpster to the jobsite and that the homeowner was to do the cleanup at the end of each day. This sounds ridiculous, but it's true. Luckily for my friend, the dispute was resolved without bloodshed! All kidding aside, Steve and the contractor discussed the situation responsibly and came to an agreement that worked for both parties. Needless to say, that new agreement was put down in writing, as were any subsequent changes.

Avoid laboring over labor costs

Even if you're hiring a contractor, you can take on a few parts of a kitchen-remodeling project to reduce labor costs and also free up the contractor to take care of another job she's working on. And, actually, that's a good thing: If the contractor has to split her time between jobs less often, she'll complete both jobs more efficiently.

Demolition can be very manageable and a real cost-saver, so many homeowners love to tackle it. Besides, who doesn't like to destroy things? Just make sure that you have all of the necessary tools and equipment for both removing and hauling the debris to the dumpster. (See Chapter 5 for a list of the most common demolition tools and equipment.) And, check with your contractor about what and how something is to be demolished so that you do it correctly. Don't forget the safety gear, either. Spending an afternoon at the doctor's office after getting a wood shaving in your eye because you didn't have any safety glasses handy is one way to defeat the money-saving aspect of doing your own demolition.

Painting is another part of the project that you can handle and that really does save the

contractor time (and you money). Most painting projects need multiple coats of paint — priming and then applying the finish coat(s). And because most paints can be recoated within a couple of hours, you can speed up this part of the project because you're at the house and not traveling between jobs, like your contractor.

Installing the cabinets is another job that really is manageable. If you have a basic knowledge of carpentry and average to advanced DIY skills, installing cabinets shouldn't be a problem. Check out Chapter 9, too, for step-by-step instructions to help you through this part of the project.

You may be able to assist your contractor on some parts of the job, for example helping haul materials in and out or even holding up cabinets while they're being installed or pulling new electrical cable through open walls. They may even knock off a few bucks from the total project price for your time and effort. But if you get in the way or become a nuisance, be prepared to be "fired" from your assistant's job! No contractor wants to be slowed down by someone who means well but doesn't know what he's doing.

Getting It All on Paper: Drawing Up a Contract

If you're hiring professionals, you need to be sure that everyone is thinking, talking, and working on the same page; in other words, you need a signed contract. In fact, you should have a contract anytime you pay someone to do work on your home. I'm sure you've heard the term but do you really know what a contract is and how it helps you?

A *contract* is a legally binding document between you and another individual, in this case a contractor or subcontractor. It stipulates the work to be done, the amount to be paid for the work, and the various responsibilities that both you and the contractor must fulfill. You need a contract to ensure that all parties involved understand their obligations and to make sure that nothing is left open to an individual's interpretation. A contract gets everyone on the same page — both literally and figuratively. As the homeowner, the contract protects you against a dishonest contractor or one who does inferior work. A contract is also the best tool for settling disputes if things should happen to end up in court.

Anyone can draw up a contract for a remodeling project. You don't need to pay a lawyer. Standard blank contracts are available at office supply stores. You can use the actual form from the store or you can use it as a guide and revise it to meet your needs and desires. Be a bit wary if the contractor has a preprinted contract for you to sign. Unless you read every word or have it examined by a lawyer, you could be opening yourself up for current or possible future liability. Draw up the contract yourself.

A contract isn't binding until you get the specifics down on paper and both parties sign it. Never rely on a verbal contract. You and your contractor may have a very smooth working relationship, but no matter how much confidence you have in him, always put things in writing and make sure both of you sign. This is the best way to handle any problems that may arise. Be sure the contractor receives a signed copy.

Your contract must include certain statements (clauses) to be legally binding. Be sure your contract includes all of the following points.

✔ **Who's involved:** Your listing of who's who on the project. Make sure you have the contractor's name as well as the name of his business listed. You also need his address and telephone number(s).

If you're hiring a general contractor, then you'll only need one contract with her. It will be her responsibility to work out the work and payment schedule with the subcontractors. If, however, you're the general contractor, then you need to draw up contracts with each of the subcontractors that you hire.

✔ **What's involved:** This lists exactly what the contractor will and will *not* do. (Remember my example in the "Getting three bids" section of miscommunication over who would clean up every day!) This section should also answer the following questions:

- Is the plumber supplying the new kitchen fixtures or are you?

- Is the electrician supplying the light fixtures?

- Who's calling for or ordering the inspections?

- Who's ordering the appliances, cabinets, and so on?

- What brand(s) are acceptable?

- What brand(s) are not acceptable?

✔ **Cost:** Be specific as you detail what the project will cost to complete. Outline the payment schedule, including the initial payment date, the second payment date, and the final payment date.

Many contractors want 25 to 50 percent of the total payment up front to pay for materials, and so on. Never put more than 50 percent down on any remodeling project. A reputable contractor should be able to obtain sufficient operating capital to order and pay for most of the materials. A good guideline to follow is to put 30 percent down at the start and define additional payment amounts and dates within the contract, for example another 20 percent after the completion of the framing inspection.

✔ **Timetable:** Give the project firm starting and ending dates. These can be adjusted as needed, for example if material delivery is delayed. Just remember to get any changes in writing and have both parties sign off on the change.

✔ **Material and equipment:** Get a detailed list of all the materials, equipment, fixtures, and so on that are purchased. List the quantity, size, color, model, and brand for each item. This could be a long section, but these details will reduce the chance of confusion or error.

✔ **Change orders:** Changes are a part of every remodeling project — DIY or pro. If you change your mind about a product, design, or anything else, get the change written down on paper. If the contractor runs into an unforeseen problem — and believe me it happens — get the necessary change/repair in writing. Make sure that the contractor is not charging for "unforeseen problems" that should have been included. Get them to explain why something changed and ask why they didn't anticipate this if you think it's something that they should have known or anticipated. Describe all changes in detail, including materials, anticipated new completion date of the project, and additional charges. Make sure both you and the contractor sign all change orders.

✔ **Warranties:** A reputable contractor will usually guarantee workmanship and materials for one year. Some materials and products will carry a longer manufacturer's warranty; so hang onto the paperwork as documentation in the event of future problems.

✔ **Arbitration clause:** Even with a contract, disputes can arise. You can avoid having to go to court, however, if you include a binding arbitration clause. If you do find yourself needing arbitration, contact the American Arbitration Association (AAA), which is a non-profit organization that helps people organize arbitration. The AAA Web site (`www.adr.org`) has downloadable forms and links and information about regional offices and on-line filing.

✔ **Avoid paying twice:** A common and unfortunate problem when dealing with general contractors is that the money sometimes gets from the homeowner to the general contractor, but not to the subcontractors. When this happens, the subs can put a mechanic's lien against your property! Avoid this by including a clause stating that the final payment won't be made until you receive a lien-release form from the general contractor, all subcontractors, and each supplier. See the sidebar "Staying off the hook — Get a lien release form" for more details.

Dealing with the Day-to-Day during Construction

After you've hired your contractor, get used to having a lot of strangers in your home. They'll be there for the better part of days, weeks, or maybe months, so do your best to get along and to stay out of their way. Not that you can't ask questions, but just don't become a nuisance.

Most contractors like to get started early in the morning, usually before 7:30 a.m. They have tools and materials to get in order for the day's work and they don't like to have to spend their regular work time hours doing it. You may need to adjust your morning schedule, too. Most folks aren't very comfortable getting ready for work when the contractors are around. But, just keep telling yourself what a beautiful kitchen you'll have when the project is finished.

If you feel comfortable with your contractor, you could give him a key to your house. This is a personal decision, however, and should not be taken lightly.

I've done this a few times when I've had work done on my home and have had no problems. But, I did it only after getting to know the person and making sure that they were insured and bonded against loss.

Also, if you don't want contractors to be at the house on a specific day or days, let them know well in advance. My wife and I had guests coming to town for a long weekend and we asked the fellows that were doing a land-scape project not work while our guests were visiting. The contractor said it was no problem because we told him about the change three weeks in advance so that he could rearrange his work schedule. He was very grateful because he was able to schedule a smaller job in over those days.

Nearing the Finish Line

Just as people are different, so are their expectation and satisfaction levels. So, as your project nears completion, you need to begin the process of examining the work of the contractors. You'll find it much easier to get things corrected, repaired, or, if necessary, changed while the contractors are still on-site on a regular basis. And most contractors want to correct things during this time, too. They hate returning to a job, especially to fix minor problems. These return trips or *callbacks* cost the contractor money because they're usually dealing with things that weren't part of the original contract and price, but they are things that need to be corrected.

Developing a punch list

While you're examining the work on the project, you need to write down the things you have questions about and the items that you feel need to be repaired or changed. The list of corrections is called a *punch list*. After you and the contractor agree on it, you'll both use the punch list to verify and ensure that the agreed upon tasks are completed. Don't feel like you're causing the contractor undue pressure or problems, either. A good contractor is very familiar with a punch list and wants to take care of the items as soon as possible. Remember, they won't get their final payment until everything's the way you want it, right?

Final sign-offs

Everyone involved is happy to participate in the final sign-off. Think of it in the same way as you thought of making the final walk-through in your house, just before you closed on the sale. This really is the last chance to bring problems to everyone's attention; however, the punch list should have taken care of most of it.

Everyone should get signed copies of the fulfilled contract. Both you and the contractor will want these for your records. Keep all other documents (lien-release forms, receipts, inspection reports, architectural drawings, and so on) with the contract, in the event of future problems or disputes.

Staying off the hook! Get a lien-release form

If a subcontractor or material supplier doesn't receive payment from the general contractor for her services or materials, she can bring a legal claim against your property by filing a mechanic's lien. If you have a lien against your home, you can't sell your house and you probably won't be able to secure financing until the lien is satisfied or the dispute is resolved.

The best way to avoid this problem is by adding a lien-release clause to the contract, mentioned in the section "Getting It All on Paper: Drawing Up a Contract". Whenever payment is made for services or materials, have the contractor or supplier sign a lien-release form. Notarizing the signed form is best, but if you can't get it notarized, just be sure to get the signatures of all parties involved.

Don't be surprised if you end up with quite a few forms for your records. Even a small payment for services or materials should have a lien-release form, which could mean dozens of receipts. Why should you get a lien-release form for every transaction? I've seen mechanic's liens for $100 and even as little as $50 filed against a homeowner. Both were the fault of the general contractor but the homeowner had to deal with the hassle and eventually pay for the materials a second time.

If you are served with a lien, don't go nuts. Most contractors don't want to file a lien, so their claim may be legitimate. Check your receipts to see whether you paid or not. Payments do slip through the cracks, so you may just need to pay up and then everyone should be happy.

Part II

Gettin' Down and Dirty: Preparing Your Kitchen for Greatness

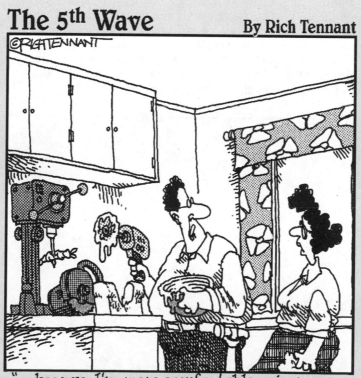

The 5th Wave   By Rich Tennant

"...because I'm more comfortable using my own tools. Now—how much longer do you want me to sand the cake batter?"

In this part . . .

This part explains what tools you need to buy and to rent to perform a successful kitchen remodel. And once you have the tools in hand, I show you how to take your kitchen apart so that you can start your remodeling project. Finally, I go over how to check and upgrade your plumbing, electrical, and ventilation systems.

Chapter 5

You Can't Have Tool Much of a Good Thing

In This Chapter

▶ Being safe

▶ Buying into quality

▶ Figuring out what tools to buy

▶ Looking into rentals

*W*ouldn't it be great if everyone had a fully stocked tool collection within reach? You could just walk over to the tool chest, grab what you need, and head back to continue on with your project, without ever having to go down to the hardware store. Okay, this is a fantasy of mine and possibly yours, too. (I'm still waiting for the "tool fairy" to visit my shop!) But whether you're an experienced do-it-yourselfer or an absolute novice at home-improvement projects, you need the right tools to make the job easier, faster, and safer.

You can find hundreds of tools available at hardware stores or home centers — which ones do you absolutely need and which ones do you need but realistically can't afford to purchase? In this chapter, I describe just about every tool you need for a kitchen remodeling and help you sort out which ones to buy and which ones you can rent.

Safety First

A pro football player doesn't ever play a game without his shoulder pads, and you never see a racecar driver start a race without strapping on her helmet and safety belts. The same is true for you if you're going to tear out your old kitchen and build a new one. To protect yourself, you need to use the appropriate safety gear. Here's a look at what you need to keep yourself safe.

Eye protection

Your sight is precious and you should take every precaution to protect it: never start a project without eye protection close by! I've seen (no pun intended) several instances where a pair of safety glasses has been the only thing that prevented a serious eye injury to someone on a construction site.

Types of eye protection include:

- **Safety glasses:** For most construction work, safety glasses are the popular choice. They fit like regular eye wear and many styles actually fit over your glasses, if you wear glasses. A good pair of safety glasses has adjustable bows that allow you to size the length of the bow to fit comfortably behind your ear. An ill-fitting pair of safety glasses don't protect you sufficiently, plus you're less likely to wear them if they're uncomfortable or don't fit properly.

- **Safety goggles:** Safety goggles are most often used when working with liquids when splashing is likely to occur. If you do go with goggles, make sure they have small vent holes on both sides to prevent fogging. If you wear glasses, goggles probably aren't your best choice; they usually fit awkwardly over the glasses and make you uncomfortable, in which case you probably won't want to wear them. And because they don't fit all that well, there isn't a tight seal for maximum protection.

Safety glasses or safety goggles are relatively inexpensive. Basic models, which provide adequate protection for most situations, sell for under $10 — a small price to pay for preserving your eyesight.

Gloves

Besides keeping your hands free of splinters and cuts, gloves provide some protection in the event of a banged or pinched hand.

- **Heavy-duty gloves:** A pair of heavy work gloves is a must. In fact, I recommend getting two pairs of heavy-duty leather gloves, so you always have a pair to wear when you accidentally misplace one of the gloves. For more comfort, I also recommend gloves that are lined because the lining keeps the seams from rubbing your hands and causing blisters and it keeps perspiration in check.

  Prices for work gloves vary widely. Unlined leather gloves can cost only a couple of dollars a pair, while kid or calfskin lined gloves can cost over $20. You'll find a wide selection of heavy-duty gloves at most home centers, usually near the outdoor hand tools section.

- **Lightweight gloves:** Get several pairs of cotton or jersey work gloves. These gloves are thinner and make it easier to pick things up. Some of the newer cotton work gloves have sticky dots on the fingers and palms that help you grip items. You'll find these gloves at many home centers and stores that sell work clothes. Regular cotton gloves sell for around $2 to $3 pair. The sticky-dot types sell for $4 to $5 a pair, but they're also made of heavier material.

Masks

A kitchen remodel (especially the demolition) creates dust, dirt, and debris — all things you don't want in your lungs. Two kinds of masks help keep you healthy:

✔ **Dust mask:** The best way to protect yourself is with a *dust mask*. These are cotton fiber devices that fit over your nose and mouth to filter out dust and dirt. I recommend getting a mask with a small, narrow metal band that goes across your nose for a better fit. These masks typically sell for around $5 for three.

✔ **Filtering mask:** If you're going to be working with materials where fumes could be a problem, such as paint stripper, invest in a *filtering mask*. These masks have one or two filtering cartridges that stop fumes. The cartridges do vary on what they filter so read the label and buy the one that suits your situation. You can find filtering masks at most home centers, hardware stores, and safety equipment retailers (check the Yellow Pages under "Safety Equipment" to find a retailer near you). Filtering mask prices start around $25 for a mask and one set of filter cartridges. Commonly used types of replacement cartridges sell for between $10 and $30, depending on what they're designed to filter.

Dumpster dos and don'ts

When you rent a dumpster, keep these things in mind.

✔ Do be prepared to let your rental company know what type of debris you're dumping. General construction debris, such as lumber, plywood, roofing shingles, and so on, is usually accepted without any additional charges. Some landfills may charge an additional fee if you need to dispose of treated lumber or old carpet.

✔ Do your best to schedule dumpster delivery and pick up when you'll get the most use out of it for your money. Most rental companies require a two-week minimum for dumpster rental (check with your individual hauler for their specific terms). This gives you a reasonable amount of time. But if things take longer, most companies will let you keep the dumpster for as long as you need it, charging for each additional week.

✔ Don't wait until the last minute to order a dumpster. You'd be amazed how long you may have to wait to get one delivered to your house, especially with the construction boom of the past few years.

You Get What You Pay for

Don't skimp on price when purchasing tools. Cheap tools usually mean less than satisfactory results and sometimes even cause damage or — worse yet — injury. Remember that you're going to spend a certain amount of money to purchase any tool, so spend the extra 10 to 20 percent (if your budget allows) for the quality tools.

Ripping Your Kitchen Apart with Demolition Tools

Have you ever wondered what it would be like to take a sledgehammer to a set of kitchen cabinets? Or how about tearing apart and ripping up that old, scarred and marred countertop? With the right tools and, most importantly, the right safety gear (described in the "Safety First" section earlier in this chapter), most folks can handle the demolition part of a kitchen remodel — and have some fun doing it, too!

Smashing and tearing tools

Visit most any construction or remodeling worksite and you're likely to find any or all of the next few tools being put to hard, aggressive use. These are the tools that really let you vent:

- **Sledgehammer:** You can tell sledgehammers apart by the weight of the head, which really makes a difference in ability to dislodge things. If you plan to buy a sledgehammer, be sure it has an 8 pound head. An 8-pound sledgehammer sells for around $15. It's usually attached to a 32-inch-long handle and breaks through wall surfaces, dislodges seemingly permanent cabinets, and manages to persuade other unmovable objects to let loose with a couple of solid whacks. Be sure to get a sledgehammer with a plastic or composite handle. They're more durable than wood and can handle the inevitable *over-strike* (that's when you miss the target with the steel head and hit the object with the handle, just below the head).

- **Three-pound maul:** This little beauty gives you the power of the sledgehammer, but only has a 12-inch-long handle so it's great for tight spaces. Besides using it for demolition, you can also use it for striking a cold chisel if you're doing mortar or brick work.

- **Crowbar:** A *crowbar* is a length of steel that's your best friend when it's time to move or lift an object to get a better grip. Crowbars or wrecking bars have a curve at one end and are flat at the other. The curved end has two smaller flattened pieces, sort of like wings, with a notch in the center for pulling nails from lumber. The flattened end is used to wedge between materials to be pried loose. Crowbars come in varying lengths ranging from 24 inches to almost 5 feet long. Most homeowners can get by with one that's between 30 and 36 inches long.

✔ **Pry bar:** Not every part of a demolition requires the force or leverage created with a crowbar. These are the times to be glad you have a pry bar on hand. A *pry bar* is similar in design to a crowbar: One end is flat but the top or head is bent at a 90-degree angle to the body of the bar. This angle lets you gain full leverage without having to struggle with a 3-foot-long piece of steel. Pry bars are usually about 12 inches long. A pry bar is the right tool, for example, for getting a countertop to break loose from the cabinets or for removing baseboards or trim around doors and windows.

✔ **Cat's paw:** Before you use either a crowbar or a pry bar, you need to remove the nails that are holding things together. A *cat's paw* is an 8-inch-long steel tool with a curved, notched end for digging into wood and getting nails started out. You set the notched end of the cat's paw just behind the nail's head, strike the cat's paw on the curve with a hammer, and then pull the nail. Without a cat's paw, you spend too much time fighting with nails.

Hauling and holding equipment

So, what do you do with all of the debris after it's been ripped up? Haul it out and put it into a receptacle of some kind. Here's what the pro's use:

✔ **Wheelbarrow:** A good, heavy-duty wheelbarrow is a must for any type of demolition job. You want one with tall, steeply sloped sides. Don't buy or rent a garden-style wheelbarrow for demolition work. Its sides are very short and generally relatively flat which allows debris to easily fall or bounce out of the bucket when you're hauling.

A *contractor's wheelbarrow* is the best choice. It has a heavy steel bucket and is usually about 5 cubic feet in capacity. Make sure the tire is a pneumatic type (one that needs air) and not a solid rubber tire. A pneumatic tire rolls more easily, especially on rough surfaces and terrain, which is usually what you're dealing with in construction. You should expect to pay around $100 (or more) for a contractor's wheelbarrow. Most home centers carry them, but you may have to ask for them because of the higher price — they're not the ones that are pitched in the sale's catalogs and flyers.

✔ **Dumpster:** Okay, no one's probably going to own or buy a dumpster. But it is a critical piece of equipment, necessary for keeping the work area in order. (I discuss other tools you can rent later in this chapter.)

A dumpster or construction container can be rented from a couple of different sources. Some companies specialize in delivering and picking up dumpsters. However, check with your garbage hauling company, too. Many of them rent dumpsters.

Charges start somewhere around $150 for a smaller dumpster (usually a 2- to 4-cubic-footer). The dumpster sizes range from 2- to 50-cubic-yard boxes. Most companies are able to help you select the size best suited for your project. Shop around, too, for the best price and don't be afraid to ask for references from previous customers. For more tips on dumpster rental, check out the "Dumpster dos and don'ts" sidebar.

Power Shopping for Tools

Every homeowner — whether getting into a remodeling project or not — should own a basic array of carpentry and power tools. These tools not only help you complete your kitchen remodel but are invaluable for tackling those inevitable home-repair projects in your future.

So, what should you already own or add to your tool selection? Let's take a look.

Hammers

Notice that the heading for this section is plural — hammers. Now you might say, "Come on, a hammer's a hammer, right?" Nope. There are different weights, claw designs, and handle materials. Besides, hammers aren't expensive, which makes it easier to justify owning several. I have no connection with any of the hammer manufacturers, so I'm not trying to drive up hammer sales. However, I'd recommend that your tool collection have three different size hammers: A 13-ounce hammer for lightweight construction and projects like hanging pictures in the kitchen after you finish up the walls, a 16-ounce hammer for general purpose construction, such as a kitchen remodel, and finally, a good-quality 20-ounce hammer if you're going to be tackling some heavy-duty projects like wall framing. Prices for the various sizes range from around $20 for the 13-ounce hammers, between $25 and $35 for a 16-ounce model and all the way up to $45 or $50 for a 20-ounce hammer.

For this project the main hammer I recommend is a 16-ounce hammer, with a straight claw and a wood or fiberglass handle because it's heavy enough to provide adequate force when swung, yet it won't tire you out too quickly or make your forearms bulk up like Popeye's. A straight claw or framing hammer is easier to maneuver in tight spaces than a curved claw hammer. And finally, both the wood and the fiberglass handles are durable enough to withstand the use (and moderate abuse) that they're going to see during this project. A fiberglass handle isn't as heavy as its wooden counterpart, plus fiberglass is more durable. Both types are priced in the $25 to $35 range.

Nailing things down — Understanding nail terminology

When someone says you need an 8-penny nail or a 16d nail, do you simply nod your head pretending to know what they're talking about because you don't want to appear stupid? Well, you're not stupid — and you're not alone! Nail terminology is thrown around like everyday conversation, but could use a little explanation. The "d" in a nail's size actually originated in Roman times and the coin called a *denarius*, relating to the cost of a specific size nail per 100

nails — an 8d nail cost 8 denaria per 100, a 10d nail cost 10 denaria per 100, and so on. Today, however, the "d" refers to a nail's length. Here are the most commonly used nails and their corresponding length in inches: 3d — 1¼-inch; 4d — 1½-inch; 6d — 2-inch; 8d — 2½-inch; 10d — 3-inch; 16d — 3½-inch; 20d — 4-inch; and 60d — 6-inch. 60d nails are often referred to as *spikes* or *pole barn nails* and used most often in landscaping projects.

The best way to select the hammer that's right for you is to pick it up, swing it, and see how it feels in your hand. Make sure the handle's diameter isn't too big for your hand and that its shape (contour) is comfortable. Also check out the length. The heavier the head, the longer the handle. Why? A heavier hammer is generally used for more heavy-duty projects and you want more momentum and force behind each swing. A longer handle provides more momentum than a shorter handled hammer.

Handsaws

When you need to make a few quick, accurate cuts in wood, a handsaw is the best way to go. It's not only fast (just pick it up and cut — no cord or power supply to worry about), but you have pinpoint accuracy on starting each cut. But with all the sizes and types available, how do you choose? I help guide you to the right one:

- **Crosscut saw:** As its name implies, the *crosscut saw* is used for cutting wood across the grain. The tooth design uses alternate teeth that go in opposite directions with the edge of each tooth cutting through the wood fibers. The number of teeth per inch of blade length is also important. The more teeth per inch, the finer the cut. An 8-point (8 teeth per inch) saw doesn't have as fine of a cut as a 12-point (12 teeth per inch) saw. For general construction use, an 8-point crosscut saw is an excellent choice.

- **Ripsaw:** A *ripsaw* is designed to cut wood in the direction of, or with, the grain. Cutting with the grain is call *ripping*, hence the name ripsaw. A ripsaw's teeth are straight across on the bottom and actually work like a chisel and push out small chips of wood.

If you own a circular saw, you don't need a rip handsaw. Ripping lumber is slower than crosscutting and a powered circular saw is the best way to go if you need to rip. (See the section "Circular saw" later in this chapter.)

✔ **Compass, keyhole, or drywall saw:** This is one type of saw (with three different names) that you can use again and again. You'll be glad you own one, especially if you're going to be cutting holes in drywall. They're not very expensive, either, so go ahead and treat yourself to this inexpensive timesaver.

✔ **Coping saw:** If you plan to install the trim work along the baseboards and around the doors and windows, you need a *coping saw*. This fine-toothed, thin-bladed wonder lets you trim and cut delicate patterns and curves in wood. Using a coping saw well, however, does take some practice. Plan to spend some time playing with it on scrap trim pieces. I gained my best experience on using a coping saw by spending three hours just trying to cut corner pieces and match *miters* (the two 45-degree cuts that form a 90-degree corner when put together). I still use this technique around my home.

Circular saw

A circular saw is the carpenter's best friend; you always see it at her side or at least within quick reach. A *circular saw* lets you crosscut or rip lumber and plywood and even, with the changing of the blade, lets you cut into concrete.

Picking a saw

The most popular size saw is called a 7¼ inch because it uses a 7¼-inch diameter blade. This size blade lets you cut through a 2-inch thick piece of lumber in one pass with the blade set at a 90-degree angle. The maximum cutting depth at a 45-degree angle is 1¾-inches.

Every circular saw that I've ever seen (or used) has an adjustable baseplate for cutting angles, a retractable blade guard (required by law), and a side discharge chute to keep chips and sawdust from blowing back on you.

Because you'll use this tool for years, spend the most you can afford to get the best saw. Go for a heavy-duty or professional-grade model that feels comfortable in your hand. I recommend a heavy-duty model because they operate more smoothly and are less likely to bog or kick back. A good quality, 7¼-inch electric circular saw runs between $125 and $175. That may seem like a lot of money for a saw, but you should expect this one-time purchase to last a lifetime. If you want to spend $50 or less, expect to replace the saw after a year or two.

Choosing blades

Words and terminology for blades are tossed around with little or no explanation and you're simply expected to understand what you're buying. And choosing the right blade can seem somewhat intimidating because of all your choices. Most well-stocked tool departments have a blade chart to help with any last-minute questions. Knowing what type of material you'll be cutting is key to purchasing the correct blade.

As a general rule, I'd advise staying away from really cheap blades. First off, you can never be sure about the quality of manufacturing. And, second, cheap blades dull quickly and you spend more time changing blades than cutting. Okay, not really, but it sure seems like it.

Here's what you have to look out for when picking out blades:

- **Carbide or steel?** Circular saw blades are made of either high-speed steel or steel with brazed-on tungsten carbide tips on each tooth. The latter are called *carbide-tipped* or *carbide blades.*

  - **Carbide blades** are best when you're cutting rough lumber, such as 2-inch thick materials, wood posts, and timbers. Use a carbide blade if you're cutting materials such as plywood, hardboard, particleboard, or wafer board. The glues used in these types of wood sheet goods quickly dull a steel blade. Carbide blades cost more than steel blades, but they stay sharper longer — up to 50 times longer, according to blade industry tests. They last so long that most homeowners never have to have them resharpened.

  - **A steel blade** is the blade to use when cutting veneered material. It's also a good choice if you're cutting through rough material like shingles. Yes, it will dull after awhile, but it's cheap enough that you won't feel too bad throwing it away and buying a new one.

- **How many teeth?** The number of teeth determines the type of cut you get. For most folks, a 16- to 20-tooth combination saw blade is adequate. This type of blade can be used for either crosscuts or rips and gives you a fairly smooth cut. A 40-tooth blade is recommended for smoother cuts. And a 60-tooth plywood blade gives you the smoothest cuts. It's best for ripping and cutting fine finish materials, such as plywood.

For splinter-free results, always place the good side of the material face down when cutting.

- **What angle?** Tooth angle varies, depending on the type of cutting the blade is designed to do. The general-purpose combination blades as well as smooth-cut plywood blades have teeth, which are angled forward slightly. This forward angle of the tooth, along with a beveled and pointed carbide tip, allows the blade to be aggressive in its cutting ability.

✔ **Prevent kickback?** The anti-kickback design is intended to prevent the saw from kicking back if it binds in the material you're cutting. The price for this type of blade is not much more than a standard blade, so pay the little bit extra for the added safety.

✔ **How wide a cut?** For general-purpose use, a thin kerf blade is a good choice. The *kerf* is the width of the cut left by the blade after the cut; it's the width of the material removed by the blade. Thin kerf blades are usually ⅟₁₆ inch thick.

If you know you're going to be cutting through lumber that's been nailed together, then your saw blade may encounter a nail or two when cutting. For this type of job, use a nail-cutting blade. The teeth on this type of blade are angled backward and each tooth's carbide tip is flat and square. This tip shape doesn't chip as easily as an angled tip does when it hits a nail. They also don't dull as rapidly. A nail-cutting blade cuts slower and leaves a rougher edge than a combination blade. It will, however, last longer when cutting through nail-embedded lumber.

Screwdrivers

Here's one category of tools where too much is never enough. I must have three or four of each size, both Phillips and straight-tipped *(slotted)*. Yet even so, I still find myself scrounging and searching through toolboxes and drawers looking for the right one. Here's some advice to help you in your screwdriver scrounging and searching.

For kitchen-remodeling projects, you need both slotted and Phillips screwdrivers:

✔ **Slotted screwdrivers:** These are available with varying tip sizes, ranging from short and narrow to wider and thicker. Slotted screws are often used for joining wood pieces together.

✔ **Phillips screwdrivers:** These come in number sizes: No. 1 (small), No. 2 (standard or medium), and No. 3 (heavy-duty). Phillips-head screws are common on electrical components, as well as on drywall screws and cabinet hardware (hinges, knobs, and pulls).

You find the best deals if you buy a screwdriver set. Manufacturers do a pretty good job of packaging what consumers actually want and need when it comes to screwdrivers. And, the sets are surprisingly inexpensive when compared to other hand tools. Just keep your eyes open for tool sales or specials. You just might find yourself picking up a couple sets of each type: Phillips and slotted.

If you don't buy a complete set of screwdrivers, then at least get a medium-sized slotted and a No. 2 Phillips. These two screwdrivers allow you to do most basic screw-driving tasks. You also want a couple screwdrivers with a rubber coating or sleeve over the handle that protects the user from electrical currents. These are called *insulated screwdrivers* and are used for electrical work, such as replacing a light switch or installing a light fixture. Most homeowners only need a couple of insulated screwdrivers: A No. 2 Phillips and a medium-sized slotted.

Use screwdrivers wisely. Here are a couple of tips:

✔ Be sure to use the correct size screwdriver for the job. Using the incorrect size screwdriver is frustrating. It takes you longer to complete the task and sometimes you damage the screw head to the point where you can no longer use it. You also stand a good chance of damaging whatever you're working on because a screwdriver tip that's too big or too small doesn't grip the screwhead properly and your screwdriver may slip out and gouge your project.

✔ Never use a screwdriver for anything but driving or removing screws. It's not a chisel and it's not a pry bar. Always remember this rule for your safety and for the best results: Use the right tool for the job.

Pliers

This may be the most widely used tool in anyone's home. There are three commonly used types of pliers you need to have on hand:

✔ **Slip joint:** Used for everything from twisting in screw hooks and eyes to holding a nut while tightening a bolt on the other side.

✔ **Groove joint or channel-type:** Used most often when the fastening nut is really large, for example on a kitchen drain.

✔ **Locking:** Used when you need a nut held really tight and don't want any slippage. Locking pliers have an adjustment nut that allows for fine-tuning of the jaw spread for gripping and holding capacity and strength.

Measuring and marking tools

You should have certain tools that allow you to take accurate measurements, mark surfaces for the installation, and then fit things together later. Here are the tools that I use all the time:

✔ **Tape measure:** Retractable tape rules come in lengths from pocket-size 8 footers to store-in-your-tool belt 30 footers with widths as narrow as ¼ inch to the heavy-duty models with a 1-inch-wide blade. Here's one time when bigger truly is better.

My advice is to buy a 30-foot tape rule. This length handles most dimensions to be measured in a kitchen remodel, plus this long of a rule has a 1-inch-wide blade. A wider blade is more stable and less likely to bend or twist when it's being extended. This is especially helpful if you're working alone. This size tape costs around $20. You can also find wider blade models (1¼-inch wide blade) for more rigidity and less flex. These sell for between $25 and $30, depending on the length.

✔ **Compass:** Not everyone keeps one in his toolbox, but everyone should. A compass is used for measuring the gap between surfaces when it's time to scribe materials against another surface, for example getting the end of a countertop to fit snuggly and evenly into a corner. (Chapter 11 explains this installation step in detail.)

✔ **Chalk line or chalk reel:** Everyone should also own a chalk line or chalk reel. It's a spool of cotton string (usually about 50-feet long) that's wound inside of a container, which holds powdered chalk. To use the chalk line, simply pull the chalk-coated string out of the housing, position and stretch the string taut between two points, and then lift it and let it snap down against the surface — this leaves a sharp line of chalk on the material surface. A chalk reel will cost around $10. An extra container of chalk costs around $3.

Levels

Every home improver needs a level. Whether you're hanging a picture or hanging cabinets, a good level is the best way to keep things straight — literally! Most homeowners choose a 2-foot or a 4-foot carpenter's level. A 2-foot model works for most projects, including a kitchen remodel. However, if you're going to be framing walls, a 4-foot level is a better choice as it gives a more accurate reading for larger projects. A 4-foot level is also better for lying across the base cabinets to check for level before you install the countertop. More on that in Chapter 11.

When it comes to levels, prices vary widely and not because one's twice as long as the other. The material that the level is made of determines whether you spend a little or a lot of money:

✔ **Aluminum:** Aluminum levels are the least expensive. A 2-foot aluminum, I-beam design level starts at around $20.

✔ **Fiberglass:** Fiberglass models are moderately priced (about the same as an aluminum model) and just as durable as an aluminum level.

✔ **Wood:** Wood levels are the most expensive and are the type that you really take care of and even pass down to your next generation. A top of the line 4-foot wood level runs close to $200.

Clamps

Here's a quick look at the clamps you need to make your remodeling project easier (check out Figure 5-1 for a visual of each):

- **C-clamps:** The very first clamps I owned were the same type that most people start out with — the good, old reliable C-clamp. They're completely adjustable and do a good job of keeping things clamped together — and they're affordable!

- **Squeeze-style bar clamps:** They've been around for about 15 years now and really set the clamping and holding world on its ear when they came out. Squeeze-style bar clamps adjust in clamping capacity from almost 5 feet to virtually nothing, depending on their size. They're easy to use and they really hold tight. They also come with padded jaws so you don't have to worry about marring surfaces. Plan on buying at least two clamps, but you probably want four or more. 12-inch or 18-inch models (which have a clamping range of 7½ to almost 27 inches) are adequate for a kitchen remodel. You can find squeeze clamps under brand names of Quick-Grip, Jorgensen, and Sears Craftsman. Prices start around $24 for a 12-inch clamp and go up, depending on size.

- **Spring-action clamps:** Everyone, and I mean everyone, who plans to remodel a kitchen needs at least six spring-action clamps. These are easy to open and use and really hold tight for temporary-holding situations. Spring clamps come in a variety of sizes with the most popular being the 6- and 9-inch models. Prices for any size are under $10 each with the smaller 4-inch versions selling for under $3. It's a lot of clamp for very little money. Invest in several of these — you'll be glad you did.

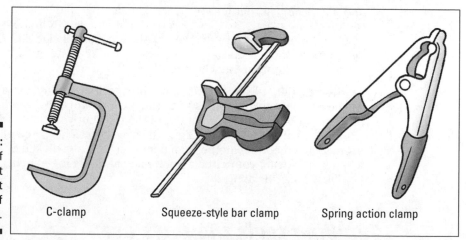

Figure 5-1:
Three of the most important types of clamps.

C-clamp   Squeeze-style bar clamp   Spring action clamp

Power drills

Just as every carpenter has a circular saw, they also have at least one and probably two or more power drills. Besides using a drill to bore holes in wood and metal, you can use it to drive screws — and even to mix paint with the correct attachment! The big decisions you need to make regarding drills involve capacity, voltage, and power source.

So, which type do you choose, especially if you don't own a drill? I guess I'd opt for a cordless, ½-inch model, which has the freedom of being cordless, plus the capacity to do larger drilling projects. A 14.4-volt or even a 12-volt cordless drill provides all the power you need for a kitchen remodel. Make sure that you buy two batteries for your drill. Some come with two but you can also buy a second battery separately. Expect to spend at least $100 and probably more like $140 to $175 for a 12- or 14.4-volt drill with two batteries. The brand to buy depends on your personal preference. Suffice it to say, my drills are either bright yellow (DeWalt) or bright red (Milwaukee).

A couple more things to have on hand

After you purchase some tools, you need a way to conveniently and easily get them from your shop or garage to the kitchen. And you'll soon find that you're always looking for a place to lay a piece of lumber so that you can cut it or somewhere to set a sheet of plywood to measure. Here are a couple of things that can make your life easier:

- **Toolboxes:** I recommend several smaller toolboxes with similar tools grouped together. For example, I have one toolbox for my screwdrivers and pliers and another for my measuring and marking tools. All of my toolboxes are plastic, so they're lightweight and easy to handle. They're also all the same color, so to avoid confusion, I simply labeled each box with a piece of duct tape and a permanent marker. One quick glance and I know which tools are in which toolbox.

- **Sawhorses:** Get at least one set of sawhorses. Two folding metal sawhorses only cost about $20 and they're well worth it. They're designed to be used as-is, right out of the box, but you can (and should) cut a length of 2 x 6 to fit the top of the sawhorse. This piece of lumber protects the metal sawhorse from being accidentally nicked or cut into when you're using your circular saw. Instead of the metal being cut, the 2 x 6 is the sacrificial piece.

Plumbing tools the pro's use

There are a number of tools that professional plumbers find necessary (for more on plumbing basics see Chapter 7). And I think it's only right that you know what these tools are so that you can decide whether to add them to your toolbox. You may find that having them makes your kitchen remodel and future improvement and repair projects more tolerable:

- ✔ **Adjustable wrench:** An adjustable wrench is handy to have because its movable jaw lets you use one tool to fit around a wide size range of nuts and bolt heads. Most plumbers have two or three different size adjustable wrenches in their toolboxes.

- ✔ **Basin wrench:** If you've ever crawled under your kitchen sink and looked up where the faucet is attached, you probably wondered how anyone could reach that spot to work. A basin wrench is the tool that lets you not only reach up there but actually tighten and loosen those nuts with relative ease. For more information on installing sinks see Chapter 13.

- ✔ **Spud wrench:** Tightening the large locknuts that secure the sink baskets to the sink is so easy, if you have the right tool — a spud wrench. Its wide, adjustable jaws fit around the nubs on the locknut, giving you enough grip to firmly tighten the locknuts.

- ✔ **Tubing cutter:** Ever wonder what a plumber uses to make those straight cuts in copper or plastic pipe? The answer is a tubing cutter.

- ✔ **Coil-spring tubing bender:** Flexible copper pipe can be bent but it takes a real touch to do it without putting a kink in the pipe. To avoid kinks, simply slip the bender over the tubing and slowly bend the pipe to the desired angle (as shown in Figure 5-2).

Getting wired: Electrical tools

Just as plumbers have their own specialty tools, so do electricians (for more on electricity basics see Chapter 7). I've identified several you may want to add to your toolbox:

- ✔ **Wire cutter/stripper:** This combination tool has cutting jaws for cutting through the sheathing and the individual wires and specially sized cutting areas for stripping off the sheathing that's around each individual wire. The pros use a pretty heavy-duty version which costs somewhere around $40, but you don't need to spend that much. I use an inexpensive, homeowner-grade cutter/stripper (under $5 each) and it works just fine. In fact, I have three or four of them just so I know I'll always have one available.

- ✔ **Needle-nose pliers:** No electrician is without a pair of needle-nose pliers and you shouldn't be either. The pliers' long, tapered jaws let you hold, bend, and shape wires when making electrical connections.

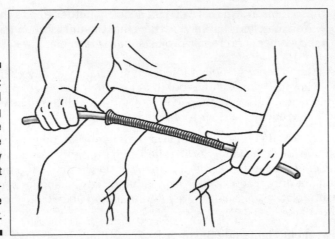

Figure 5-2: Avoid kinking flexible copper pipe by gradually bending it with a coil-spring tube bender.

- ✔ **Shock preventers:** I discuss these tools earlier in the "Screwdrivers" section, so take a look there for more information.

- ✔ **Multi-tester:** A multi-tester is a battery-operated tool that measures electrical voltage, continuity in switches and fixtures, and can even measure current ranging from 1 to 1,000 volts. Just remember that weak batteries can and will affect the unit's testing and diagnostic capabilities.

Renting Your Way to Tool Heaven

It doesn't make a lot of sense for you to try to own every tool needed for a kitchen remodel, especially when you can rent some of them instead!

A cut above: Saws

In all likelihood, the only saw you need to buy is a circular saw; the rest are probably so specialized you don't need to own them. Some are designed for heavy-duty demolition, although others are made for accurately cutting larger or longer material. Take a look at three saws that you may need to rent during your remodel:

- ✔ **Reciprocating saw:** This workhorse is a contractor's number-one friend when it comes to heavy demolition. It's not intended for fine cuts. It's main function is cutting apart and through everything from shingles to plywood to dimensional lumber. You can also cut through metal, plastic, and other materials by using the right type of blade. Rent one for around $25 to $35 a day — you'll only need it during the demolition. You'll spend at least $200 if you buy one.

✔ **Saber saw:** Often called a jigsaw, this type of power saw uses a small, thin blade and is excellent for cutting curves or circles (for example, if you need to cut a hole for your sink in your new countertop). It usually has an adjustable baseplate, similar to the type on a circular saw. You can cut metal, wood, plastic, and plywood simply by changing to the appropriate type of blade. A saber or jigsaw rents for under $20 a day.

✔ **Portable table saw:** If you need to cut sheets of plywood or paneling or rip long boards, renting a portable table saw makes a lot of sense. The size of the saw is determined by the size of the blade, much like sizing a circular saw. Most rental stores have 10- or 12-inch portable table saws. The blade can be moved up and down to control the depth of cut and it can also be set at an angle of up to 45 degrees. A 10- or 12-inch portable table saw rents for between $45 and $75 per day, depending on the size and capacity.

A table saw also has a moveable *rip fence*, which you can adjust to varying distances from the blade. The rip fence helps you guide the material along, keeping it the same distance from the blade through the entire cut. A rental saw, as well as all portable table saws, should have a moveable blade guard in place when you rent it. If it doesn't, don't rent the saw. If it does, don't remove the guard! It's there for your protection regardless of whether or not you think it interferes with your ability to operate the saw.

Power nailers

Visit most home construction sites today and the sound of a hammer striking a nail has been replaced by the sound of nail being shot out of a nailing gun. Power nailers have made construction easier and faster for the contractor. But, why should they have all the fun? You can get in on it, too, by renting a power nailer. Here's a look at your options:

✔ **Framing nailer:** If you want to nail lumber together fast and easy, then a framing nailer is the tool to rent. Most framing nailers can handle nails ranging from 1¼ inches to 2½ inches long so they're ideal for connecting wall studs and plates. Another neat feature about using a framing nailer is that the nails are joined together, usually in a strip, with glue that acts as an adhesive as the nail is shot into the wood. The sudden driving of the nail instantly heats and melts the glue, and, when the nail's in place, the glue dries to help hold the nail in the wood. Framing nailers use nails with heads and are intended for general or rough-carpentry jobs such as building a stud wall when you open or close up a section of the kitchen wall. A framing nailer usually rents for around $35 a day.

✔ **Finish nailer:** When it's time to install trim, renting a finish nailer saves lots of time and quite possibly some material, too. Finish or brad nailers drive nails or brads similar in size and shape to finishing nails. These nails do not have a large, flat head. Instead, the head is only slightly larger than the diameter of the nail, providing enough holding power without being too noticeable when driven into the wood. The head is cupped slightly, which allows you to drive or *set* the nail slightly below the surface of the material to help hide the nail. Finish nailers rent for between $25 and $35 per day, depending on the size (capacity).

Both framing nailers and finish nailers require an air compressor for operation. Most nailers don't need more than a 1½- to 3-hp (horsepower) air compressor. Your rental equipment dealer should have a compressor and nailer matched together to help with what you need. Rental compressors, especially the sizes I mentioned, can be powered by a standard 120-volt electrical circuit. No special wiring or plugs are needed. Just plug it in, fill up the tank, hook up the nailer, and you're ready to go. Just be sure that the rental dealer explains how to operate the compressor for maximum performance. The rental price for the compressor is not included in the nailer rental fee, although many rental stores give a discounted or package rental price when renting both.

Tile tools

Removing, installing, and cutting floor tile is no walk in the park, but renting the following tools can help you get the jobs done in no time! For more information on installing tile floors, see Chapter 21.

✔ **Electric power stripper:** Removing old floor tile can be a real struggle. An electric power stripper gets underneath the tiles and uses a chiseling motion to break them loose. It's noisy to operate, but it's a real time-saver — and backsaver! Just wear hearing protection (also available at most rental stores) and you're all set. Don't forget eye protection, too.

✔ **Slammer bar:** This is a thick-bladed steel bar that removes stubborn floor tile. It's manually operated (your muscles are the power!), but it does the job.

✔ **Ceramic tile snap cutter:** This rental tool is perfect for making straight cuts on ceramic tile, and a great help when installing new tile. The handle has a small cutting wheel that scores the tile as you pull the handle across. You then apply downward pressure on the handle, which forces the tile down and snaps it clean.

✔ **Tile nippers:** If you need to make round cuts in a tile, you want to use tile nippers. They're sort of like hybrid pliers with curved jaws that bite or nip off small pieces of tile a little at a time. Be sure to wear safety glasses when using any tile cutting tools because small pieces of tile fly around.

✔ **Wet saw:** A snap cutter handles most tile cutting jobs. But if you're installing thicker floor tiles (more than ½ inch thick) or slate flooring, you need to rent a wet saw. It's called a wet saw because the blade of the saw is in a small reservoir of water which keeps the blade and tile cool and wet during the cutting.

If you do rent a wet saw, make sure you use it outside or where you won't mind some water spray and dirt. The spinning blade throws a heavy mist mixture of water and tile residue that gets things quite messy. Again, you need eye protection for this one. Goggles work well, although safety glasses are okay, too.

A few more good rentals

Here are four tools that aren't widely known about or thought of as rental tools. However, if you do rent them, you'll be glad you did, because they're real timesavers and problem solvers.

✔ **Drywall lift:** For most DIYers, lifting and installing — called *hanging* — sheets of drywall is a wrestling match that they don't enjoy. But there is a piece of rental equipment that saves time and your back, too. A drywall lift lets one person install drywall on walls, ceilings, and even sloped areas (see Figure 5-3). After the unit's set, you simply turn the wheel to raise the drywall into position and then secure it to the framing studs. Drywall lifts have telescoping arms that let you use both 8-foot and 12-foot long drywall for your drywall project. The tripod base keeps the unit steady and the *casters* (pivoting wheels) make it easy to maneuver into position. Rental prices vary on this piece of equipment, but you should expect to spend around $75 a day.

Figure 5-3:
A drywall lift makes hanging sheets of drywall easier, even for one person.

✔ **Auger:** Cleaning an existing drain line is always recommended before installing a new sink. The best way to make sure the line is as clean as possible is to use an auger or *snake*. A snake is a long steel cable that you feed into the drain line to break through clogs and any debris in the line. There are both hand-powered and motorized drain augers available to rent. A hand auger is sufficient for most kitchen drain cleanings, but a motorized auger is better suited for cleaning the main drain line of the house, especially if tree roots are a problem. For more on sink installation see Chapter 13. Power augers rent for around $20.

✔ **Fish tape:** Installing new electrical cables can be tricky, especially if you have to pull them behind a finished wall surface. Using a fish tape makes this job easier and a little less frustrating. A *fish tape* (shown in Figure 5-4) is a long spool of thin steel with a hook on one end for holding the cable as you pull. You feed the tape through the areas where the cable needs to run, and then attach the cable to the hook and reel in the tape (and cable) until the cable is in place. For more on installing electrical cable, see Chapter 7. You can rent a fish tape for around $10.

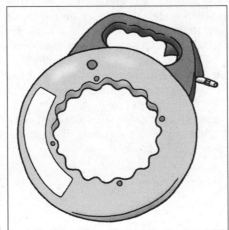

Figure 5-4:
Fish tape.

✔ **Flooring nailer:** No, I'm not talking about more power nailers. You operate this nailer by striking it with a specially designed and weighted mallet, which always comes with the nailer. The mallet has a rubber head for striking the nailer and a metal weight located directly behind the rubber part for force and drive. This tool not only drives nails faster, but its design helps ensure that the nails are driven in at the correct angle every time. Don't use a regular hammer or maul to strike the nailer. See Chapter 21 for more information on installing floors with a floor nailer. Flooring nailers rent for between $35 and $75 per day, depending on the size and model. Fasteners (either nails or staples, depending on your flooring's requirements) may or may not be included in the rental cost.

Chapter 6

Getting Your Kitchen Ready for Construction

In This Chapter

▶ Clearing out your kitchen

▶ Tearing your kitchen apart

▶ Looking at what's left

*Y*ou need to follow a logical progression of steps in any major remodeling project to keep things moving smoothly and efficiently. So, before you start tearing off the old cabinets and countertop and ripping up the floor, develop a solid understanding of what to expect, including a timetable and a plan. Start by packing up all of the stuff that's currently in the cabinets and on the countertops. Then, remove the existing cabinets, countertops, flooring, and whatever else you plan on replacing. Finally, install the new materials and equipment. Lucky for you, I've remodeled a few kitchens in my time, and in this chapter I share the inside scoop on how to tackle the packing and demolition duties. I cover installing new materials in Parts III and IV.

Packing Up the Kitchen

Getting started may be the most exhilarating part of the project. After all, you're taking the first step toward creating your dream kitchen! But before you start tearing things out, take steps to protect items that you don't plan to replace and that you want to reuse. And remember that the kitchen probably won't be the only room affected by this project. You need to find places to store all of the stuff normally kept in the kitchen drawers and cabinets — your dishes, your silverware, and all of those reusable plastic containers you've accumulated over the years.

Storing all of the kitchen items won't turn into a nightmare if you use common sense and think things through. Check out the following list of tips to help you clear your kitchen for remodeling:

✔ If a new refrigerator isn't part of the plan, move the old one out of the kitchen. That way, your fridge is protected from the inevitable scratches or dings and you get as much working room as possible.

✔ Removing the stove or range isn't quite as easy or practical as removing the fridge. Instead, leave your stove in place for as long as possible. Cover it up with a tarp, blanket, or drop cloth to protect it from scratches and dings during the remodeling.

Not all ranges or stoves can be left in your kitchen while you remodel. Drop-in style models — where the lip of the stove actually rests on and is supported by the countertop — have to be removed. A free-standing unit (sometimes referred to as a *slide-in*) can be left in place.

✔ Pack kitchen items in sturdy boxes in several different sizes:

• The smaller boxes are great for holding items you plan to use regularly even when the kitchen's torn up such as spices, condiments, and silverware.

• The medium-sized boxes work well for holding plates, bowls, glasses, and the like.

• The large boxes are best suited for items that you don't use on a regular basis. And the large boxes can double as temporary tabletops, where you can eat meals over the weeks (or months) that your kitchen is under construction.

You may find that using more boxes with fewer items in each box makes it easier to locate things; you don't have to spend hours each day digging through a really full box looking for the same stuff. Don't forget to mark the boxes — as you're packing them!

So now that everything's out of the kitchen, take a look at what's ahead for your kitchen-remodeling project.

Removing Everything Including the Kitchen Sink

After you've removed and packed away all of your kitchen items, you're ready to start tearing the kitchen apart. Don't go too overboard and try to get everything out as quickly as possible. Work at a steady but manageable pace, and you can accomplish a lot!

Lifting a heavy sink or countertop is awkward, and handling cabinets is tricky. Don't try to do either alone; these steps are accomplished more safely by two people. Make sure both you and your helper wear heavy gloves and use other appropriate safety gear, especially eye protection. Chapter 5 describes the safety gear you need for this type of project.

Taking out the cabinets

I haven't discovered a set-in-stone order for removing cabinets and counter-tops. But based on my experiences in demolishing kitchens, I recommend removing the upper or wall cabinets first and then removing the countertops (I discuss this in the "Removing wall cabinets" section). The lower or base cabinets come out after the countertops are removed.

Start by removing the cabinet doors, drawers, and shelves to make the remaining cabinet body or shell as light as possible. Removing the doors also gives you more clear working space.

Removing wall cabinets

Most wall cabinets are secured with 3-inch-long screws and may also be supported by a wood *cleat* (a length of 1 x 4 board that's as wide as the cabinet and also screwed to the wall). Remove the screws that hold the cabinet, but don't remove the screws that secure the cleats. You'll need some help steadying the cabinets while you remove the screws. Start removing the screws located inside and along the bottom of the cabinets, working your way up the back edges. Remove the screws at the top of the cabinet last.

You also need to disconnect adjoining cabinets so that you take down only a single cabinet at a time. Look for screws that are located on the front frame of the cabinet and go from one cabinet frame to another.

If your cabinets were installed during the 1960s or earlier, they may be secured to the wall with nails. If your cabinets are nailed to the wall, you need to carefully pry them off using a pry bar. (See Chapter 5 for a discussion about demolition tools.)

If you need to use a pry bar, be sure to place a short length of 1 x 4 board against the wall where you'll be prying. The board not only gives you extra leverage, but it also prevents the pry bar from breaking through the wall's surface.

Removing base cabinets

Removing base cabinets is pretty straightforward, but you need to watch out for a couple things:

✔ If the base cabinets are attached to the existing floor either with adhesive or with grout, you need to gently but firmly persuade the cabinets from the flooring. Usually, a firm rocking or working back and forth does the trick. If not, use a pry bar. If you aren't going to replace the floor in your kitchen, just make sure that base cabinets aren't attached to the old flooring when it's time to remove the cabinets. And by attached, I don't necessarily mean secured with screws or nails. Over the years, cabinets and flooring can be joined together with coats of floor wax and other preservers. Use a utility knife to cut *(score)* through any buildup connecting the two materials. Remember, too, to lift the base cabinets straight up and don't try to tip or tilt them and drag them up and over the lip of the flooring.

✔ If the base cabinet that holds the sink has a back on it (usually a ¼-inch thick piece of plywood), you also need to disconnect the plumbing connections from the water supplies to the sink (I discuss this in the "Getting rid of countertops and sinks" section) to remove the cabinet without destroying the back panel.

Getting rid of countertops and sinks

Before you can remove the countertop, you must remove the sink and faucet. And before you can do that, you must shut off the water. Here's how:

1. **Close the valves.**

   If your sink's existing plumbing setup has shutoff valves on both the hot- and cold-water supply lines, then the first step is easy. If your sink doesn't have shutoff valves, your progress was just slowed and a step was added. You need to install shutoff valves. (Individual shutoff valves for both cold and hot water supplies are now required by code for all sinks.) For instructions on how to install shutoff valves, see Chapter 7.

2. **Disconnect the water supply lines that are connected to the faucet.**

   When the valves are closed, simply unscrew the supply lines that run from the shutoff valves to the underside connections on the faucet. A little water may drain out or drip, so keep some rags handy. Don't plan to reuse the water supply lines on your new setup. They'll probably be the wrong length. New connections are a good idea, anyway.

3. **Remove the sink and faucet.**

   If you're not planning to reuse either the sink or faucet, feel free to use whatever tools and force is needed to free the sink from the countertop. If you are planning on reusing the sink and faucet, use a utility knife to break the caulk seal between the sink and the countertop and then lift out the sink.

And just so you know that home improvement writers do have real-life problems, here's a horror story of my own: My home, which was built in 1979, had no shutoff valves at any of the sinks because shutoffs weren't required by code in our area at the time that the house was built. When I needed to repair a leaky faucet in one of the bathrooms, I had to shut off the water to the entire house just to work on the bathroom faucet. Needless to say, the complaints I received from my family about not having any water in the kitchen (or anywhere in the house for that matter!) while I worked in the bathroom persuaded me to install shutoff valves at each sink. Trust me, you want shutoff valves on the supply lines so that only the water to the kitchen is shut off during the demolition and remodeling processes.

Tearing up the old floor

Removing old flooring is a job that most homeowners can handle. If your floors are made of sheet flooring, you'll need a long-handled, wide-blade flat scraper, available at rental stores for around $20. If you're taking up ceramic tile, you'll need a sledge hammer, a 3-pound maul, and a thick-bladed scraper bar, sometimes called a *slammer*. You can rent the slammer, too. Don't forget to wear eye protection, no matter what type of flooring you're removing!

Be sure to remove as much of the old flooring's adhesive as possible and get the subfloor plywood (or boards, depending on the age of your home) as smooth as possible. You may need to scrape or even use a belt sander to get rid of real tough spots of adhesive residue left behind by sheet flooring or vinyl tiles. Ceramic tile used to be set in mortar; if this is the case in your house, you need to be sure to remove all of the small chunks of mortar that are usually left on the subfloor after the tile is removed.

Disposing of your old cabinets, countertops, and appliances

Please don't assume that because you're replacing your kitchen fixtures and cabinets that everything needs to head to the dump. Many of the items, especially cabinets, can be reused, as long as they're in decent, useable shape. Check with local housing agencies or church affiliated agencies that rehab houses to see whether they can use your old cabinets and other materials. You can usually write off the cabinets on your taxes as a donation, plus you don't add to our already overfilled landfills. One other solution for disposing of cabinets is to use them in your garage or as basement storage. And don't forget about your neighbors, either. Ask them if they could use some or all of the cabinets.

Disposing of old appliances can be a bit trickier, but not impossible. Some used furniture stores accept appliances, but they must work. Many appliance stores will haul away your old appliances when the new ones are delivered. If neither of these options are available, check with your trash hauler. They usually have some sort of appliance pickup/disposal service, although there is a fee associated with it.

Opening Up the Walls and Seeing What's Inside

Most kitchen remodeling jobs require some sort of hard construction. This can mean everything from tearing out damaged or deteriorated drywall and wall studs (and then reframing and finishing the area) to closing up or opening an existing wall area and installing new drywall. Either way, this adds several days to the overall length of the project. Just be sure to allow enough time, not only for the removal (the quick part) but also for the rebuilding, which includes the taping of the drywall joints and the drying time required between coats of drywall joint compound.

Opening up walls is tricky because it involves framing the new wall and hanging drywall (also called wallboard, plasterboard, and Sheetrock). You may want to hire a professional. If, on the other hand, you think you can handle the job, check the Internet for Web sites on home construction. A quick search for "framing a wall" or "hanging drywall" on any of the popular Internet search engines will give you several sites to investigate.

Before you begin tearing down a wall, determine whether the wall is a *partition* wall — which merely separates rooms — or a *supporting* or *structural* wall. Supporting walls separate rooms just like partitions walls do, but their primary function is to support and hold up the house. Partition walls can usually be modified with added openings and so on without causing any structural damage to the house's support system. Supporting walls, on the other hand, cannot be altered without having the proposed change evaluated and approved by your local building inspector or a structural engineer. As a general rule, partition walls run parallel to the direction of your home's rafters or trusses, and supporting (structural) walls run perpendicular to the rafters or trusses. All exterior walls are structural.

When the new framing is in place, make any necessary electrical, plumbing, or ventilation changes before hanging the drywall. (I talk more about these specific changes and upgrades in Chapter 7.) Open stud walls give you complete, convenient access for pulling cable and running water lines, plus you can see what you're doing.

If this is your first remodeling project, the previously mentioned demolition and rebuilding steps added together probably seem overwhelming. Any remodeling takes longer than expected and remember that living without a kitchen is more of a hardship than you may imagine. Don't be afraid to reevaluate your plans and scale-back, if necessary. Maybe replacing an old appliance or painting the walls and cabinets is enough for now. I've seen projects go on for years because the homeowners were not willing to admit they took on too much.

Chapter 7

Evaluating Your Plumbing, Electrical, and Ventilation Systems

In This Chapter

▶ Figuring out what to do with your plumbing

▶ Venting out moisture and odors

▶ Bringing your electrical system up to code

Your existing kitchen already has water supply lines, drain lines, and electricity, and in most homes ductwork for ventilation. However, your new kitchen design may include repositioning the sink, which means moving water supply and drain lines. And if your plan calls for new lights or maybe adding a microwave oven or other new appliances, the electrical requirements will be greater and you may need to add a new circuit or two. This chapter provides an overview on how to assess your existing plumbing, electrical, and ventilation setups and decide what changes are needed.

If your kitchen remodel is smaller in scope, or if it's more of a makeover or freshening up than a complete remodel, you probably won't need the information in this chapter. But, if you're planning a larger remodel, many of the necessary upgrades described in this chapter require the experience of a licensed professional. Look for the "Call A Pro" icons throughout this chapter — this icon highlights the tasks better left to a professional. Also see Chapter 4 for information and advice on hiring a pro.

Preparing Your Plumbing

Every kitchen plumbing system has two components: The supply side that brings the water to the kitchen; and the drain, vent, and waste (DVW) side that carries water and waste away and vents odors (such as sewer gas) to the outdoors. Making changes and upgrades to the kitchen plumbing system is one of the first things to do after you've finished the necessary demolition or gutting described in Chapter 6 — new plumbing lines go in and the old ones come out more easily when the walls are open. And whether you've stripped everything back to the bare wall studs or simply removed cabinets and flooring, you need to understand what's required to supply your new kitchen with water and what changes to expect. Lucky for you, this section explains it all.

Repositioning drain lines

Most homeowners — even novice do-it-yourselfers (DIYers) — can install a new sink or faucet at the existing location. I explain how to install new sinks and faucets in Chapter 13. However, if you're planning on moving the location of existing plumbing fixtures, chances are almost 100% that you'll have to move or at least modify the location of the *drain line* — the large pipe that typically goes through the wall underneath the sink and is connected to the configuration of smaller pipes (usually plastic but sometimes plated chrome) that are connected to the bottom of the sink. This system of pipes carries away waste water and, if you have a garbage disposer, food waste, too.

Whether you plan to move the drain line several feet or across the kitchen, you probably need to hire a plumbing contractor to make the move for you. When you move the drain line, a lot of technical stuff must be done according to plumbing code regulations, and most homeowners don't have the expertise or knowledge to ensure that the major changes are done correctly. Things like making sure the drain lines are properly sloped to ensure that water and waste drain completely and don't stand inside the pipe, and that you're using the correct size (diameter) pipe are just two of the many reasons to bring in a professional for this part of the remodeling project. You will probably spend a sizeable amount on labor, but it will be worth the peace of mind knowing that the installation was done up to code.

Don't cast out cast-iron pipes

At one time, cast iron was the only type of pipe used for the drainage part of a plumbing system, but cast iron's been replace by PVC or ABS plastic pipe where code allows. If your house was built after the mid-1970s, you probably won't find cast iron used as the main drainage pipes from the sinks, showers, tubs, and toilets. If your home does have cast-iron pipe, however, don't be alarmed. Cast iron is strong and durable and lasts a long, long time. I've seen homes that are over 50 years old with original cast-iron pipe and everything works just fine.

Installing new water lines (and moving old ones, too)

Repositioning drain lines is extremely difficult, but the opposite can be said for installing most new *water supply lines* (the pipe that gets the water from the main water line to the shut-off valve under the sink). Why? Because the most commonly used material for water supply lines is copper pipe and fittings and it's very DIY-friendly. It's easy to cut, learning how to solder the joints and fittings is not difficult (see the "Trying your hand at soldering copper pipe" sidebar), and the materials are not expensive, either. I've repositioned both hot and cold water supply lines in my home for various projects, and once I mastered the technique of sweat soldering copper pipes and fittings, I felt like I could handle just about any water supply plumbing project. And just where would you need to add a new water line? One example is if your new kitchen island is going to house a sink (as shown in the color insert).

After you install new water supply lines, you need to connect them to the new faucet with the appropriate size and type of faucet supply line. Chapter 13 explains this process in detail.

Moving a water supply line involves shutting off the water supply to the entire house, so make sure you have all the necessary tools and materials ready to go. While your water's shut off, go ahead and install shut-off valves on any water supply lines that don't have them. The following sections explain how.

Locating the main shut-off

Make sure that you know where your home's water meter and main shut-off are located. Unless you know this, you won't be able to do any water supply plumbing repairs.

- ✔ If your house has a basement, the water meter and main shut-off will be located there, usually close to all of the mechanical equipment such as the furnace, water heater, and water softener. The meter is about 12 to 16 inches tall and is installed where the water main pipe enters the house. The pipe may come through the floor or through an exterior wall, depending on your home's set up. Look for the main shut-off valve beyond the meter, usually within a couple of feet of the meter and usually on a vertical pipe.

- ✔ If you have a slab home (without a basement) or you live in a region of the country that doesn't have a freeze season, chances are good that your water meter and shut-off valve are outside. They're usually located on a corner of the house near the street, because the water main from the city comes to the house from the street. The meter and valve will still be within a few feet of each other. If your home has a well, the meter will probably be located near the other service entrance items, such as gas or electric.

Shutting off the water supply is easy, but the process can differ depending on the type of valve on the meter. Many meters have a round handle that looks like the ones on the outside spigots of your house. This type of shut-off valve is called a *gate valve*. Simply turn the handle clockwise until it stops. Other meters have a handle that you move so that the handle is perpendicular to the water pipe that it's attached to in order to shut off the water flow. This valve is called simply a *shut-off valve*.

Adding shut-off valves

The water flows from the main supply coming into your house and then through the various runs of narrower supply pipes. But before the water gets to the fixture of use, it needs to run through a shut-off valve. Believe it or not, up until just a few years ago, shut-off valves weren't required on water supply lines leading to sinks. The supply line could simply be hooked up directly to the faucet and considered ready to use. Today's codes require shut-offs at all fixtures, which makes perfect sense because when you do need to shut off the water at a particular fixture, you don't want to have to shut down the entire water system while you work on the single fixture with the problem.

Shut-off valves come in two different styles or configurations. Selecting the right one for your setup means figuring out where the water supply lines enter your sink area.

✔ An *in-line shut-off valve* is used when the water supply comes up through the floor of the kitchen and the bottom of the sink base cabinet. The water supply line is connected to the bottom of the valve, and the water feed line to the sink runs directly out of the top of the valve — everything is in-line.

✔ A *right-angle shut-off valve* is used when the water supply pipe comes straight out of the wall at the back of the sink base cabinet. The valve is set up so that the bottom fitting connects to the pipe coming out of the wall. The valve's body then makes a 90-degree (right-angle) turn up with the shut-off handle and water feed connection in-line to the sink. (The 90-degree bend is what makes this a right-angle valve.)

Valves are made with either solder or compression fittings or a combination of both. The easiest type of shut-off valve to install is a compression-fitting valve. If the old supply lines are copper or plastic, plan on using compression fittings. If the supply pipes are galvanized, use a combination fitting, which is threaded on one end to fit the galvanized pipe and has a compression fitting on the other end. If you can't find this fitting at the store, ask for some help. They're readily available, but sometimes hard to locate especially if you don't know exactly what you're looking for.

Although the soldered joint valves seem to last longer (as long as the solder joint was done properly), compression joint valves give you good service and they're easy to install and uninstall. Take a look at Figure 7-1 to see how they look. No special tools are required and you don't have to learn a technique, as you do with soldering. Should you need to uninstall a compression fitting, simply unscrew the compression nut and pull the pipe or supply line out of the joint. With a soldered joint, you need to use a propane torch to heat the joint and melt the solder in the joint. And reconnecting the compression joint is easier, too. You can reuse the compression fitting pieces, as is. However you need to clean, flux, and reapply solder to a soldered fitting.

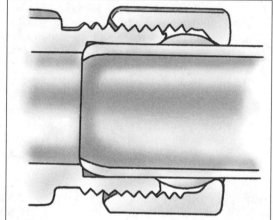

Figure 7-1:
A compres-
sion valve.

But be warned: Some cities forbid the use of compression fittings on the main water supply lines, so check with your city's plumbing inspector.

When you install new shut-offs, try to make the supply lines close to the same height, not only for appearance but for keeping things uniform underneath the sink. I've seen shut-offs that where almost a foot different in height, which not only looked bad but the handle on the lower valve was in the way when it came time to store things. Uneven valve heights are the sign of a lazy plumber. Also, when matching a shut-off valve to the type of pipe, make sure you're using the correct pipe diameter dimension. All copper pipe diameters are based on their *I.D.* or *inside diameter (dimension)*. So, when you're matching the valves to the pipe, make sure to check the valve's specs, too.

Preparing the existing water supply lines for the installation of shut-off valves is easy, especially if they're copper lines. The old set up should have a soldered connector/reducer between the copper supply pipes and the supply lines to the faucet. With the water turned off, use a tubing cutter (described in Chapter 5) to cut the supply pipe just below the connector. Make sure the cuts are straight. Slip the compression nut over the supply pipe with the nut threads facing up toward the cut end of the pipe. Then, slide the brass compression ring over the pipe. Believe it or not, you're more than halfway home. Next, slide the shut-off valve onto the pipe and apply a bead of pipe joint compound around the top section of the compression ring. The ring has a seam in the middle dividing it in half so you can see which is the top section. Now, hold the valve and slide the compression ring and nut up to the threads of the valve. Hand-tighten the nut onto the valve and finish tightening it with an adjustable wrench. Follow these steps for both the cold and hot water supply lines and then turn the water back on to check for leaks.

Before turning the water back on to check for leaks, make sure that the valve is closed by turning the handle clockwise until it stops. Doing this keeps the water pressure on full at the valve and will immediately let you know if the valve joint is leaking or leak-free. A helper really comes in handy at this stage. You'd be amazed at how much water can rush out even from a small leak before you can get the main water supply shut-off if you're working alone. With a helper at the main water shut-off, the flood should be minimal.

If the fitting leaks around the bottom, you need to turn off the water and redo the whole thing. A leaking compression fitting is usually caused by the compression ring not being seated (forming a complete seal against the pipe) correctly. You can't seat it properly without taking the connection apart and doing it again.

If you have galvanized supply pipes, it's a good idea to replace them with copper pipes. Galvanized pipes become clogged with sediment buildup over time, which reduces water flow and pressure. If your system has a plastic type of main water supply system (popular in the late 70s and even the early 80s), contact a plumber to run new supplies. You must have the correct type of fittings and not all home centers and hardware stores stock these parts.

Examining your pipe type choices (Here's a tip: Choose copper)

Copper is hands-down the most widely used type of pipe for new water supply lines. Highly resistant to corrosion, copper also has a smooth interior surface that provides good water flow with little resistance. Copper is affordable, and most folks can handle it with a little practice. Take a look at the various categories of copper pipe and their recommended usage.

- ✔ **Rigid copper:** Simply the best material for water supply pipes. Rigid copper's smooth interior surface lets water flow freely and the soldered copper joints are very durable. You can also use compression fittings for the joints. However, a soldered joint will outlast any compression-fitting joint. Rigid copper is sold in 10-foot lengths and comes in ⅜, ½, ¾ and 1-inch diameters. You can cut rigid copper with a tube cutter, hacksaw, or jigsaw. The tube cutter is the most accurate tool and the easiest to use.

Rigid copper pipe comes in three types or ratings: M, L, and K. All are determined by their thickness. Type M is the thinnest, the least expensive, and is a popular choice for residential plumbing systems like your kitchen.

✔ **Flexible copper:** Most cities won't allow the use of flexible copper tubing as your main water supply line. They will, however, let you use it to supply water to a refrigerator icemaker, dishwasher, or from the rigid copper pipe to a faucet. Flexible copper is easy to shape around corners. It can handle gradual bends and curves but it's also easily kinked, so be careful. Flexible copper pipe is sold in coils or by the foot. It comes in ¼-, ⅜-, ½-, and 1-inch diameters. And because you're not using it for your main supply, you can generally use compression fittings. Check with your local plumbing authorities, however, to be sure. Flexible copper can be cut easily with a tube cutter or hacksaw.

Although most homeowners choose to install copper supply lines, not all water supply lines are copper pipe and fittings. Your house could have

✔ **Galvanized steel pipe:** Galvanized steel is very strong and lasts a long time. In fact, galvanized steel was the pipe of choice before copper became popular. However, it gradually corrodes and is difficult to work with and cut.

You don't see galvanized pipe used much anymore on new installation. However, if your home has galvanized supply lines and you don't want to replace them with copper, you can use rigid copper with galvanized pipe by using the correct transition-type fittings.

✔ **CPVC pipe:** Chlorinated polyvinyl chloride (CPVC) pipe has become the pipe of choice for water supply lines in some regions. CPVC is easy to work with and can be used for both hot and cold water supplies. The pipe and fittings are relatively inexpensive and highly resistant to heat and chemicals. On the downside, earlier generations of CPVC had major failure rates, with pipes splitting and joints failing, even when properly fitted. CPVC uses solvent glue and plastic fittings or grip fittings — a kind of friction/compression-fit fitting. The current generation of CPVC doesn't seem to have the problems of the earlier stuff, but it's still not accepted for use everywhere. Check with your local plumbing inspector *before* you install it. If it doesn't meet code in your area, you'll have to tear it out. CPCV comes in ⅜-, ½-, ¾- and 1-inch diameters.

✔ **PEX water supply pipe:** A new type of water supply pipe that is establishing a very strong track record is PEX (cross-linked polyethylene). PEX is flexible and resistant to heat and chemicals and also withstands the high pressure found in the water supply lines in a home. PEX uses compression fittings for the joints, making it easy to use, and it gives you leak-free joints virtually every time. One big downer is that PEX hasn't been around long enough for all areas to believe that it will hold up over time. Check with your local authorities to see whether PEX pipe is code compliant before you install it.

Trying your hand at soldering copper pipe

If you're running new copper water lines, you need to solder. A properly soldered joint will last for years (in many cases decades), and soldering a joint is pretty easy:

1. Clean the pipe.

2. Apply flux paste (which ensures a clean surface for the solder).

3. Heat the fitting.

4. Finally, using a soldering iron, melt the solder so that it flows into and fills the joint between the pipe and the fitting.

Soldering copper pipe isn't difficult, but it takes practice. I mastered sweating solder (often called simply soldering) copper joints, however it wasn't without one or two joints that weren't quite watertight on my first attempt. Be patient! Your first couple of attempts may not look beautiful, but soon you'll be soldering copper that not only doesn't leak but also looks good.

All three of these types of pipe use threaded couplings and fittings to join sections together. Although threaded joints are easier to assemble, threading the pipe is difficult without the proper equipment, and most homeowners don't own or have access to the type of pipe cutter that's required. You can have the ends threaded at most home centers and full-service hardware stores, but it's really inconvenient and it eats up a lot of time.

PB, or polybutylene, is a flexible pipe that was used for water supply lines for a while — maybe even in your home. PB was prone to leaking and deterioration and is not installed anymore. If your house has it, chances are good that the inspector will require that you replace it. And even though replacement adds cost and time, you'll be better off in the long run.

Vetting Ventilation Needs

I can almost guarantee that your new kitchen will have you spending more time cooking. And with the extra cooking will come additional ventilation needs. Why? More cooking means more moisture and odors in the air, both of which you'll want to remove efficiently. If you're lucky, this part of the project will take no extra time, because you'll already have a ventilation system in place.

But unfortunately, if you don't have a ventilation system, or if your system needs a lot of work, you have hours of work and much construction ahead of you to make things fit properly. But making these changes will be a good investment in the long run. For the best job and to have it completed in a reasonable timeframe, hire a pro.

Whether you need to make minor adjustments to your ventilation or add or move ductwork, the fastest and certainly the easiest way to install ductwork is when the wall studs and ceiling joists are exposed, which is usually right after demolition (described in Chapter 6).

Locating existing ductwork

If your old kitchen had an over-the-range microwave oven or an exhaust hood, chances are good that you already have ductwork in place. The exception would be if the old exhaust hood was one that simply recirculated the air in the kitchen, only removing odors and not venting the air out of the kitchen. If your old kitchen didn't have an exhaust hood or an over-the-range microwave oven, then chances are good that no ductwork is in place over the range area for venting fumes and moisture. If your new kitchen plans include either of these appliances, ductwork will need to be installed and it must be vented to the outside. I discuss adding ductwork later in this chapter.

The easiest way to check for existing ductwork is to open the doors of the cabinet located over the range. Any ductwork will be visible inside of that cabinet.

Fitting the old ductwork to the new appliances

If your kitchen does have ductwork, make sure that its current position will work with the new range hood or microwave oven. Look for the existing section of ductwork that is connected to the old vent hood or microwave oven. You'll need to measure the length and the width of this section, called the *boot*. Exhaust boots are usually about 12 inches long and about 2 inches wide. You also need to check the boot's location in relationship to where it fits inside the cabinet. I've seen these boots positioned 2 or 3 inches from the back of the cabinet or flush against the back wall. If it's away from the wall, you have some leeway to reposition the boot, if necessary. More on that in a minute. If it's flush against the back wall, the new unit must have the exhaust opening in the some location or you're in for a lot more work. Take these measurements and information with you when you're shopping for your new range hood or microwave oven to make sure that the new equipment fits. (See Chapters 15 and 16 for more information about shopping for and installing new ductwork for appliances.)

If your current ductwork doesn't fit your new appliances, you'll have to move the ductwork around. Moving ductwork can be tricky and sometimes seems impossible. I had personal experience with just this problem when upgrading our over-the-range microwave oven. The existing ductwork boot had to be moved forward almost two inches so that I could line it up with the vent in the new microwave. Fortunately, I was able to cut a 2-inch-wide strip out of the bottom of the cabinet and then pull the boot forward to align the two without disconnecting the boot from the rest of the ductwork.

But if you aren't so lucky, and your kitchen requires you move the existing ductwork, this job falls into the "major kitchen remodeling" category and often requires removal and replacement of wall and ceiling surfaces. If your heart is set on a particular appliance and new framing and drywall is the only way to get it, you'll be willing to do the extra work (or hire someone who can).

The good news is that in most cases, existing ductwork will work with the new exhaust hood or microwave oven. Today's appliance manufacturers design their product's exhaust area specifications, both location and size, to work with equipment that may have been installed 20 or more years ago. They understand that many times their new products are purchased to replace existing equipment and the installer wants the installation to be as easy as possible.

Adding ductwork

If your old kitchen didn't have any mechanical exhaust equipment, your new one will (or at least it should!). You must be able to remove the moisture from all of the extra cooking you'll do and you'll also want to get odors out of the kitchen. Installing new ductwork adds a sizeable chunk of time and labor (and money!) to the remodeling project because all exhaust ductwork must move the air to the outside of the house.

Depending on the location of the range and oven, you could be in for some major construction work tearing into the walls and ceiling. The ductwork runs up and between the ceiling joists and then exits out through the side of the house. The direction the joists run in relation to the location of the stove determines how much work will be involved. If the joists run perpendicular to the exterior wall where the ductwork will exit, you're in luck because the ductwork can be placed between two of the ceiling joists.

If the stove is positioned on the exterior wall, you should be able to run the ductwork up through the cabinet and out the exterior wall. If, however, the joists run parallel to the exterior wall, you won't be able to run the ductwork straight out. And you can't cut holes in the joists for the ductwork, either. The ductwork is either 5 or 6 inches in diameter and even though most ceiling joists are 2 x 10s, cutting a 5 or 6 inch diameter hole in either of these size joists destroys the joist's structural integrity. If you're faced with this situation, consult with your building inspector or an architect to explore your options. Once again, if major changes are needed, you'll probably want a contractor to handle that part of the project.

Keeping Current: Electricity Concerns

Your old electrical setup may not fit your new kitchen's design or it simply may not supply the amount of electricity you need. This section helps you assess your current electrical situation and determine what upgrades, if any, are necessary to bring your new kitchen to life!

Running or *pulling* a new cable from the main electric service panel to the kitchen or even changing receptacles and switches is faster and easier when the wall framing is open. So if your kitchen remodel requires you to replace drywall, make all necessary adjustments to your electrical supply (or hire a pro to do the work) before the new drywall is installed. Pulling or "fishing" electric cable behind a finished wall is not only difficult but very time consuming.

Conforming to code

You (or an electrician) need to assess your kitchen's electrical supply and plan to make the necessary changes and upgrades in order to make your new kitchen more efficient and enjoyable to work in.

Your kitchen's electrical setup must be up to snuff according to the National Electrical Code (NEC), which is the minimum requirements for safe installation of electrical service in your home, and local electrical codes, which are often more strict than the NEC, so check with your local electrical inspector for your city's electrical requirements. (See the "Getting a thumbs up from the NEC" sidebar in this chapter for detailed information about NEC requirements.)

If you have circuits that continually blow fuses or trip the circuit breaker in the main service panel, have the entire electrical service checked out. Start by contacting your local electrical inspector to find out what the most current NEC requires are. Then, get at least three bids from licensed electricians for the necessary upgrades or repairs.

Ground Fault Circuit Interrupter (GFCI) protection is required for all kitchen outlets (especially any receptacle within 6 feet of the kitchen sink). A GFCI monitors the balance of electrical current moving through the circuit. When an imbalance occurs, the GFCI cuts off the electricity. Its purpose is to prevent fatal shocks. As you know, water and electricity are a deadly combination. Because both are necessary in a kitchen, all switches, sockets, breakers, and circuits for the kitchen should be GFCI protected for your family's safety.

Getting a thumbs up from the NEC

The National Electric Code (NEC) requires three types of circuits in a kitchen: general purpose/lighting, small appliance, and individual appliance. The current NEC requires an individual circuit for each electric stove/range, microwave oven, or dishwasher in your home. Additionally, you will need two separate circuits for countertop or small appliances. The NEC also has specific voltage requirements for each appliance. The range requires a 120/240-volt circuit (120 volts for the clock and timer and 240 volts for the heating elements), the microwave oven and dishwasher circuits must be 120-volt and 20-amps. The two small appliance circuits must also be 120-volt, 20-amp service and they must be protected with a Ground Fault Circuit Interrupter (GFCI). If your plan doesn't include these electrical upgrades, it should or your kitchen won't pass inspection.

The lighting circuit doesn't have to operate only the kitchen lights. The code requires at least one lighting circuit for every 600 square feet of floor space. And because many kitchens aren't that large, the kitchen lighting can be on the same circuit as lighting for additional rooms. (The NEC requires a minimum of three lighting circuits, no matter how small the house.)

GFCI protection can be handled by either installing a GFCI-equipped circuit breaker in the main service panel or by installing a GFCI outlet (see Figure 7-2) as the first receptacle on the circuit in the kitchen. Installing the GFCI outlet as the first outlet provides GFCI protection to all receptacles downstream that are on the same circuit.

If you're comfortable doing electrical work, then installing a GFCI receptacle is doable. If you're uncomfortable, hire a pro to do the work.

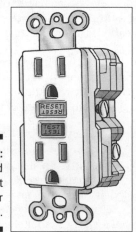

Figure 7-2:
A ground fault circuit interrupter (GFCI).

Upgrading with additional circuits and outlets

One of the most common complaints from homeowners about their old kitchens is the lack of electrical outlets. I've been in some older kitchens that have only one outlet on each wall. I really can't imagine how any cooking ever got done without having the cook go nuts looking for more power! For me, the more outlets the better. The code requires a receptacle every 6 feet, but having them every 4 feet would be better. Remember, however, that each circuit can only handle a maximum of eight receptacles. Adding three or four outlets to the overall electrical layout could require running an additional small appliance circuit to the kitchen, and adding circuits means that your home's main electrical service has to have the capacity.

If your existing electrical service is only 60-amps, plan to upgrade the service to at least 100-amps and preferably 150- or 200-amps. The difference in cost, again, is minimal with most of it coming in materials. Most homeowners can find out their home's electrical service rating by opening the door on the main service panel and looking for the rating capacity of the box. It should be stamped either on the inside of the door or near the top of the panel that houses the circuit breakers or fuses. Some boxes may have a label rather than a stamp.

Speaking of fuses, if your home still has them, consider upgrading to circuit breakers. Not that fuse-equipped systems aren't safe — they've been used for decades and have a good safety record. But breakers are designed to react more quickly to power fluctuations, thus protecting your home more efficiently. Plus, breakers can be reset and they're ready to go again. After a fuse blows, it must be replaced.

Hire a licensed electrician to upgrade your home's main service because you're dealing with disconnecting and reconnecting the high voltage lines that come from the power pole to your house. Besides, your home's entire electrical supply will be shut off while the switch is being made and you want to be without power for as short a time as possible.

If you do decide you want to do the electrical upgrade yourself, or any major electrical wiring work on your home, check with your homeowner's insurance provider to see if they allow you to do the work. If you do the work and it's inspected and signed-off by your city electrical inspector, you should be okay. But, to be on the safe side, check with your insurance company first.

Running electrical cable

If you've ever had the chance to see how electrical cables get from the main panel to the various locations in the house, then you know that the cables run through holes drilled in the wall studs. Drilling through the studs is not very difficult, as long as you use the right tools. An electric right-angle drill is the power tool you'll need. The drill's *chuck* (the piece that holds the drill bit) is set at a right-angle to the drill body, which allows you to drill without having to get the entire drill and spade bit within the space between the wall studs (see Figure 7-3).

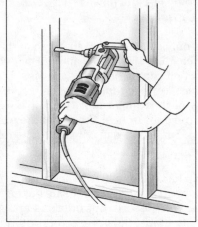

Figure 7-3:
Run cable through holes drilled in the wall studs.

Drill the holes in the middle or back third of the stud. Accessing this area is usually not too difficult either because wall studs are supposed to be placed every 16 inches or 16-inch-on-center (16 o.c.). This 16-inch spacing is enough to let you get the drill and paddle bit started into the stud. Don't worry if the bit is started at a slight angle. After you get the first ½ inch or so of the bit into the wood, you'll be able to level the drilling angle. The NEC doesn't require that the holes be drilled exactly straight, either.

You also should install a protective steel plate on the face surface of the wall stud where you drilled the hole (see Figure 7-4). The plate is nailed onto the stud and prevents you from drilling into the stud at that point, for example to hang a picture, and accidentally nicking the electrical cable with the drill bit.

After the holes are all drilled, you can pull the electrical cable from the service panel to the first box of the circuit run. You'll pull shorter lengths of cable from each box to each box, as needed, to connect the entire circuit.

Always pull more cable than you'll need. You can always cut it off, but you can *never* add a short jumper section if the cable is too short. That's a code violation and it's dangerous!

Figure 7-4:
Install a
protective
steel nailing
plate.

Installing smoke detectors: The best locations

The National Electric Code (NEC) does not require smoke detectors, however, most local codes do, and I recommend that every home have at least one smoke detector on each level of the house. The National Fire Protection Agency (NFPA) works closely with the NEC in developing guidelines for the electrical code and is the key force behind getting people to install smoke detectors in homes.

The NFPA states that the best location for a smoke detector is on the ceiling near a doorway or stairway. As a fire burns, the smoke rises and seeks the highest point and easiest route of escape, which is usually at the stairway leading to the next higher level in the house. The NFPA also recommends a smoke detector on the hallway ceiling outside of sleeping areas (bedrooms). Remember to install a separate smoke detector in each sleeping area if you have multiple sleeping areas located in different areas or different levels of the house. The NFPA also recommends individual smoke detectors in each bedroom, as well.

The NFPA doesn't recommend installing a smoke detector in or just outside the kitchen. If you do put one there, you'll have many nuisance alarms caused by smoke when you're cooking. Nuisance alarms cause people to temporarily disconnect or remove the battery from the offending smoke detector. Unfortunately, people too often forget to reconnect the alarm or reinstall the battery; that's often what you hear reported after a tragic fire.

Check with your city's fire department for their regulations and requirements for the number of smoke detectors you should have and the best locations for installation. But, most importantly, install smoke detectors in your home — *now!*

Part III
Selecting and Installing Cabinets and Countertops

The 5th Wave   By Rich Tennant

"This whole kitchen needs remodeling. The oven doesn't stay hot, I don't have enough storage space, and this kitchen island just never made any sense to me."

In this part . . .

Get out your checkbook and roll up your sleeves —
it's time to pick out some cabinets and countertops!
But before you plunk down your hard-earned cash, you
need to know what you're shopping for and how to tell the
difference between the good and the not-so-good products, so you can get the most kitchen for your dollar.

In this section, I arm you with all the information you need
to select the best countertop and cabinets for your needs.
Then I guide you through installation.

An open floor plan offers large work areas in medium-sized kitchens. A ceiling fan provides sufficient air movement and keeps the entire space comfortable while you're cooking.

Carry a geometric shape throughout the space. This small kitchen uses squares on the floor and the back-splash behind the stove.

A large kitchen space allows long work areas as well as room for a large, central island. Hanging pots and pans overhead increases available space in your cabinets.

Corner cabinets don't have to have square corners. This round contour provides a smooth-looking flow and maximizes useable storage space.

The richness and warmth of dark wood cabinets give a kitchen a feel of elegance.

Light colored wood cabinets brighten up this room, and glass doors in the wall cabinets provide a showroom-type feel.

Inlaid stainless steel rods next to the stove or cooktop let you move hot pots and pans from the burners onto the countertop without damaging the countertop surface.

Sandwiching a dark layer of material between two lighter layers is a striking way to add a color accent to solid surface countertops.

Routed drain channels in a solid surface countertop provide a built-in draining area for dishes and glassware.

Fashions in sink shapes are always changing. This unit has a built-in cutting board, a round bowl for washing food, and several extras including a soap dispenser.

A single two-bowl, undermount sink combined with this solid sur-face countertop gives the appearance of two separate sink bowls.

Undermount sinks provide uninterrupted flow on the countertop and allow you to space faucet handles wider than the traditional 8-inch-on-center spacing allows.

A pullout spout lets you move the water supply to wherever you need it. A filtering faucet puts better-tasting water at your fingertips.

Two workstations in a kitchen provide multi-cook households a separate sink and faucet for cleaning and preparing food.

A sink and faucet in a center island provide you with additional workspace.

A skylight allows plenty of overhead natural light and illuminates a large area in the kitchen.

Three types of lighting provide maximum illumination: natural light through the window, undercabinet lighting for the counter-tops, and recessed lights in the ceiling.

Track and pendant task lighting allows you to position and focus each individual light to whatever area or surface you want illuminated.

Formica Corp.

Gridley & Graves with permission from Women's Day Special Interest Publications

Embossed textures in this resilient sheet flooring give the floor the look of ceramic tile.

Different types of flooring help to visually separate spaces. The contrast between hardwood and ceramic tile–style resilient flooring provides a definite room break.

NOFMA (The Wood Flooring Manufacturers Association)

A red oak hardwood floor brings a country look and the warmth of real wood to this kitchen.

An island doesn't have to be square or rectangular. This island's shape mirrors the other cabinet configuration. This island also contains a cooktop and a wine rack.

An island provides an area for work or serving food. The two-tiered countertop surfaces (lower right) give added countertop room without requiring extra space.

An island can also serve as an eating area.

Chapter 8

Your Old Cabinets: Spruce 'em Up or Scrap 'em?

In This Chapter

▶ Updating your old cabinets

▶ Looking into new cabinet options

▶ Maximizing storage capabilities

Cabinets have a tremendous impact on a kitchen's look, so deciding whether you want to replace your existing cabinets or simply spruce them up with a new finish or some fancy knobs is a big decision. One factor that may help you decide is cost.

New cabinets will use up a huge chunk of your remodeling budget — nearly half of the cost of a complete kitchen remodel, according to a survey by the National Kitchen and Bath Association (NKBA). And you can easily spend more than half if you choose hardwoods or exotic veneers. If you're working with a generous budget, get the best quality cabinets that your budget allows to ensure the best endurance and performance. If you're working with a small budget, consider giving the cabinets you have a face-lift.

So with all the choices and decisions you'll need to make, just how should you start shopping? This chapter explains cabinets, inside and out. I also go over some alternatives to replacing cabinets that will give your kitchen a new look, yet aren't as expensive or as time consuming as a complete remodel.

Renovating Your Cabinets

I remember the first powerboat that my sister and brother-in-law purchased. The boat was a small 16-foot outboard that didn't look like anything special. My brother-in-law, however, is someone who knows how to take something ordinary and, with very little work, turn it into something special. In this case, he simply applied some pin striping along three areas of the hull. The striping not only classed up the look of the boat, but it also made the boat look like models that were two years newer. Okay, so what does pin-striping a boat have to do with a kitchen remodel? That boat's new look is a perfect example of what a little change or upgrade can do to make an old item look new or different. This section looks at some different levels of cabinet renovation that can get your kitchen looking just as great as my brother-in-law's boat.

Handles and hinges make a huge difference

One relatively easy and fairly inexpensive way to give your kitchen cabinets a new look is to replace the existing hardware. New knobs or pulls cost anywhere from $2 to $10 apiece, depending on style and finish. You can choose from simple, clean looking knobs to handles that are shaped like vegetables to match your kitchen's theme! You can also install new hinges, which usually run somewhere around $4 to $5 each. (See the "Making the 'hard' ware choices" section later in this chapter for more information about selecting hinges.)

If you plan to replace the drawer knobs or pulls, be aware of a couple of things. First, if the old handles are pulls, they'll have two legs that make the pull stand away from the drawer face. This means that you'll have two holes in the drawer face, approximately 3 to 4 inches apart (or on-center — o.c.). If you want to switch from pulls to a drawer knob, you'll have to deal with the two holes, because a single knob has one hole for the screw and is centered in the drawer face. Don't worry, though. You can still install a knob by putting a faceplate on the drawer front and then installing the knob. Faceplates are usually between 4- to 6-inches long so that they cover the holes created by a drawer pull. They also have a hole in the center for the knob. The reverse is true if you're going from knobs to pulls. You'll need to drill two holes for the pull's legs and cover the old centered hole from the knob. Faceplates for pulls are also available with two holes.

If you want to replace hinges, you'll first need to know the construction type of your cabinets and doors so that you purchase the correct type of hinge (I discuss cabinet types in detail later in this chapter). You need to know whether your cabinets have mortise hinges or non-mortise hinges:

- ✔ **Mortise hinges** are installed into the cabinet or door and require boring holes or cutting notches where the hinges attach.

- ✔ **Non-mortise hinges** simply attach to the cabinet face or back of the door panel with screws. No boring or notching is required, however, the hinges are more visible than the mortise type.

You also need to know whether your cabinets require fully-concealed or semi-concealed style hinges.

- ✔ **Fully-concealed hinges** are completely unseen when the doors are closed. Doors that completely or partially cover the cabinet's face panel use concealed hinges.

- ✔ **Semi-concealed hinges** show the moving hinge or knuckle of the cabinet hinge. Doors that are inset, which means they have ⅜-inch notch or lip along the edge and close inside the cabinet face panel, use semi-concealed hinges.

If you can't figure out what type your old hinges are, take one with you when you shop for replacements. A sales associate should be able to help you categorize your hinges.

Refinishing existing cabinets

If your old cabinets still seem to be solid but you're just tired of their look, then consider changing the finish by either painting or staining them. This allows you to leave the cabinet bodies in place, so you don't need to clear out the cabinets and live out of boxes for weeks. However, you will want to make sure that the items in your cabinets are back from the front edges of the cabinet faces when you paint or stain that area.

Painting

We painted the cabinets in our first home, mainly because our budget didn't allow for new cabinets. Painting the old blonde wood cabinets a very light sky blue transformed the kitchen into a much more inviting place to work, talk, or just hang out.

Before you paint, be sure that all the surfaces to be painted are smooth and clean. Use a fine grit sandpaper (150-grit or higher) to smooth any rough areas and fill any nicks, digs, or other imperfections with a latex wood filler or wall filler before priming. Follow the directions on the filler label.

You'll also want to apply a good-quality primer to cover the old finish. The primer ensures that the old stain and varnish is completely sealed, plus it provides a good surface for the new finish-coat. Use a good-quality oil-based primer. And, if possible, use the same brand primer that you use for the top-coat. Like-brands are formulated to work together.

Finally, apply a paint finish tough enough to stand up to the daily wear-and-tear, dirt, and grease every kitchen inflicts on cabinets. Go with a latex (water-based) semi-gloss (remember the old painter's rule: latex over oil, but never oil over latex). The latex base makes it easy to apply and clean up. Besides, today's generation of latex paints is just as durable as alkyd (oil-based) paints.

Painting will take a few days, primarily to allow for sufficient drying time between coats. Don't rush the application between coats. If the first coat isn't dry, the next won't adhere properly and you'll eventually have bubbles and blistering and a very unattractive finish. Remember, too, that you should paint only when you can provide adequate ventilation to remove fumes. Also be aware that the higher the humidity is, the longer paint takes to dry.

Staining

If you're someone who just can't stand painted wood or woodwork (and I know plenty of you are out there!), consider restaining the cabinets and doors. This involves more work than painting and takes longer, but when the job's completed you have the rich color you want and the natural look and grain of the wood showing through.

To refinish your cabinets, first strip off the old stain and varnish. You have options when it comes to paint and finish strippers. Some are much more user-friendly and less smelly and can actually be used indoors. These latex-based strippers are especially nice when you're stripping cabinets in the winter, when you can't open the windows for ventilation. Follow the directions on the stripper container.

Don't try to rush the process. Let the stripper work for as long as directed — if directions tell you to apply it and leave the stripper on for 24 hours, then do what they say!

After you strip the cabinets, select a stain. If you're trying to match the existing trim, which often is the same color as the old cabinets, it helps to bring along a sample piece when you buy the stain. If you like the existing color stain and you want to match it or you're just trying to reinvigorate the existing color, bring an unstripped door or drawer front panel. If you're changing color, be sure to know what species of wood the cabinets are so that you're looking at stain samples on the same species of wood as the cabinets. Different species can make stain lighter or darker, depending on the wood species.

When you start staining and varnishing, allow enough drying time between coats. Apply varnish to the doors in as dust-free an area as possible. Most kitchen doors will need two coats of varnish for best protection and endurance. Sand lightly after the first coat of varnish, usually with a 0000-grade steel wool, to remove any small blemishes. Use a tack cloth on the doors after sanding to remove all dust and sanding residue before applying the second coat. A *tack cloth* is a piece of wax-impregnated cheesecloth that grabs and holds even the finest dust particles. You'll find tack cloths wherever paint products are sold.

Refacing your existing cabinets

The true cabinet face-lift is when you replace the old doors and drawer fronts with new ones. This process is called *refacing* and is a perfect choice when the existing cabinet bodies are sound and you just want to change the style of the doors and drawers. You apply *veneer* (a thin self-adhering layer of wood) over the exposed cabinet fronts (the thin "faces" of the cabinet body itself) to match the doors. The companies also sell ⅛-inch thick plywood veneer panels in the same wood species as the new doors and drawer fronts that are installed on the exposed side panels of the end cabinets. You can buy the doors, drawer fronts, veneer, and plywood panels stained or unstained. The price difference is not great, but buying them unstained gives you more color options.

I can speak from experience on this project because I refaced the cabinets in my current kitchen. The old cabinets were solid and didn't need any repairs. I replaced the rough-sawn grain oak cabinet doors and drawer fronts with raised-panel maple doors and drawer fronts and boy, what a difference! The total cost for materials (doors, drawer fronts, stain, and varnish) was about $800. Thousands less than if I had replaced the cabinets. It also only took about two days to install the veneer strips and side panels and install the doors and drawers and another five days to stain and varnish the wood (because high humidity slowed drying conditions).

Most home centers can order the refacing materials for you. One vendor of refacing products is the Quality Door Company in Cedar Hill, Texas (800-950-3667). They make any size door in oak, maple, or even cherry. They also sell the veneer and the plywood end panels. They drill the holes in the doors if you're using concealed hinges, and they even sell the hinges, too. All wood products can be ordered natural (unstained) or they're available in a variety of the more popular stain colors. It takes about three weeks to fill an order — much less time than it takes to order cabinets, which usually takes between four to six weeks.

Replacing the old cabinets with new

Now we come to the most involved and expensive option — replacing the old cabinets with new ones. Choose this option if your old cabinets are too few in number, in need of a lot of repairs to make them serviceable, or if you want everything in the old kitchen replaced.

Selecting new cabinets isn't too difficult, as long as you have a decent understanding of cabinets and what to look for and as long as you do your homework. Accurate measurements are essential for when you order your new cabinets. Remember, even being off by as little as 1 inch can create major headaches when it comes time for the installation (which I discuss in Chapter 9). With those reminders, go ahead and dive into the world of kitchen cabinets — fill your head with the information that you need to shop smart.

Checking Out New Cabinet Choices

Get out your pencil and paper or your highlighting pen. This section is chock-full of information that you really need to know so that your cabinet shopping experience will be frustration free. Understanding the various types of cabinet construction, your range of choices in materials, and your style and finish options will make you one smart shopper. After you read this, you'll have a better understanding of the differences in the various cabinets on display at your home center or cabinet store. Check out the color insert, too, for many examples of cabinet styles and color options.

Comparing stock versus custom-made

There are two basic types of cabinets to choose from: stock and custom-made. Budget will play a big part when deciding which type you choose, as will whether you're planning on doing the installation or hiring someone to install the cabinets for you. Let's look at both types to help you decide which ones fit best in your new kitchen and budget.

- ✔ **Stock cabinets** are sold at home centers. Their quality of construction and materials range from somewhat below average to as good as a custom-made set, depending on how much you spend. The biggest advantage of stock cabinets is that they're designed for DIY installation. They also come finished (if you choose), or you can order stock cabinets unfinished if you don't like any of the manufacturer's color options.

  A drawback to stock cabinets is that they're constructed in 1-inch increments, so if your cabinet run comes up an inch or two short of your wall space, you'll need to fill the gap with filler strips (described in Chapter 9). Though not unattractive, filler strips do sometimes look like they're just, well, filling space.

- ✔ **Custom-made cabinets** are the best of the best because they're built to fit and fill an exact space — they can be sized down to $\frac{1}{16}$ of an inch! They're also constructed as one continuous structural unit, which makes them stronger than the individual boxes of stock cabinets.

> The drawback to custom cabinets is that you probably won't be able to do the installation. Custom cabinets are usually only guaranteed by the maker if they do the installation for you, to ensure proper alignment and operation.

You might be surprised to find that custom-made cabinets are not much more expensive than stock styles, and, in some cases, can even cost less, depending on the style and materials you select.

Stock cabinets still need to be ordered, built, and shipped, but you usually can expect to receive them six weeks from the time you order them. No home center has the space to store all the different sizes and finishes needed to complete a kitchen. You may have to wait a little longer for custom-made cabinets, depending on how fast the carpenter works and how busy he is with other jobs. Be sure to inquire about the construction and delivery timetable before giving a cabinetmaker the go-ahead. No one wants to wait six months for their new cabinets.

Shopping sites

Now that you have a better understanding of cabinets and hardware, you'd probably like some tips on where to shop for cabinets. You have three options: a kitchen design center, a custom cabinetmaker, or a home center. Here's some info on each one to help you decide where you might want to start shopping.

Kitchen design centers

As I mentioned in Chapter 2, a kitchen design center employs experts whose only job is designing kitchens. You'll be able to get advice on current cabinet trends, assistance in designing your new kitchen, help in selecting all the materials and hardware, and access to companies or individuals who can do all or part of the cabinet installation for you. These centers aren't inexpensive to use, but you get top-quality information that's usually worth the cost. You can find kitchen designers in the phonebook under "Kitchen Cabinets & Equipment". Or check the NKBA Web site (www.nkba.org) for a designer in your area.

Cabinetmakers

If you want cabinets that are truly unique and made just for your kitchen, a cabinetmaker is worth considering. Most have years of experience in construction and most install the cabinets themselves. However, although a cabinetmaker may have building and construction knowledge, she may lack a similar knowledge in total kitchen design. Don't be afraid to ask her for her background and experience in designing kitchens. Also, ask for references and a list of current clients. Give the references a call to see what they think of the quality of work, promptness, neatness, and even prices. If they liked the cabinetmaker's work, they'll probably be more than willing to talk. If not, they'll probably be closed-mouth — which should send up a red flag. Check the phonebook under "Cabinets & Cabinet Makers" for cabinetmakers in your area.

Big-box stores

Okay, you know who I'm talking about. They're the big home centers that are in all the major cities, most with multiple locations. Actually, this type of store is getting better and better in terms of assistance, both in materials and design help. Most are trying to cater to contractors in addition to their target market of homeowners and DIYers. Most home centers have a full-service kitchen department and offer kitchen design services. They usually have fairly current CAD (computer assisted design) equipment and trained designers and other staff to answer your questions. You'll also probably get the best cabinet prices, along with a decent selection of cabinet brands and styles. What you won't get is unique or custom items. Home centers carry specific brands of cabinets and can only offer what the various manufacturers make. So, if want custom, you'll have to go elsewhere.

Considering cabinet construction

Kitchen cabinets are generally divided into two construction types: framed or frameless. Both styles have one thing in common: each cabinet, regardless of the construction style, starts as a box. After that, things happen that give the cabinets different looks. Framed cabinets have a more traditional appearance, and frameless cabinets, often referred to as European-style cabinets, have a more contemporary look. Remember, too, that the type of material and the style of the doors and drawers and the hardware you choose will affect the look of the cabinet, no matter what type you choose.

Framed cabinets

In framed cabinets, the face frames are attached to the front edge of the box. The frame reinforces the box, making it a stronger cabinet than a frameless type. It also keeps the box square, which ensures that the doors open and close smoothly and that the drawers go in and out with little effort. The doors are mounted to the face frame. The face frame on each cabinet is also slightly wider than the actual box. This provides a tight seam when two cabinets are joined together.

Because each box is reinforced and very sturdy, framed cabinets can be made in wider widths than frameless cabinets. You'll find stock as wide as 48 inches (usually used as a sink base cabinet), and custom-made framed cabinets can be even wider.

The major drawback with framed cabinets is that the face frames overlap into the opening of the box, making the clear space to shelves and drawers narrower than the actual cabinet width. You only lose a few inches of clear space per cabinet, but even that small amount makes a real difference in storage space.

Features of a framed cabinet include a mounting rail at the back of the cabinet, corner blocks in the top corners to keep the cabinet square, and drawer box fronts that are attached to the drawer box itself. The shelves in a framed cabinet are stationary or *fixed* and rest on clips. The drawer glides are generally attached to the insides of the box and the drawer runs on the glides. The doors are usually attached with exterior hinges; however, concealed hinges are an option. Figure 8-1 shows the features of a framed cabinet.

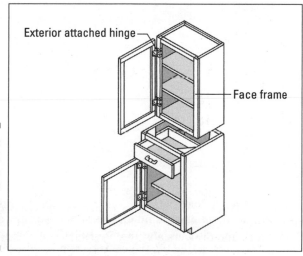

Exterior attached hinge

Face frame

Figure 8-1:
Framed cabinets are sturdy and have a more traditional look.

Frameless cabinets

Frameless cabinets are a relatively new design that came about primarily because of the development of a hinge that lets you attach the door directly to the box and not to a frame. The biggest drawback with frameless cabinets is that they're usually more expensive than framed cousins. Sometimes as much as 20 to 25 percent more, depending on the manufacturer.

Storage is easier in frameless cabinets and the amount of clear-space access is greater than with a framed cabinet, because the frame doesn't block off any space. They have a smoother, cleaner appearance than framed cabinets. Rollout shelves, drawers, and even stationary shelves are the full width of the box. Frameless cabinets use wood dowels and pins to connect the walls of the box. The shelves in a frameless cabinet are much more adjustable in height. Shelf pinholes are drilled every inch, which allows you to decide where to position the shelves. The drawers in frameless cabinets have the glides attached directly to the sides of the drawer. The front face of the drawer is also the front side of the drawer box; you don't have a drawer front like with a framed cabinet drawer. Figure 8-2 shows what a frameless cabinet looks like.

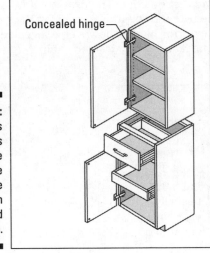

Concealed hinge

Figure 8-2:
Frameless cabinets provide more storage space than framed cabinets.

After they're installed, frameless cabinets are as solid as framed cabinets. Before they're installed, however, they're much less sturdy and need to be handled more carefully so that the joints aren't weakened. Take your time when installing them, however, and you'll have a rock solid, tight-seamed run of cabinets that will be the envy of your neighbors.

Taking note of cabinet types and sizes

Regardless of whether you select stock or custom-made cabinets, the types of cabinet you select from are the same. Sizes will vary, especially with custom-made cabinets, because they're being built to fit a specific area or dimension. Stock cabinets come in standard heights, widths, and depths, and any leftover spaces or gaps between a run of stock cabinets are filled with filler strips.

✔ **Base cabinets:** These are all of the cabinets that sit on the floor and are of standard countertop height. (A pantry cabinet that's full height is not considered a base cabinet.) The height of a standard base cabinet is 34½ inches, so that the counter top height will be no more than 36 inches after everything's installed. The standard depth is 24 inches, again, to accommodate the standard depth of counter tops (see Chapter 10 for more about countertops). Widths range from 9 to 48 inches in 3-inch increments. The 3-inch increment is standard for all stock cabinet manufacturers.

One specific base cabinet you need is the sink base cabinet. It's the widest base cabinet and comes in 36-, 39- 42- and 44-inch wide versions, depending on your design needs. All widths come with two doors for wide and clear access to not only the things you store in the cabinet, but also for any work that is done under the sink. One other specialty base cabinet you may need is one that has drop space in it to allow for a gas-fueled, drop-in cooktop (see Chapter 15). If you plan on having this type of appliance, make sure you or the kitchen designer orders the correct cabinets.

✓ **Utility cabinets:** This category includes cabinets for storage or for housing a wall oven. The standard heights are 84, 90, or 96 inches; depths are 12, 18, 21, or 24 inches for storage cabinets and 24 inches for an oven cabinet. Widths for storage cabinets are 12, 15, 18, 24, 30, or 36 inches; oven cabinets are 24, 27, 30, or 33 inches wide.

✓ **Wall cabinets:** These are the cabinets that are hung on the wall and considered to be at eye-level. You usually store your glasses and plates in wall cabinets. Standard wall cabinets come in heights of 12, 15, 18, 24, 30, 36, and 48 inches depending on where the cabinet is used in the kitchen design; for example, certain wall cabinets are made to fit over a refrigerator or range. Typically, a wall cabinet is either 12, 15, 18, or 21 inches deep. The widths range from 12 to 48 inches, also in 3-inch increments.

Mulling over material choices

As you begin shopping for cabinets, you'll find one thing for sure — few manufacturers make solid-wood cabinets. And if you do find some, the price tag will probably send you into shock. Most cabinets are made of several different materials — some for strength and durability and some for appearance. Many cabinets have solid wood face frames and solid wood doors with the box (body) of the cabinet being made of plywood. These materials determine how long you can expect the cabinets to last and how good they look. Take a closer look at your options.

Side substrate

The *side substrate* refers to the material that is underneath the veneer or outer surface of the cabinet, but it's the heart and strength of the cabinet.

✔ **Particleboard:** The most widely used product for making the inside or core of each wall of the box is *particleboard*, which is made of sawdust, wood shavings, and other small-sized wood by-products that are glued together under pressure. It's very cost-efficient and has amazing screw-holding capabilities. One drawback to particleboard is that it can warp over time, especially if the cabinet is overloaded.

✔ **Plywood:** Cabinets made with a plywood core were the original alternative to solid wood cabinets. Plywood is made by laminating thin layers of wood plies to each other and is engineered for strength by running each layer of the wood plies perpendicular to the one directly above or below it. The plywood surface is usually very rough and one that you wouldn't want as your outward surface. For that reason, a thin layer of actual wood, called *veneer,* is glued to the outer surface or face of the plywood. A cabinet made with a veneer-plywood is actually referred to as a solid-wood cabinet. Plywood is very strong and also has great screw-holding strength.

✔ **Medium-density fiberboard (MDF):** A high-quality product gaining ground in the cabinet construction world, MDF is made of wood particles that are even smaller than the ones used in particleboard. Like particleboard, MDF is glued together under pressure. However, MDF has a smooth, clean, paintable surface, and the edges can be shaped.

Surface materials

Surface materials refer to what you see. I'm talking about the outside of the cabinets. Your choice usually falls into one of four categories: laminates, melamine, vinyl films, and wood veneers.

✔ **Laminate** (actually called high-pressure laminate or HPL in the industry) has been around for years. High-pressure describes how the laminate is affixed to the substrate. The back of the laminate is coated with adhesive and then pressed onto the substrate under high pressure to bond the two materials together. All types of laminate, regardless of brand, are referred to as Formica. (Formica is an actual brand; using the name to refer to all laminate is like calling all facial tissues Kleenex.) Laminate is very durable, highly stain resistant, and available in the widest range of colors. A major drawback is that laminate is difficult to repair, and scratches, nicks, or gouges are hard to hide.

✔ **Melamine** is a newer type of laminate surface, a low-pressure laminate or LPL, which is attached with adhesive but not bonded under high pressure, but it's still very durable. Be warned that LPL may chip or crack if applied over a low-quality substrate such as waferboard or a poor grade of particleboard.

✔ **Vinyl films,** also known as thermo-foil films, are heat-laminated to the substrate. They're impervious to water and moisture, however, their appearance is less expensive looking (some actually almost look like drawer-liner contact paper!) than any of the other types of surface materials. Plus they're not as durable and can be nicked or ripped, much like vinyl drawer liner paper can be ripped.

✔ **Wood veneer.** Wood veneers give you the most elegant, expensive look for a cabinet surface, and they allow you to select any stain or paint color you want. It gives cabinets warmth, color, and texture and is actually very durable.

Dealing with doors and drawers

Now it's time to make the most important choice — style-wise: What will the door and drawer fronts look like? The doors are the largest exposed surface of the cabinet and they give cabinets their style. You can find everything from a flat-panel or slab door, to square raised-panel, to a Shaker style flat- and recessed-panel door. Figure 8-3 shows you some of the most popular door styles. Check out all the current styles at a home center or a cabinet-maker's shop. The color insert section also shows a variety of door and drawer styles.

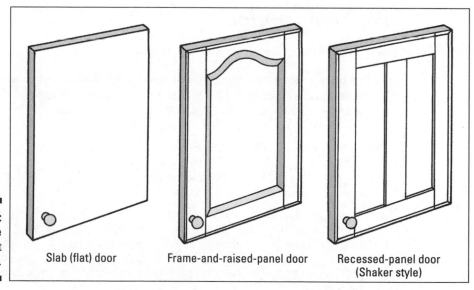

Figure 8-3:
Some cabinet door styles.

Slab (flat) door   Frame-and-raised-panel door   Recessed-panel door (Shaker style)

You also need to consider drawers. Cabinet drawers probably take the most abuse of any of the moving parts in a cabinet. The best way to know whether your cabinet is good quality is to check how long the drawers are guaranteed for — better-quality drawer construction and hardware (drawer glides) will be guaranteed for ten years or more.

To guarantee quality in the overall drawer construction, check to see what type of joint is used. *Dovetail joints* (where the two sides have fingers that interlock) show quality construction. *Dowel joints* (where wood dowel pins are glued into holes in the adjacent drawer side) are the next best type of joint. A *dado joint* (where the end of the face or back of the drawer fits into a slot in the side) is also okay, but not as good as the dovetail or dowel joints. (See the "Making the 'hard' ware choices" section later in this chapter for information about choosing drawer glides.)

Avoid joints that are simply stapled together. They're rarely very secure and certainly won't last long.

One other type of drawer design that some manufacturers use is a pre-formed metal pan with the drawer front screwed to the pan. This design is very sturdy. Naturally, they're more noisy due to their metal bodies, however most people use some sort of drawer liner or insert to keep various utensils separated.

Finishing options

You usually have three options for the finish:

- ✔ Factory-applied finishes actually are among the best and most consistent. Major cabinet manufacturers have automated finish application systems that ensure even application as well as controlled temperature and humidity levels for the best drying results.

- ✔ Natural or unfinished cabinets cost a little less than prefinished cabinets but not a lot less — usually only about 10 percent or so. However, buying unfinished cabinets and applying the finish yourself lets you gain a real connectedness to the project.

- ✔ Having the finish applied by a custom cabinet shop, especially if they didn't make the cabinets and are only finishing them, is fairly expensive. In most cases, the finish won't be any better than the factory-applied finish because the smaller cabinet shops can't afford the expense of the automated application and drying systems like the major cabinets companies can.

So, which is best? Well, if want to do more of the hands-on stuff, order unfinished cabinets and do the finishing. If you want to save time, or if you have a custom color picked out, have your cabinets come with the finished applied.

Making the "hard" ware choices

An often-overlooked part of selecting cabinets is deciding what type of hardware to use. Take a look at the four different types of hardware:

- ✔ **Door catches:** The hardware that keeps your doors closed isn't a biggie, but is still worth mentioning. Magnetic catches hold well, but sometimes take some effort to open. This may be a problem for younger children or adults with physical limitations. Nylon rollers with spring-steel catches are easy to use and still keep the cabinet door securely shut. Changing from one type to the other is a cheap project — either type of catch shouldn't cost more than $1 or $2 each.

- ✔ **Drawer glides:** A good-quality drawer glide makes the difference between a good drawer and a great drawer. Drawer glides come in three installation varieties (see Figure 8-4):

    Under-mounted slides that are installed on the bottom of the drawer.

    Bottom-mounted slides that are installed on both of the lower sides of each drawer.

    Full-extension slides that are mounted on the sides of the drawer. Full-extension slides are the best of the three for a couple of reasons. Because they allow the drawer to be pulled out fully, they must be heavy and durable enough to support the full weight of the drawer. And they allow you full access to the entire length of the drawer — outside of the cabinet! Because they're the best (and most desirable), they're the most expensive, often two or three times more expensive than under- or bottom-mounted glides.

No matter what type of drawer glide you choose, make sure the glides either have nylon rollers or a ball bearing and sleeve assembly. Both types move drawers in and out with little effort and, more importantly, little or no noise.

- ✔ **Handles and knobs:** Solid metal — especially brass — handles and knobs are preferred. They're heavy and solid and last for years. You'll probably replace them because you're tired of the style long before they show any signs of wear. Again, inexpensive knobs and handles (under $2 each) won't last forever. However, if you're someone who changes cabinet hardware every five years, then inexpensive stuff may be just fine. If you want these pieces to last as long as the cabinets, then expect to spend $4 to $8 (or more for solid brass) each.

    If you're going to install handles, make sure that the shape of the handle is easy to get your hand around. I've seen several cases where a homeowner had to change styles because the fancy curved shape was very difficult to grip. Also, avoid handles that stick out an inch or so beyond each mounting leg. These little stub-ends are great clothing catchers and can actually cause accidents in the kitchen. Imagine catching a shirt-sleeve on one when you're carrying a pot of boiling water over to the sink! It does happen.

✔ **Hinges:** As I mentioned in the "Handles and hinges make a huge differ-ence" section earlier in this chapter, the two major types of hinges are fully-concealed and semi-concealed. Hinges also differ in the material used and the finish. Most semi-concealed hinges are solid metal with plating applied and most fully-concealed hinges are usually stainless steel. Stainless hinges are the most durable because they don't add an applied finish that may come off. Expect to pay $4 to $10 for a high-quality, durable hinge. Hinges that cost only a buck or two are probably made of low-grade metals and will either wear out, break, or peel before too many years.

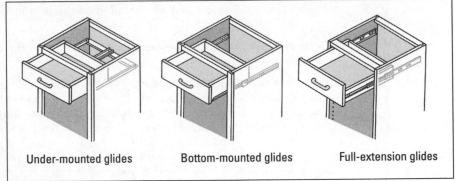

Figure 8-4: Drawer glide options.

Under-mounted glides   Bottom-mounted glides   Full-extension glides

Storage Design Options

Sure, most folks only see the outside of your cabinets, but how cabinets are designed and how they function on the inside is just as important to you as how they look on the outside. Check out the choices available to maximize your storage capacity.

Efficient interior designs

Years ago, the only options people had for how the interior of a cabinet was set up was how many shelves they wanted and where to position them. Well, not any more. Several new accessories make the inside of cabinets easy to use and give you maximum storage. These handy interior upgrades can be ordered already installed in your new cabinets, or you can buy them and install them yourself.

- ✔ **Appliance garage:** Hiding countertop appliances is easy when you have an appliance garage on the counter. They're usually placed in a corner, although I have seen them right in the middle of the counter run. A pull-down door hides the appliances when they're not needed, yet allows for quick, easy access when you need to use them.

- ✔ **Pullout shelves:** This may be the most popular design change to kitchen base cabinets to come along. Pullout shelves allow easy access to everything in the cabinet, especially items that are typically buried or lost in the back. They're also a great upgrade for folks nearing or in middle age. Remember, as we get older it gets harder and harder to bend down and reach into the back of the cabinets.

- ✔ **Rollout baskets and bins:** Rollout baskets are a great way to handle garbage containers and recycle bins. Rollout wire bins are very popular, especially for storing vegetables, because they allow air circulation, which reduces spoilage. They're also great for storing linens because you can see exactly what's in the bin without having to dig through everything.

- ✔ **Spice racks:** One of the most popular options in the kitchen, according to an NKBA survey, is a separate, tilted spice rack in a drawer. Its design allows for maximum storage space and easy reading of and access to the individual bottles.

- ✔ **Tilt-out drawer fronts:** Another neat add-on or upgrade is a tilt-out hinge and holder for the back of the drawer front that's directly below the sink. Most often this is a stationary drawer front. The tilt-out bins or holders are great for holding scrub brushes, pads, and other small cleaning items used for cleaning dishes.

Avoiding dead corner spaces

Everyone wants to maximize kitchen storage space, and letting a dead corner go unused is almost considered a sin. But you can gain as much useful space and access as possible with the following options:

- ✔ **Full-access doors:** The best way to eliminate multiple door hassles in a corner is to have a 90-degree, full- or easy-access corner door. This door style opens with both sections of the 90-degree door swinging open, giving you a clear view and full access into the corner cabinet. Full-access doors are available on both base and wall cabinets.

- ✔ **Lazy Susan:** You can have things at your fingertips with just the turn of a shelf. Install a Lazy Susan. The revolving shelves of a Lazy Susan bring items to the front of the cabinet by simply spinning the unit. A Lazy Susan works best with full-access doors, although it also works okay even with a corner cabinet with two separate doors. Figure 8-5 shows a Lazy Susan in a corner cabinet.

The biggest drawback with a Lazy Susan is that it's easy to overload, which can deform shelves and cause the unit to drag or rub on the cabinet bottom. Use it wisely and you'll be fine.

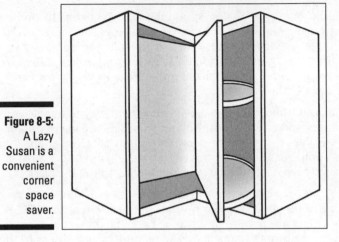

Figure 8-5:
A Lazy
Susan is a
convenient
corner
space
saver.

Chapter 9

Making Old Mother Hubbard Proud: Putting New Cabinets Up

In This Chapter

▶ Getting your tools together

▶ Figuring out where to put your cabinets

▶ Installing wall cabinets

▶ Fitting base cabinets to the wall

*I*f you bought new base and wall cabinets, you know how expensive they are. In fact, you probably spent the biggest chunk of your remodeling budget on them, so you want them installed correctly.

Installing kitchen cabinets is a project that most intermediately skilled DIYers can handle. But if you decide to do this yourself, make sure you allow yourself enough time — and don't rush through any of the steps. Rushing leads to mistakes and mistakes lead to frustration and an unsatisfied homeowner (that's you!). Remember, these cabinets may be in your home for many, many years. And if you're not happy with the installation or their operation, you'll only be reminded of your dissatisfaction every time you reach for a glass or a saucer; only you know how often that is, but in most homes it's at least once a day.

Plan your work schedule *before* you begin the installation. Set aside the better part of a weekend to install the cabinets. The project may not take the entire weekend, but better that you have extra time in the event of a problem or two.

Gathering the Right Tools

Always gather all of the tools together that you need before you start a project. You need them at various stages of the project; however, it's better and faster to be able to walk (or send a helper) to your tool area and grab what you need to keep the job moving. If you're not familiar with all of the tools mentioned in this chapter, flip back to Chapter 5 for a quick review or explanation. Here's a list of the tools you need on hand in order to install new cabinets:

✔ One 2-foot and one 4-foot level. (The 2-footer is good for checking level and plumb in tight areas, but use the 4-foot level whenever possible for checking level and plumb; you can also use the 4-foot level to determine the high point of your floor.)

✔ A straight, long (6- or 8-foot) 2 x 4 (used with the level for checking the floor's level and high point)

✔ An 8-foot-long 1 x 4 pine board (used as the ledger support board when installing the wall cabinets)

✔ A chalk line

✔ A tape measure (25 foot minimum)

✔ A stud finder

✔ A 6-foot stepladder (a 4- or 5-foot ladder will work, but I prefer a 6-footer)

✔ A variety of clamps (squeeze, wooden screw, and spring clamps of various sizes)

✔ A $\frac{3}{16}$-inch diameter, countersink drill bit

✔ Some 3-inch-long drywall screws

✔ Several No.2 Phillips screw bits

✔ A $\frac{3}{8}$-inch drill/driver (corded or cordless)

✔ A hammer

✔ A package (or two) of wood shims

✔ A jigsaw

✔ A heavy-duty extension cord for a corded drill or jigsaw (a 25-foot cord is best, especially if you need to draw power from another room)

Once again, you'll need these tools throughout this part of the project but not for every step. Just make sure you have them handy.

Marking Reference Lines and Mounting Locations

Marking reference lines is the first step you need to take when installing cabinets and it's the most crucial step for this part of the remodel. If you don't have accurate reference lines, your cabinets will most likely be misaligned, which will affect their operation and appearance.

Checking your floor for level

Don't assume that your floor is level. Most floors are off by a little bit, but not so much that an installation is impossible for a DIYer. To check your floor for level, lay a long 2 x 4 on edge against the wall where the base cabinets will be installed and set the 4-foot level on the edge of the 2 x 4 as shown in Figure 9-1. The long 2 x 4 measures a greater distance of the floor giving you a more accurate reading with the level, plus the level is higher than floor-level making it easier to read. Perform this check against the wall and also about 2 feet out from the wall. (Two feet out is approximately where the front of the cabinets will be located.) Look at the bubbles in the vials. The bubbles should be inside the two lines marked on the vials. After you've determined level, find the highest point of the floor and mark that spot on the wall. The high point of the floor is where the floor and wall actually meet. This is the starting point for all of the height measurements.

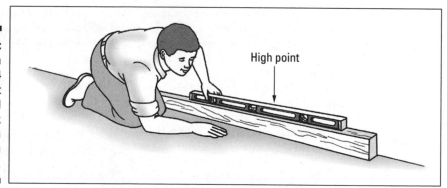

Figure 9-1: Use a straight 2 x 4 and a 4-foot level to find and mark the high point on the wall.

High point

Adding cabinets before new flooring is the way to go

Here's one question that a lot of people ask: "Should I run my new floor from wall-to-wall and then install the cabinets on the new floor, or should I install the cabinets first and butt the new floor up to it?" Honestly, either method works, but installing new cabinets before new flooring is best.

Installing flooring over the entire area and then installing cabinets on it seems like a waste of money, because you're covering flooring that will never be used. In addition, installing cabinets on a finished floor raises the height of the top of the base cabinet, though not that much. In my kitchen I lost about ½ to ¾ of an inch of space between the countertop and the bottom of my wall cabinets because my base cabinets are on the finished floor. Not a lot of space to lose, but it is less than I'd have had if the cabinets had been installed on the kitchen's plywood subfloor. I discuss flooring and subfloors in Chapter 21.

If you choose to install the cabinets first and then lay the floor, you will save money by using less flooring material. Plus you can work on the subfloor and not have to worry about damaging a new floor when you're installing cabinets. I know if I have a choice, I install the cabinets first and put the flooring down second. And if you're even moderately skilled, you can make your flooring cuts close enough to the cabinet so that any small gap can be covered by a toe-kick trim strip.

Measuring cabinet heights

Measuring cabinet heights may be the most crucial step in the entire cabinet installation because, if your reference lines aren't accurate, the entire installation will be incorrect. Here's what to do so that your installation is perfect.

First, measure the height of your base cabinets. If your cabinets are standard height, they should be 34½ inches tall (before a countertop is installed). This is the height I refer to in this chapter. Next, measure up the wall from the high point mark the height of your base cabinets — 34½ inches for me — and mark the wall. Mark this height in three or four spots down the length of the wall for easy and accurate height marking on the wall.

Next, measure the height of your wall cabinets. The most common height of wall cabinets is 30 inches, so that's the measurement I use in this chapter. 30-inch cabinets are common in kitchens with 8-foot ceilings. If your ceiling is taller, you may choose to have taller wall cabinets. Shorter wall cabinets of 18, 15, and 12 inches tall are used around appliances; however, you should use the measurement of your tallest wall cabinet to mark a mounting line.

You need to measure and mark the height of the top and bottom of the wall cabinets. For a 30-inch wall cabinet, start at the high point and measure up 54 inches, and mark this height on the wall in three or four places. This line notes the bottom of your wall cabinet. Next, measure up 30 inches from the bottom line, and mark this height on the wall in three or four places. This line notes the top of your wall cabinet.

After you mark the top and bottom of the wall cabinet, check the distance between the bottom of the wall cabinet and the top of the base cabinet — this distance should be 19½ inches. Also, check the distance from the floor's high point to the top of the wall cabinet — this distance should be 84 inches. Figure 9-2 shows these standard measurements marked on a wall.

When you have your measurements marked on the wall, have a helper assist you and snap chalk lines at the top of your base cabinets and the bottom of your wall cabinets. These are your reference lines for installation. Perform this procedure on each wall where cabinets will be installed. Be careful as you chalk the lines — make sure your lines are staying level around the entire room.

If you do the math for the previously mentioned height marks, you'll come up with a total cabinet height of 84 inches or 7 feet. This leaves you approximately 12 inches of space above the cabinet for open storage or for a soffit, if your kitchen has one. A *soffit* is the square, boxed-in shape above many kitchen cabinet installations.

Again, I say these dimensions are approximates. For example, my kitchen has wall cabinets that are 32-inches tall and a soffit that's 12½ inches high. The space between my countertop and wall cabinets is 16 inches, and the distance from the floor to the top of the countertop is 35 inches. Add those figures together and you get 95½ inches. So, where's the other ½ inch for my 96-inch (8-foot) tall ceilings? It's made up of the ½-inch-thick ceramic tile floor. See, I told you a lot of these measurements are approximates, but they still need to add up to 96 inches for a standard 8-foot-tall ceiling.

Locating the wall studs for mounting

Wall cabinets must be secured to the walls with screws that are driven into wall studs. Hanging cabinets with hollow wall anchors is asking for a disaster! Even the most heavy-duty hollow wall anchor can't support the weight of the cabinets plus the weight of all of the items stored inside.

Use a stud finder to locate each wall stud. In most construction, especially in homes built after the 1960s, the wall studs are spaced every 16 inches or 16-inches-on-center (16-o.c.). In older homes, spacing could vary or be inconsistent. Mark each wall stud in the measured areas for the wall cabinets and the base cabinets. No need to draw lines in the space between the cabinets, because nothing will be anchored to them there. Make sure the stud marks go to the ceiling or where the top of the cabinet will hit, so that you can secure the cabinet at the very top.

A quick, slick way to verify your marks and ensure that you have, indeed, located the wall studs is to pound a finish nail in an area hidden by the cabinets. If you've found the stud, the nail will be hard to drive after it has penetrated the drywall.

After you've marked the wall stud locations, attach a temporary *ledger board* to help support the upper cabinets during installation. I suggest using an 8-foot-long 1 x 4 pine board. Secure the ledger board along and below the line that marks the bottom of your wall cabinets. Use 2½ inch long drywall screws driven into every other stud to secure the ledger board to the wall (see Figure 9-3). Cut the ledger board to length, depending on the length or *run* of your wall cabinet sections. After the wall cabinets are up and secured, you remove the ledger board, patch the small screw holes, and paint the walls when ready.

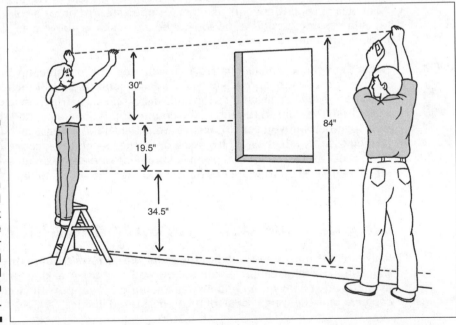

Figure 9-2:
Measure from the floor's high point and mark reference lines for base and wall cabinets on the wall.

Figure 9-3:
Attach a ledger board to temporarily support wall cabinets.

Checking your walls for plumb

You need to check to see if your walls are *plumb* or vertically level. The best way to check is to place a 4-foot level vertically on the wall. If the wall where the cabinet end butts against is either way in or out of plumb (walls can go in either direction — I've seen both), you may need to add a *filler strip* between the cabinet end and the wall to compensate for the difference. (Sometimes you also need to add a filler strip between two cabinets if the widths of the cabinets don't quite add up to the dimension they're trying to fill.) I tell you when and how to install a filler strip later in this chapter.

If the wall is more than ½-inch out of plumb or if you feel this is more than you want to attempt, hire a contractor to install the cabinets.

Noting cabinet position

Before you start hanging cabinets, mark each cabinet (both base and wall cabinets) position along the chalk lines. This means measuring each cabinet's width and transferring that dimension onto the wall at the appropriate location. Marking the cabinet positions now allows you to see if the cabinets will line up vertically, especially around appliances. Believe me, you want to do this dry-layout of marks to detect any problem, rather than finding out that something doesn't line up after you've started installing the cabinets.

If you have face-framed cabinets (see Chapter 8 for an explanation), the frames or faces extend beyond each side of each cabinet by ¼ inch. Make sure that you allow for this distance (a total of ½ inch or ¼ inch on each side of the cabinets) when marking the cabinets' positions on the wall. The side panel marks for each cabinet should not butt up to each other. There should be ½ inch between each cabinet or box side. If you have frameless cabinets (again, see Chapter 8), the front and rear width dimensions will be the same.

Now is also the time to test-fit the corner cabinets. A *blind corner* is where two cabinets butt to each other forming a right angle as shown in Figure 9-4. Move the two cabinets into position and adjust their location as needed so that they line up correctly and the doors of each cabinet operate properly without interfering with each other. You can avoid blind corners by ordering a blind corner cabinet unit, which is one large cabinet that extends to both walls in the corner eliminating the panel that causes the blind corner.

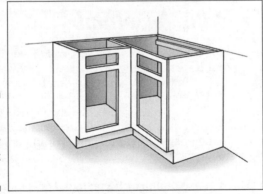

Figure 9-4: A blind corner cabinet unit.

Hanging Wall Cabinets First

I recommend installing the upper or wall cabinets first because you won't have to be working above the base cabinets. The open area of the floor allows you, your helper, and your stepladder clear access.

Before you actually mount the wall cabinets, get organized. Uncrate or unbox each cabinet and remove the doors. Mark each door and cabinet so that the door that came off a specific cabinet goes back on the same cabinet. They may look the same, but each door and cabinet box was matched, drilled, and attached to fit only the cabinet it came with. Mix them up and you could be in for misalignment, poor operation, and less than desirable appearance. Identify each cabinet and door with a piece of masking tape. I start with a corner cabinet as Number 1 and then work out in each direction using the Number 1 cabinet as my starting point for each direction. This system works for me, however, you can develop a system that works for you.

Note: This section describes installing framed cabinets. Installation instructions for frameless cabinets are similar except when connecting adjoining cabinets, as I explain in the "Finishing the cabinet run" section.

Installing the first cabinet

Well, it's time to install the first cabinet. And once you start, you'll be amazed at the quick progress you'll make by following these steps:

1. **Set the first cabinet (I suggest starting with a corner cabinet) on the ledger strip and secure the top and bottom of the cabinet to the wall with 3-inch long screws (as shown in Figure 9-5).**

   First drill two $\frac{3}{16}$-diameter pilot holes in the upper and lower hanging rails of the cabinets (the two horizontal pieces of lumber along the top and bottom of the back of the cabinet). Pilot holes make it easier to drive in screws because you've removed some of the material that you need to drill through. Always make pilot holes slightly smaller in diameter than the diameter of the screw you'll be driving. If they're larger, the screw won't hold.

   Go ahead and snug up the screws as you go, but don't tighten them completely. You'll go back later for a final tightening of all the screws.

   If you have a helper, have her hold the unit in place while you secure it with screws. If you're working alone, cut some lengths of lumber and make a V-shaped notch in one end. Use these pieces as braces by placing the notch against the bottom of the cabinet and wedging the lumber up to hold the cabinet in place. Put a rag or piece of cardboard over the cabinet where the notched lumber will go to protect the cabinet's finish.

Figure 9-5: Position the wall cabinet on the ledger board and drive 3-inch-long screws into the top and bottom hanging rails.

2. Check the cabinet for plumb.

You shouldn't have to worry about the cabinet being level if your reference lines and chalk lines were level when you measured and marked them. However, if the cabinet happens to be out of alignment by more than an ⅛-inch, use shims to adjust its position. Most often you'll need to bring the bottom of the cabinet out away from the wall, as most walls bow in the middle.

3. If a shim is necessary to plumb the cabinet, gently tap the shim behind the outer edge of the cabinet using a hammer (see Figure 9-6).

Be careful not to mar the wall surface with the hammer. Keep the level against the face of the cabinet so that you know when the shim has corrected the problem.

4. After the cabinet's plumb and level, drill a pilot hole through the cabinet's hanging strip and the shim and then drive a 3-inch drywall screw into the hole to hold the shim in place.

Figure 9-6:
Use shims to make the cabinets plumb.

5. Break off the excess length of the shim.

Score the shim along the bottom of the cabinet using a utility knife with a new blade. (A new blade makes a clearer cut and works more easily.) Make several score cuts and then snap off the excess shim.

6. Install a filler strip if one is needed between the cabinet you just installed and the one next to it.

Clamp the filler strip in place and drill ³⁄₁₆-inch pilot holes through the cabinet face frame and filler strip, using a countersink bit to recess the screw head into the face frame. Secure the strip with 3-inch drywall screws.

Finishing the cabinet run

Continue installing each adjoining cabinet, but work outward in only one direction at a time. Don't work back and forth from the corner. You'll have better results finishing one entire length of the run.

1. **After you've set the first cabinet, position the second cabinet next to the first one.**

2. **Check the second cabinet for plumb along the face frame and secure it temporarily to the adjacent cabinet with squeeze or wooden screw clamps.**

   I recommend these types of clamps, because their faces won't mar the cabinet finish. However, if I had to choose one over the other, I'd go with the squeeze clamps (described in Chapter 5). They're easier to use.

3. **After the cabinet is clamped, recheck it for plumb and then attach the cabinet to the wall using the hanger strips inside the cabinet.**

4. **Connect adjacent cabinets to each other with 3-inch drywall screws — one about 6 inches from the top and one about 6 inches from the bottom of the cabinet.**

   First, drill a pilot hole in the face frame of one cabinet and half way into the adjacent face frame to make connecting the cabinets easier.

5. **Continue these steps to complete one side of the cabinet run, then start back at the corner (Number 1) cabinet and install the other direction of the cabinet run.**

6. **After the entire run of cabinets has been installed, remove the ledger board and recheck the entire run for plumb.**

7. **Make any necessary adjustments with shims.**

   You may need to loosen some of the screws to make the adjustments.

8. **Tighten all the wall screws completely.**

9. **Reinstall the doors, and check each one for clean operation.**

   Doors have a tendency to misalign after they've been removed. However, many styles of hinges allow you to make minor adjustments to get doors operating smoothly. Be careful when redriving the screws for the hinges. The screws are generally made from a fairly soft metal, which makes the heads easy to strip and the shafts of the screws easy to snap off. A stripped screw can be replaced. A snapped off screw will need to be extracted, because you need to use the same hole that currently has the broken screw in it. To remove a broken screw, use a screw extractor. Extractor kits are available at home centers and hardware stores for under $20.

If the end of the cabinet run has an exposed end panel, you may want to use a trim molding to cover any gaps between the cabinets and the wall. Sometimes a wall is just too wavy or weird to get an end panel to fit snug, and a piece of trim molding not only looks nice but covers up the imperfection.

Now is the time to install a decorative valance, if your design has one, over the sink. You need to position the valance between the two cabinets that flank each side of the sink, secure the valance temporarily with clamps, drill pilot holes, and then secure it to the adjacent cabinets with 3-inch screws.

The steps listed in this section are for face-framed cabinets. Frameless cabinets are installed in much the same manner except when connecting adjoining cabinets. To join frameless cabinets, use wood screws that are just shorter than the thickness of the two cabinet sides. Secure each cabinet with four screws placed about 1 inch in from the front edge of the cabinet. If you drill pilot holes, be very careful not to drill completely through both of the cabinets.

Adding the Lower Level — Base Cabinets

Now you get to fill in the bottom half of the kitchen and install the base cabinets. You start the same way you did with the wall cabinets — unbox each cabinet and remove all doors and drawers, marking each one as you go, to make sure the right door or drawer returns to its intended spot.

Installing the first cabinet

Start your base cabinets in the same way you started the wall cabinets:

1. **Position the first cabinet (I suggest starting with a corner cabinet) so that the top is flush with the reference line.**

2. **Check the cabinet to make sure that it's plumb and level.**

   The first unit that's installed must be level. If you start with a level base, the countertop will be much easier to level.

3. **If necessary, gently tap wood shims under the front or exposed side of the cabinet to get it level and between the wall and cabinet back to get it plumb (see Figure 9-7).**

   Keep the level against the face of the cabinet so that you know when the shim has corrected the problem. Also, if you use a shim between the wall and cabinet back to plumb the cabinet, make sure the shim is placed over a wall stud so that the screw that holds the shim in place can later be screwed into a stud.

Figure 9-7:
Use shims as needed to level the base cabinet.

4. **After the cabinet is plumb and level, drill pilot holes through the mounting (called a hanging strip in a wall cabinet) strip and then secure the cabinet to the wall with 3-inch drywall screws.**

5. **Break off the excess length of shim protruding out from the front or side of the cabinet.**

   Score the shim along the bottom of the cabinet using a utility knife with a new blade. (A new blade makes a clearer cut and works more easily.) Make several score cuts and then snap off the excess shim.

Finishing the cabinet run

Finishing the base cabinet runs is less strenuous than hanging the wall cabinets because the cabinets rest on the floor and don't need to be supported while you secure them to the wall. It's still a good idea, however, to have a helper nearby to help make adjustments.

Before you install your sink-base cabinet, you may need to make cutouts for the plumbing pipes if the cabinet has a back (see Figure 9-8). Measure from the side of the adjacent cabinet to the center of each plumbing supply or pipe (drain line and water supply lines). Transfer those measurements to the back of the cabinet and use a jig saw to cut out enough of an opening for your plumbing pipes to fit through. Make sure the measurements are accurate — you'll be making an expensive mistake if you have to replace the sink base cabinet. Remember the old rule: "Measure twice, cut once." If you do happen to screw up big-time, you can cover the errant holes with a piece of ⅛-inch-thick Masonite plywood/paneling. Paint the piece to match the inside of the cabinet and no one will know that you goofed!

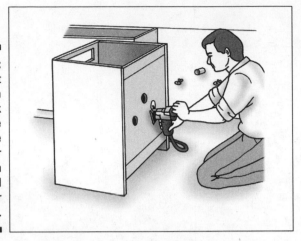

Figure 9-8:
Cut
openings in
the back
panel of the
sink base
cabinet for
the drain
line and
water
supply lines.

Follow these steps to finish the base cabinet run:

1. **Place the second cabinet into position and check it for plumb and level.**

2. **If a shim is necessary, gently tap it into place using a hammer.**

   Don't trust your eye to check for level. Just because the two cabinets are flush along the top edge doesn't mean they're both level and/or plumb. Check it and adjust as necessary. You may need to place shims under the front or exposed side of the cabinet and between the back of the cabinet and the wall.

3. **After both cabinets are level and plumb, clamp them together and drill ³/₁₆-inch pilot holes through the mounting strip and secure both cabinets to the wall with 3-inch drywall screws.**

4. **Connect adjacent cabinet face frames by first clamping them together.**

5. **Drill ³/₁₆-inch pilot holes through one of the adjacent face frames but not through the other face frame.**

   Use a countersink bit so that these screw heads will be hidden after they're installed.

6. **Secure the cabinets together with 3-inch drywall screws (see Figure 9-9).**

7. **Break off the excess length of the shim.**

   Score the shim along the bottom of the cabinet using a utility knife with a new blade. (A new blade makes a clearer cut and works more easily.) Make several score cuts and then snap off the excess shim.

8. **Continue adding cabinets until the entire run is connected in both directions.**

Figure 9-9:
Connect
the base
cabinets
with 3-inch
screws.

9. **Recheck each cabinet individually to make sure it's level and even in all directions.**

10. **Then, secure each cabinet to the wall studs with 3-inch drywall screws.**

   If a shim was necessary to plumb the cabinet, be sure to screw the shim into a stud. If it isn't secure, the shim could work loose over time.

If your new cabinets include a separate pantry unit, install it the same way you installed the first cabinet of either the wall or base run: make sure it's level and plumb and secure it to the wall with 3-inch drywall screws.

After the cabinets are secured, you may find that you have a gap along an end panel and the wall or along the floor where shims may have been needed. Use a decorative trim molding to cover the gap between the end panel and the wall in the same manner as with the wall cabinets. To cover the gap at the floor along the area called the toe-kick, install a strip of matching hardwood.

Don't reinstall the doors and drawers on the base cabinets until after the countertop has been installed (see Chapter 11). You need to have access to the underside of the countertop to secure it to the cabinets. Leaving the doors off and the drawers out gives you as much clear access as possible.

Chapter 10

Considering Creative Countertop Options

In This Chapter

▶ Perusing countertop possibilities

▶ Figuring out the best place to buy a countertop

part from the kitchen cabinets, countertops have the most influence and effect on the overall appearance of your kitchen, especially if you have a large area of counter space. A wide variety and selection of countertops is available in an array of materials, colors, and even textures. Each one has unique design and function properties.

As you plan your kitchen, you need to determine how much of your budget you're willing to devote to countertops. Go nuts and you can easily devote 30 to 40 percent of your budget to the countertops. (Remember that you may have spent 50 percent of your budget on cabinets, so between the cabinets and countertops you may have used up to 80 percent of your budget!) But even if you have to make some compromises on materials to stay within your total budget, you should still be able to get countertops that will make your kitchen look fabulous.

Considering Your Countertop Options

Replacing an out-of-date or damaged countertop is one way to upgrade the look of your kitchen without replacing everything (I tell you how in Chapter 11). Several friends of mine have done just that and, boy, do the new countertops jazz up their kitchens. If you hadn't known that they only replaced the countertops, you'd swear that they remodeled the entire kitchen.

Reusing existing countertops when you're replacing cabinets, however, is not a cost-cutting or money-saving option in my book. Countertop materials and colors seem to become dated more easily than cabinet styles, and your new cabinets will make the old countertops look just that — old — even when installed on new cabinets.

Choosing what you want your countertops to be made of isn't difficult, after you know what your choices are and understand the pros and cons of each type of material. The next sections describe the most commonly used materials for countertops and go over the positives and negatives of each one.

Countertops you can install yourself

Don't let countertops frighten you — some are actually intended to be installed by DIYers. That's why so many are sold at home centers. If you have even average DIY skills, you should be able to tackle and finish installing the countertops described in the following sections.

Plastic laminate

The number one material used for kitchen countertops is plastic laminate. You may hear some professionals refer to the countertop as Formica, but this is actually a brand name. Some folks use the word Formica generically just as some people refer to all sodas as Coke. Formica does make a nice plastic laminate countertop; Wilsonart is another popular brand name plastic laminate manufacturer.

Plastic laminate is very popular because it's

✔ Inexpensive (ranging from $3 per foot and up, depending on style and color)

✔ Easy to maintain (just wipe it down and go!)

✔ Available in many colors, textures, and patterns

✔ Easy to install

But plastic laminate does have some drawbacks:

✔ Shows scratches and chips (doesn't stand up well to sharp knives).

✔ Tricky to repair if you nick or scratch the surface (all repairs should be handled by professional countertop technicians).

✔ Burns or scorches if a hot pan is placed directly on the surface. Burns and scorches can't be removed.

One way you can reduce the chance of seeing a scratch is to order solid-core or color-through laminate. This type of laminate has the color running completely through it, top to bottom, so when you scratch the surface, you don't have a white substrate showing in the scratched area. You may have a scratch, but it's the same color as the laminate, making it less obvious. The color on less expensive laminate is only on the surface. Color-through laminate is also better at hiding the dark lines at seams and along the edges.

Plastic laminate countertops come in two forms: prefab or special order (cut and shaped to your specifications). The prefab sections are called premolded or post-formed and are formed by bonding sheets of laminate over a ¾-inch thick substrate of either particleboard or plywood. These post-formed sections are what you commonly see standing upright in the tall racks at home center stores. In-stock lengths range from 4- to 12-feet long and come in the standard depth of 25 inches. Longer lengths and special angles, corners, or seam-cuts can be ordered. The price difference between in-stock and special order post-formed countertops is not very great. You'll have to pay for special angle cuts or unusual sizes, for example, if you want the countertop to be deeper than the standard 26-inch depth. But aside from the special cut or size charges, the straight sections of either prefab or special order countertop will be about the same size. The reason some sizes have to be special ordered is because no home center has enough room to keep every length in stock.

The backsplash of a plastic laminate countertop is usually one of two types:

✔ **Post-formed** at the factory as part of the substrate. This style has a seamless piece of laminate covering the entire backsplash, flat surface, and front edge.

✔ **Self backsplash** where a separate piece of the substrate is attached on-site. The self backsplash has a seam at the back of the flat surface where it meets the backsplash.

Personally, I like the post-formed style because of the seamless look.

The front edges on all laminate countertops are part of the flat surface with no seam along the length of the edge. From there, your countertop may have one of three styles or shapes of edges:

✔ The **radius edge** has rounded shoulders on both the top and bottom and a flat front surface.

✔ The **waterfall** uses a broader, rounded top edge and flat front.

✔ The **round-over edge** has rounded top and bottom shoulders but has a protruding or bumped out front surface.

The cut edge of the laminate and the edge of the substrate are exposed on the ends of laminate countertops. These ends need to be covered to prevent damage, such as chipping, plus they're ugly if left exposed. Adhesive-attached end caps are available.

TIP

A popular design option that really dresses up plastic laminate countertops is to use a contrasting edge material, such as wood, tile, or even stone, along the front edge. If you choose this option, the manufacturer leaves the front edge of the countertop open, just like the ends. You'll need to attach the edging after the countertop is installed.

Ceramic tile

Another extremely popular material for kitchen countertops is ceramic tile. Why? Because you can do so much with it, especially when you incorporate different colors and textures in the design. You can make your kitchen look rustic or urban, traditional or contemporary. Just don't make the colors or patterns too busy design-wise. A few colored tiles used wisely on the counter surface or the backsplash is usually all that's needed to add zip and zest to a ceramic tile countertop. You can also add color by using colored or lightly shaded grout between the tiles.

Take a look at ceramic tile's pluses:

- ✔ Durable
- ✔ Affordable, starting at around $2 a square foot and going up from there, depending on tile style
- ✔ Available in many colors, sizes, and textures
- ✔ Moisture- and heat-resistant
- ✔ Easy to clean
- ✔ Can be installed by moderately-skilled DIYers

But ceramic tile has some cons to consider too:

- ✔ Grout lines are prone to staining, especially if you don't wipe them down often
- ✔ Food, dirt, and debris can become encrusted on grout surface
- ✔ Can chip or crack, which means replacing damaged tile(s) and grout
- ✔ Not a good chopping surface due to the unevenness between tiles and grout lines

If you plan to install a ceramic tile countertop, your tile choices are seemingly endless. You can use either wall or floor tiles. Wall tiles are usually smaller in size and thickness. Floor tiles are thicker so they're more durable. Either way, your choices are wide ranging.

REMEMBER

Make sure that the tile(s) you select don't absorb water. And choose tile that has a gloss or matte glaze finish. The glaze prevents water from penetrating and damaging the tile, plus smooth surfaces are easier to clean.

Butcher-block

Yes, you can still actually use real wood in the kitchen. And not just for small cutting boards. Butcher-block countertops are made of thin strips of hardwood that are glued together. Hard maple is the best wood for a butcher-block counter. Its tight, fine grain makes it very durable. Red and white oak as well as beech are also suitable countertop woods. The most common use of a wood or butcher-block surface is as a cutting-board insert or as the surface of a center island. The warm richness of the wood can be paired with other countertop materials to enhance a kitchen's visual appeal.

Wood is a wise choice for several reasons:

- Perfect for providing a warm appearance
- Easy to repair — scratches can be sanded out with sandpaper
- Easy on knives (doesn't dull them)
- Easy to install

But it does have drawbacks:

- Hard to maintain (must be oiled regularly with vegetable oil or a non-toxic finishing oil, such as pure tung oil)
- Not a good choice near the sink or other wet areas due to possible water absorption and staining
- Expensive, depending on the size

Wood was once thought to encourage bacteria growth more than other materials. Actually, recent studies have shown that synthetic countertop materials are more bacteria-friendly. Just keep the food and crumbs wiped up and periodically wipe the surface with a non-toxic finishing oil such as pure tung oil and you'll be fine.

Countertops that require a professional's touch

Some countertops look great but should only be installed by professionals. The materials can be tricky or difficult to cut and making clean, smooth joints takes a lot of experience. And there's usually no second chance to correct a mistake. Here's a look-see at the stuff that should be installed by the pros (which will jack up the cost of your project).

Solid surface materials

This category of building materials is really gaining popularity. Solid surface countertops are made of polyester or acrylic resins, or a combination of both — they don't have a substrate base. These countertops give the appearance of stone. They're sold under such brand names as Corian, Cambria, Avonite, Gibralter, and Surrell. They come in solid colors and patterns that really do look a lot like stone. See the color insert for examples of these elegant looking countertops.

Sadly, this style of countertop isn't DIY-installable — only a trained and certified contractor can get his hands on this stuff right now. So if you decide you want a solid surface material countertop, remember to budget a little extra for installation costs.

Despite the added installation expense, solid-surface material countertops have many redeeming qualities:

- ✔ Very durable
- ✔ Available in many colors and stone patterns (even granite)
- ✔ Self-supporting (doesn't need center bracing support)
- ✔ Used with an *integrated sink* (or a sink that is part of the countertop, which eliminates seams or joints — see the color insert)
- ✔ Easy to clean
- ✔ Fairly easy to repair (smaller cuts and nicks can be sanded out with sandpaper or an abrasive pad)

But be sure to keep the following disadvantages in mind as you make your decision:

- ✔ Doesn't stand up well to hot pans (although better than laminate)
- ✔ Expensive (anywhere between $50 and $120 a square foot, depending on the brand, color, and edge treatment)
- ✔ Requires installation by a licensed contractor/installer
- ✔ Not available to DIY market

Solid-surface countertops are either ½ or ¾ inch thick and come as wide as 36 inches and as long as 144 inches. If a joint is needed, the two pieces are bonded together with color-matching adhesive. After the joint has dried, it's sanded and burnished — making the joint nearly invisible. Another neat feature is that these countertops can be cut and shaped (because they're a solid material and don't have a substrate base). Many folks like to have a custom or styled edge routed along the surface's front edge and ends.

If you do have a solid-surface countertop installed, don't be alarmed at the small (usually about a ⅛-inch) gap along the walls. Solid-surface materials expand when heated so the gap is needed to avoid damaging the material or your wall.

Granite

If you absolutely want to have real stone in your kitchen, then granite is the way to go.

Take a look at granite's good points:

- ✔ Durable
- ✔ Comes in small pieces and large slabs and every size in between
- ✔ Really classy
- ✔ Makes a good insert for pastry prep (a small area, maybe 24 x 24 inches or smaller, where you prepare or roll out dough for pastries, and so on)

Granite's disadvantages include:

- ✔ Glossy stones can be hard to keep looking nice — they show water spots quite readily.
- ✔ Very expensive (figure at least the cost per square foot of a solid-surface countertop).
- ✔ Should be installed by a contractor (an added expense).
- ✔ Cabinets need to be reinforced to support the weight of the granite.

To select a slab of granite for your countertop, you must see the actual slab and not a small sample. The colors and grain vary throughout the slab, so make sure that you like the piece that will be used. Remember, granite is very expensive and you won't want to replace it after a year if you just can't live with the look. Visit the stone yard and view the cut slabs up close.

Marble

All those veins and streaks that you see in marble tabletops may look beautiful, but they actually weaken the marble. And the last thing you want for a kitchen countertop is weak material. In addition to being a weak material, marble stains easily, scratches easily, and is very, very expensive. If your heart is set on having marble in the kitchen, consider using marble tiles or marble-looking laminate. Either one will be more durable, yet still give you the look of marble.

Marble's cool, smooth surface is good as an insert for preparing pastries, but frankly that's the only good point it has.

Concrete

Who wants a gray kitchen? Probably not too many people. And you won't have to have one, either, even if you go with another new material that's making its way into the kitchen. Concrete countertops are actually becoming quite popular. Okay, a very small percentage of people have them. But only because most homeowners aren't aware that they're available and don't realize how versatile they are.

A concrete top offers several advantages:

 ✔ Can be colored and textured to create many different looks
 ✔ Can have small decorative tiles inlaid giving you a mosaic look
 ✔ A point of conversation with your guests

But don't forget to weigh the disadvantages:

 ✔ Should be installed by an experienced contractor for a potentially high labor cost
 ✔ Very heavy, requiring your cabinets to be reinforced
 ✔ A rough-hewn texture makes cleaning more time consuming

Concrete countertops, until recently, were used mainly in upscale homes, but you're probably going to see them used more frequently in years to come.

Where to Shop for Countertops

Ah, another perplexing problem in the kitchen-remodel project. My basic advice is to look for countertops where you purchase your cabinets. You probably enjoyed working with your cabinet salesperson and she should be just as knowledgeable and helpful with your countertop shopping as she was with your cabinets.

Kitchen design studios have samples and catalogs for you to browse through. They'll probably also have a wider array of the newest and, in some cases, most unusual kitchen countertop scenarios. That's not all bad, either. You can see what others are doing (or not doing) and maybe, just maybe, ease your mind if you think you're making a wild or unusual decision.

As for the big-box stores, if you get your cabinets through one of them, stick with them for the countertops. They can offer just about any of the materials we've discussed, with the exception of concrete. These stores also have ceramic tile and can special order just about any size plastic laminate countertop you need. They can probably recommend a contractor or two who works with solid-surface materials. Remember, you can't buy it direct but they can sell it to you through a contractor.

Chapter 11

Making Sure Your Countertops Are Level

In This Chapter

▶ Getting your tools together

▶ Attaching a pre-formed countertop

▶ Hip to be square: Installing tile

A new countertop can add the finishing touch to a total kitchen remodel, or it can stand alone as an upgrade that makes an outdated kitchen look like a million bucks. A new countertop doesn't cost that much, either. Stock, preformed countertops cost as little as $3 to $4 a linear foot, and even custom-made or ceramic tile countertops and backsplashes aren't that expensive — at least when compared to the cost of remodeling an entire kitchen. Besides the relative affordability, a moderately skilled DIYer can handle the installation of a post-formed countertop. And a ceramic tile countertop isn't too much beyond the skill level of most average to experienced DIYers, either, if you take your time and have some patience.

The main focus of this chapter is on installing a *post-formed countertop,* which is a laminate surface with a particleboard substrate (see Chapter 10 for more details). However, I also show you the basic steps for installing a ceramic tile countertop and backsplash. I won't get into every possible problem or situation, but I will give you a solid, basic primer on what to expect and where to go for assistance if you decide that installing a tile countertop is a project that you want to tackle.

Gathering the Right Tools

I can't stress enough how much easier you can make your task by getting all the tools together for the entire project before you even start. Set up a pair of sawhorses and a half sheet (4 x 4 feet) of plywood to act as the staging area for all the tools. With that set up, you have all the tools laid out so that they're easy to see and grab when you need to use them. A well laid out staging area also makes things easier for your helper if you send him off to get tools.

Here are the tools you need for installing countertops:

- Levels (both a 2-foot and a 4-foot)
- A ½-inch open-end wrench
- A compass (check your kid's geometry gear before you run out and buy one!)
- A belt sander (an 18-, 21-, or 24-inch model will work)
- Coarse (60-grit) and medium (100-grit) sanding belts (sized for your belt sander)
- A medium-sized, straight-tip and a No.2 Phillips screwdriver
- A ⅜-inch corded or cordless drill
- A ¾-inch spade bit
- A powered jigsaw
- Circular saw
- Fine-tooth steel plywood blade
- A heavy-duty extension cord
- A short length (a 4-footer works) of scrap 1 x 4 board
- A clothes iron (for applying end caps to post-formed countertops)
- Carpenter's wood glue or liquid hide glue
- A tube of silicone caulk and a caulk gun
- A tube of construction adhesive
- Various length drywall screws (1-, 1¼- and 1½-inch)
- Two sawhorses
- C-Clamps
- Squeeze clamps (at least one pair)
- Rags or cardboard
- Masking tape
- Pressure sticks (short lengths of 1 x 1 or 1 x 2 board or trim)
- Utility knife
- A ¾-inch thick wood strip for support behind the laminate end cap
- Hand file

> ✔ Pencil
>
> ✔ A package of wood shims
>
> ✔ Heavy-duty work gloves and eye protection

Installing a Pre-formed Countertop

Pre-formed countertops are great for the DIYer, because so many options exist. But even though these countertops have been cut to standard specifications, you still have a bit of work ahead of you to perfect the fit (few walls are perfectly straight!). And you need to carve out a hole for your sink — certainly enough sawing and drilling to give you that DIYer's high!

Before you begin, remove the cabinet doors as well as the drawers from the base cabinets. You need as much clear access as possible to make the countertop installation as easy as possible.

Ensuring a perfect fit: Scribing and trimming

Wouldn't it be great if the walls of your kitchen were as straight and true as the edges of the countertop? Well, I haven't seen a house yet where this is the case.

The best way to check to see if a corner is square is to use the 3-4-5 method. It's a simple geometry formula:

1. **Start in the corner (it has to be a 90 degree corner) and measure out 3 feet and mark that spot.**

2. **Measure out from the corner in the other direction 4 feet and mark that spot.**

3. **Now use a tape rule and measure the distance from the end marks of the 3 and 4 foot marks.**

   The distance between the marks should be 5 feet, if the walls are square.

If the corner of the kitchen where the countertops fit is out of square even by as little as ½ to ¾ of an inch, you're likely to damage the countertop trying to make it fit. If you find that your walls are not close to square, hire a contractor to do the installation.

To shape the edges of your countertop, you need to transfer the contour of the wall onto the countertop's edge surface. You need to use a compass to *scribe,* or transfer, the wall's contour onto the laminate.

1. **Set the countertop in place where you're going to eventually install it.**

   When installing any section of countertop, be sure to check that it's level. Use a 2- or 4-foot level. If the countertop is not level, you should slide shims between the countertop and the support struts of the cabinet frame to level the countertop. The shims will remain in place and won't move once the countertop is secured to the cabinets.

2. **Set your compass to fit the widest gap between the countertop and the wall.**

3. **Then, move the compass along the wall to draw a pencil line on the countertop's surface that matches the wall contour (see Figure 11-1).**

   Do this for both the backsplash and any edge that is against a wall.

Figure 11-1:
Scribe a
line on the
countertop
surface.

4. **Remove the countertop and set it on a pair of sawhorses.**

5. **Secure the countertop to the sawhorses with squeeze clamps.**

   Be sure to place a rag or a piece of cardboard between the clamp jaws and the countertop's surface to protect the surface. If you're using squeeze clamps or wooden screw clamps, you shouldn't need the rag or cardboard.

6. **Remove the excess countertop (up to the pencil line) with a belt sander and a coarse (60-grit) sanding belt (see Figure 11-2).**

A coarse belt works best because it removes laminate and the substrate quickly, yet neatly. If you have a lot of excess countertop, say ⅛ inch or more, cut off most of it with a jigsaw and then use the belt sander to finish up to the pencil line.

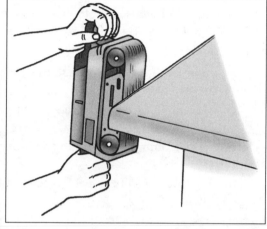

Figure 11-2:
Sand off excess laminate and substrate up to the scribed line.

Run a couple of strips of masking tape on the top of the countertop to avoid scratching the surface or possibly chipping the laminate when cutting with a saw.

7. **Reposition the countertop in place and check for any tight spots.**

8. **Touch up any tight spots with the sander and recheck the fit again.**

   You want the countertop to fit, especially if you're installing it during the humid summer months when the wall will be "fatter" with humidity. If you're installing the countertop in the drier winter months, leave a gap of about ¹⁄₁₆ inch along the wall to allow for movement due to changes in temperature and humidity. Fill the gap with a bead of silicone caulk as one of the final steps in the remodel.

Installing a mitered corner

If your countertop turns a corner, it probably has two pieces, each one with a 45-degree angle, or *miter cut,* which meet to form the 90-degree corner. Chances are good that you'll have to do some scribing and trimming to make the front edge of the mitered angle flush without any of the substrate showing.

1. Place one of the countertop pieces into the corner to assess the fit.

2. Scribe and trim the back edge (as descried in the previous section) so that the rear mitered point fits exactly into the corner of the wall.

3. Set the second piece in place and check its position in relation to the piece that fits.

4. Scribe and trim the back edge enough so that the two front edges meet exactly. Do not trim the mitered edge that forms the joint.

5. Pull out both pieces of countertop.

6. Apply yellow carpenter's glue or liquid hide glue to both edges of the joint and reposition the two sections.

   Either glue works well, however, the carpenter's glue sets up more quickly; if you use it, you need to work faster.

7. Connect the two pieces from the underside with toggle bolts that were supplied with the countertop.

   Position the wings of the bolt into the slots on each piece. Tighten the bolt with an open-end wrench.

8. Check the joint on the surface to make sure the seam is flush. If it's not, adjust the countertop position and retighten the toggle bolts.

9. If the joint still isn't flush, shim one of the sections to make the seam flush, and then tighten the toggle bolts.

10. To ensure that the joint stays flush while drying, place a C-clamp on the front edge joint and place pressure sticks on each side of the joint (see Figure 11-3).

    Pressure sticks are simply two equal lengths of board (usually 1 inch x 1 inch) that are slightly longer than the distance between the countertop and the bottom of the wall cabinets. They need to be longer than that distance so you can wedge them in place to force pressure onto the countertop.

Attaching countertops other than corners

After you've scribed and trimmed all the straight countertop pieces, you can finally begin the job of securing them to the base cabinets.

Don't start securing the countertop to the cabinets until the mitered joint has dried. Allow a few hours for the glue to dry or overnight if the weather is humid. It's better to wait a little longer than rush the job and have the seam break because the glue hadn't set up. If the seam does break, you need to go back, remove the old glue, and redo the process.

Figure 11-3:
Create a smooth seam with pressure sticks.

1. **Start by positioning the straight countertop pieces on the cabinets.**

2. **Tip the countertop up and apply a bead of silicone caulk or construction adhesive along the top edge of all the cabinet parts that support the countertop.**

   The silicone caulk or construction adhesive will hold things in place after drying. Don't forget to apply the caulk or adhesive to the top of the triangular mounting blocks in the corners, too.

3. **Now, lower the countertop back into place.**

4. **Place pressure sticks every 12 to 18 inches to help the adhesive bond the countertop to the cabinets.**

   Be sure to place pressure sticks along the back corners (where the corner blocks are located) to get the countertop down tight.

The caulk connection: Knowing your adhesives

I mentioned that you can use either silicone caulk or construction adhesive to secure the countertop to the cabinets. Most people think of caulk as only a gap filler or sealer, but caulk also works as an adhesive for holding things in place.

The advantage of silicone caulk versus construction adhesive is that the caulk stays flexible, allowing materials to move slightly when the temperature and humidity changes. This flexibility lets the caulk retain its holding power without breaking apart as construction adhesive will do if things shift after drying. My recommendation — use silicone caulk for both sealing and holding.

5. **Finally, seal any gap between the backsplash and wall or along the edges and the wall with a clear, silicone acrylic caulk.**

If you're going to paint the walls and you want to paint the clear caulk, make sure it's labeled as being paintable! Most acrylic silicone caulk is paintable, whereas regular silicone caulk isn't. Check the label to be sure.

Cutting the hole for the sink

You can order your countertops precut, including the hole for the sink, but you should only do that if you know your measurements are absolutely, positively dead-on, with no chance of being off by even a little bit. And if you're like me, that's very unlikely. Cutting a hole in a post-formed countertop isn't difficult. Just follow these steps and take your time for professional-looking results.

Using a template

Most sinks come with a paper or cardboard template to help outline the area to be cut out. Quite often the cardboard template is part of the shipping box for the sink. Use a utility knife to cut the template from the box. Just be careful not to cut yourself and be sure to follow the dotted or solid line so that the template is as straight as possible.

If your sink doesn't come with a template or if you bought a good-looking closeout-sale sink without a box, you can still make your own template:

1. **Take the sink and lay it upside down on the countertop where you're going to install it.**

2. **Measure from both corners in the back to make sure that the sink is evenly positioned.**

3. **Now just trace around the outer edge of the sink with a pencil.**

   Have a helper hold the sink in place to ensure that it doesn't shift while you're tracing.

4. **Next, measure the lip on the underside of the sink.**

5. **Mark the dimension of the lip in from the line you traced around the sink.**

   Mark it on the counter at several points inside the traced line and then draw straight lines connecting the marks. You can freehand the corners — just follow the same shape as the corners you traced using the sink.

   The distance between the two lines forms the lip on the countertop to support your sink. The inner line is the cutting line.

Cutting the countertop

To cut a hole for a sink, I've always used a jigsaw, because it gives me great control when cutting. (*Note:* Always, always, always use a new jigsaw blade. An old or dull blade can chip the laminate along the cutting line.) Some people use a circular saw; however, that involves making a plunge-cut with the blade because you don't have a starter hole to work with. Most folks find that the jigsaw is the easiest, most reliable, and safest saw to use. Don't forget to wear heavy gloves and eye protection when making this cut.

1. **Drill two starter holes in opposite corners just inside the cutting line. Use a ¾-inch spade bit and drill through the laminate and substrate.**

   Don't worry if you chip the laminate, either. You're cutting into sections that will be cut out and tossed.

2. **Place the blade of the jigsaw in the starter hole and line up the blade exactly on the cutting line (see Figure 11-4).**

3. **Cut slowly along the line.**

   Don't be in a rush — let the saw do the work. Again, don't worry about any little chipping that may occur. The sink lip will cover it.

Figure 11-4:
Insert the jigsaw blade in the starter hole and cut around the entire inner or cutting line.

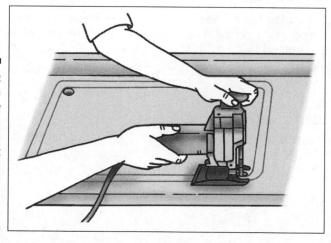

To make a clean, safe cut, ask a helper to support the cutout area so that the piece doesn't drop and cause the saw blade to bind. Make sure your helper is wearing heavy gloves and eye protection.

Believe it or not, that's all there is to cutting a hole for a sink in a laminate countertop. When it's time to install the sink and faucet, move on to Chapter 13 for all the information you need.

Sizing and finishing your countertop

Stock countertops are sold in 2-foot increments, so most folks will have excess to cut off. Because most situations call for cutting, most post-formed countertops are manufactured without end caps, which you need to apply — I tell you how, read on!

Cutting off excess

The easiest way to cut off any extra length of a post-formed countertop is with a circular saw and fine-tooth steel plywood blade. Do not use a carbide-tipped blade. Carbide-tipped blades have larger teeth, which increase the chance of chipping the laminate.

1. **Place the countertop upside down on a solid, protected surface to avoid scratching the laminate.**

   A pair of sawhorses works well. You may want to clamp the countertop to the sawhorses for extra security; however, the weight of the countertop should be enough to keep it from moving.

2. **Measure the length of the countertop that's needed and mark a cutting line on the substrate.**

3. **Line up the blade of the saw with the marked line and then place a scrap length of 1 x 4 board against the edge of the baseplate of the saw (see Figure 11-5).**

4. **Clamp the board to the countertop. The board is your cutting guide.**

Figure 11-5:
Cut the countertop along your cutting guide.

5. **Start cutting from the back or rear of the countertop, through the backsplash toward the front.**

Support the cutoff end or have a helper hold it while you're cutting. Failure to do that will cause the piece to fall away before it's completely cut and will break the laminate unevenly, ruining the countertop. If you have trouble finishing the cut with the circular saw, stop about 1 inch from the end and finish the cut with a jigsaw or handsaw.

Applying end caps

If your countertop has an exposed end that doesn't butt against a wall or into a corner, you need to finish it by applying a laminate *end cap* (a piece of the laminate surface that covers the exposed end of the countertop substrate).

End caps are differently designed to cover either left- or right-hand counter ends, so make sure you get the correct variety. You determine which hand you need by simply facing the cabinet — the end to your left needs a left-hand end cap and the end to your right needs a right-hander. End caps are slightly larger than the end piece that they'll be covering, so you need to do some trimming with a hand file. End caps also come with applied, heat-activated glue or adhesive, which makes installation a snap.

1. **Start by gluing a ¾-inch thick wood strip to the bottom edge of the countertop.**

   This strip supports the end cap because the substrate isn't thick enough by itself. Make sure the strip is flush with the outer edge.

2. **Position the end cap on the cut end of the countertop and align the angle and corner with the contour of the countertop's surface.**

3. **Use a clothes iron to heat and activate the adhesive (see Figure 11-6).**

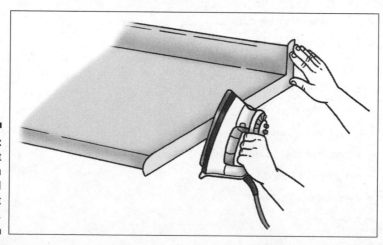

Figure 11-6:
Run a hot clothes iron over the end cap to heat the glue.

4. **After the glue and end cap have cooled, finish the edges. A hand file works best. Push the file toward the countertop.**

   Never remove excess by pulling the file — always push! Pulling will break the glue bond and the end cap will come off.

5. **Reinstall the cabinet doors and put the drawers back in place, and you're set.**

Installing a Ceramic Tile Countertop

One other type of countertop that is quite popular and is also a manageable DIY project for most homeowners is a ceramic tile countertop. Ceramic tile is not only attractive, but also very durable and resistant to spills and stains. The tile is available in a wide range of colors, sizes, and styles. A ceramic tile countertop is more expensive than a post-formed top, but the beauty of ceramic tile is usually enough to offset the extra cost.

Gathering additional tools for tile

Here's what you need in addition to the tools listed at the beginning of this chapter:

- A tile cutter (available at rental stores)
- A tile nipper (special pliers used for cutting/nipping small pieces)
- A notched trowel
- A rubber grout float
- Latex underlayment filler
- Framing square
- Tiles, straight and bull-nose
- Tile adhesive (mastic)
- Plastic tile spacers
- Grout and grout sealer
- ¾-inch exterior grade plywood
- 1 x 2 board (used for filler strips)
- Cement backerboard
- A sponge

Constructing your ceramic countertop

A ceramic tile countertop is made up of ¾-inch exterior plywood and cement *backerboard* (a drywall-like product that's made of cement instead of gypsum) cut to the same size as the top of the cabinets. The edges of the plywood and backerboard sandwich are built up with 1 x 2 strips of wood. The tiles are applied directly to the backerboard and secured with the mastic. The gaps between the tiles are filled with grout, which you must seal to prevent moisture from getting under the tiles and loosening them.

Two styles of tiles are needed for a countertop: straight-edged or *field tiles* and rounded-edge or *bull-nose tiles*. Bull-nose tiles also come in two styles: a single rounded edge for use along a straight edge, or a *double bull-nose* (two adjacent rounded edges) for use on outside corners. The backsplash on a ceramic tile top can be installed over a separate plywood core (backerboard isn't needed) or directly to the wall. Figure 11-7 shows how a ceramic tile countertop fits together.

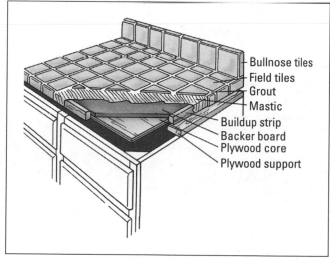

Bullnose tiles
Field tiles
Grout
Mastic
Buildup strip
Backer board
Plywood core
Plywood support

Figure 11-7:
The many layers of a ceramic tile countertop.

Here's a quick look at the basic steps for building your ceramic tile countertop:

1. **You need to add extra support pieces to the top of your cabinets to support the weight of a ceramic tile top. Cut 3-inch-wide strips of ¾-inch exterior plywood the same depth as the cabinets.**

2. **Position them every 24 inches; use 1¼-inch drywall screws to secure them.**

3. **Position the plywood and backerboard core tightly against the wall and secure it to the cabinets with drywall screws. Screw it along the edge supports and on the added crosspieces.**

4. **Fill in the screw head holes with a latex underlayment filler.**

5. **Allow the filler to dry and then sand it smooth.**

6. **Measure the length of the countertop and mark the centerline of the countertop.**

7. **Establish a perpendicular line to the centerline using a framing square as shown in Figure 11-8.**

   Align the square with the front edge of the plywood core to establish the right angle.

8. **Dry-fit rows of tile along the lines (see Figure 11-8).**

   Be sure you're left with at least half a tile at the end of a row. If not, adjust your line positions and dry-fit the tiles again along the new lines. Mark the cutting line on any tiles that need trimming.

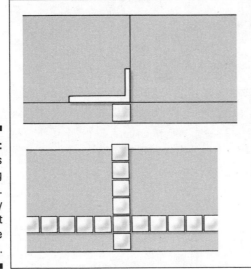

Figure 11-8:
Dry-fit rows of tile along the lines. Mark any tiles that need to be trimmed.

9. **Use the tile cutter to make straight cuts on field and bull-nose tiles (see Figure 11-9).**

10. **To make curve cuts, freehand score the area on the tile to be removed. Then use the tile nipper to break off small pieces until the cutout is complete (see Figure 11-10).**

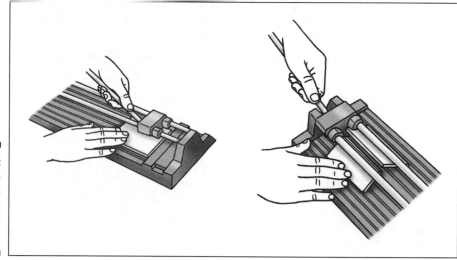

Figure 11-9:
Use a tile
cutter to
score and
cut the tiles
to fit.

11. **After all the tiles have been cut and dry-fit, secure them to the sub-strate with mastic.**

Use plastic tile spacers between each tile to ensure even spacing. Allow the mastic to set up for at least 24 hours.

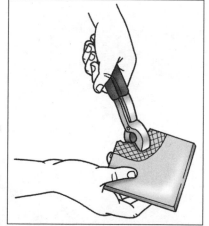

Figure 11-10:
Remove
small pieces
of tile with a
tile nipper.

12. **After 24 hours, fill the gaps between the tiles with grout using a rubber grout float.**

Hold the float at a 45-degree angle to the tiles and use a sweeping motion to force the grout into the gaps. Wipe off any excess grout with a sponge.

Let the grout dry for about one hour and then wipe off any haze that's on the tile. After you clean the surface, allow the grout to dry per the instructions on the package.

13. **Finally, seal the grout with a penetrating silicone grout sealer.**

    Although sealing the grout may seem like a tedious job (and it is!), it's critical that you do it to keep the grout from staining and to extend its useful life.

Part IV

Selecting and Installing Sinks, Faucets, Appliances, and More

The 5th Wave   By Rich Tennant

Eschewing the indoor covered and more traditional stovetop varieties, Stan opts for a 1946 Chevrolet Fleetline grill.

In this part . . .

Shopping for new appliances, a faucet, and a sink should be a blast! But you have so many choices, you may be intimidated. In this part, I give you pointers on how to pick out top quality merchandise that fits your budget.

I also show you how to install your new sink and faucet — with no leaks! And don't let installing appliances scare you off, either. I demystify this whole area so that you at least know what the installers are talking about if you decide to have someone do the work for you.

Chapter 12

"Pouring" Over the Choices for Sinks and Faucets

In This Chapter

▶ Deciding what your sink should be made of

▶ Selecting a stylish sink and faucet

▶ Opting for a few good extras

▶ Remembering to keep your warranties in a safe place

The kitchen sink is one of the busiest spots in your home. A recent study shows that the sink and faucet are used, on average, 20 times a day — and in some homes, as many as 40 times a day! Because the sink is in plain view, just about everyone who visits your home sees it, so you want your kitchen sink and faucet to look good and function well.

Selecting the right sink and faucet combination can seem like a complicated and even daunting task, especially if you've noticed the huge number of items on display down the sink and faucet aisles in your local home center or plumbing supply store these days. That's why I provide this chapter to help you better understand the choices and options available to you. So, grab a paper and pencil and get ready to explore your sink and faucet options!

Selecting the Best Sink Material for Your Needs

Sinks are generally made from four types of material: metal, enameled cast iron or steel, solid surface, or composite. Prices, as well as quality, are wide-ranging in all four categories, so do your homework before you start shopping. If you don't, you could be buying a beer sink at champagne prices. (Be sure to check out the sink photos in the color insert for sink material and style ideas.)

Metal: Affordable and easy to clean

Metal sinks, also known as stainless steel sinks, are the most popular type for a few reasons: They're durable, they're really easy to keep clean, and they're affordable. You can buy a decent stainless steel sink for around $150, but expect to pay anywhere from $200 to $600 for a quality stainless steel sink. Low-end sinks sell for under $50. This may be okay for your cabin, but you won't be happy with its performance for day-to-day use because they're noisy and the bowls are very shallow. And the low-end models have the least amount of character or charm because of the plainness in color and appearance. But designs and styles have really made some great strides forward, so you do have more choices than in the past.

Stainless steel won't chip, crack, stain, or corrode, and is fairly forgiving about not breaking dropped dishes. If you're worried about your stainless sink showing scratches over time, buy a brushed or satin finish model — the satin's less-shiny surface does a good job of hiding the scratches.

Metal sinks are made of a mixture of chromium and nickel. The best mixture is 18 percent chromium for strength and 8 percent nickel to fend off corrosion. The best quality and most durable stainless steel sinks are made of 18-gauge or heavier steel. Medium-grade sinks (usually 20-gauge) can have this 18/8 mixture, but the lighter gauge makes them less durable. When shopping, remember the lower the gauge number, the heavier the sheet and the better the quality. You can find out what the metal content is by checking the label, asking a qualified sales attendant, or visiting the Web sites of the various manufacturers.

The better quality stainless sinks also have a *sound-dampening coating* on the underside of the bowl, which I recommend. The coating is usually a gray or black colored sprayed-on product that has a rough, bumpy texture. It doesn't look pretty, but it can help deaden the noise created when you set plates, glasses, and utensils in the sink. An uncoated stainless steel sink is really noisy!

Two manufacturers you can trust are American Standard and Sterling. Ask a sales associate to recommend other quality stainless steel sink manufacturers, and keep in mind you get what you pay for.

Enameled: The power of cast iron and steel

If you want a brightly colored sink, then an enameled (sometimes called porcelain-enameled) cast-iron or steel sink is the way to go. Enameled sinks are available in vivid colors and are also extremely durable. Today's enameled sinks are less likely to chip than older models. However, even the best quality enameled sink will chip if a heavy item, such as a cast-iron skillet, is dropped onto it. Lighter colored enameled sinks also have a tendency to stain more easily than darker sinks and may require frequent scouring.

An enameled cast-iron sink is quieter than its steel counterpart and it retains heat better when washing dishes by hand. But cast iron is more expensive: A quality enameled steel sink costs roughly $300–$600, and a quality enameled cast-iron sink can set you back $400 or more. Kohler and American Standard are a couple of manufacturers you'll find when shopping for an enameled sink.

A cast-iron sink is thicker than either an enameled steel or stainless steel sink, so it may not fit into the same size opening if you're replacing an existing sink and not changing the countertop.

Solid surface: So sleek and smooth!

Solid surface sinks are frequently an integral part of a solid surface countertop, creating a seamless, watertight assembly that looks sleek and smooth. The material is a mixture of mineral compounds and polyester or resin. These sinks are easy to clean, and you can buff out scratches. They rarely stain or chip, but they won't tolerate a hot pan, so make sure you cool a hot pan by running cold water over it before you set it in the sink.

These sinks must be fabricated and installed by trained and licensed trades people, so they're not a do-it-yourself (DIY) project. Prices range from $300 to $700, with installation sometimes running higher.

You may hear craftsmen refer to Corian sinks. This is DuPont's trademarked name for its brand of solid surface material sinks. Solid surface sinks are becoming more popular primarily because of the wide choice of colors and designs. Actually, asking for a Corian sink is a bit like asking someone for a Kleenex when what you're really asking for is a tissue. Gibraltar and Avonite are two other brand name solid surface sink manufacturers.

Composite: Making it fancy with faux marble

Though relatively new in the industry, faux marble or composite sinks are gaining popularity. They're molded from acrylic resins and quartz compounds and, much like a solid surface sink, can be an integrated part of a countertop. Composite sinks are much more heat- and stain-resistant than solid surface products and offer more color choices. On the downside, composites are more likely to scratch and you should *never* use an abrasive cleaner on the surface. A sharp knife also leaves a mark on the surface if you forget to use a cutting board.

Composite sinks are typically priced between $350 and $800. Brand names include Quartzite, Cristalite, Asterlite, and Silacron 200.

Choosing the Right Sink Design for Your Space

A sink's a sink, right? Wrong! There's more to picking the right sink than just deciding on a color and a material. In the following sections, I discuss the options you need to consider when choosing a sink.

Looking into sink bowls

The first question you should ask when replacing your sink is: How many bowls do I need or want? (*Bowl* refers to the water holding or food and waste collecting compartments of the sink.) The second question you should ask is: What bowl depth and shape do I prefer?

One, two, or three bowls — you do have a choice

A kitchen sink can have one, two, or three bowls of various shapes and sizes (see Figures 12-1, 12-2, and 12-3). The National Kitchen and Bath Association (NKBA) recommends a single large-bowl sink for kitchens under 150 square feet. A double-bowl sink is recommended for larger kitchens. The two bowls give you two work areas, so you can clean vegetables in one bowl while someone else is washing his hands in the other. Try doing that in a single-bowl sink! You may even want to add a smaller third bowl, especially if you have a lot of counter space. The third bowl is often called a *salad-prep sink* because you generally use it during food (usually salad) preparation and not for washing or rinsing dishes. Most kitchens have a two- or three-bowl sink.

The number of bowls your sink can actually support usually depends on the available countertop space. The NKBA recommends a minimum of 36 inches of open counter space on one side of a kitchen sink and at least 18 inches on the other. Meeting these space requirements is not a problem in most kitchens. Don't forget, too, that you can add a second sink in a kitchen island.

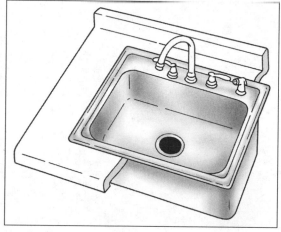

Figure 12-1:
A single-bowl sink is a good choice when overall counter space is limited.

Choosing a bowl shape

You can find bowls that are square or round, but I recommend going with a rectangular bowl for a couple of good reasons. First, the rounded corners found in most rectangular sinks are easier to clean than square corners. Second, and maybe more important, a rectangular bowl holds more stuff than either a round or oval-shaped bowl.

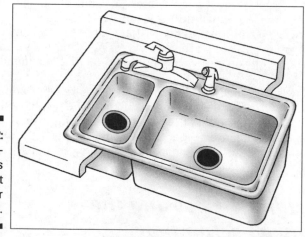

Figure 12-2:
A double-bowl sink is the most popular design.

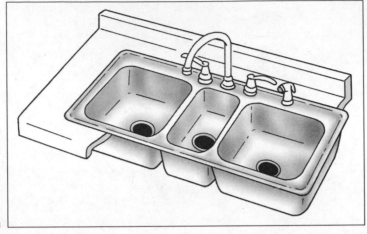

Figure 12-3:
Triple-bowl
sinks are
gaining
popularity.

The depth of kitchen sink bowls has gradually increased over the past decade or so. Your existing sink may be only 5 or 5½ inches deep, although today's sinks are usually between 6 and 8 inches deep. Sinks as deep as 10 and even 12 inches are not uncommon because deep sinks have their advantages. For example, a deeper sink keeps splashing to a minimum. But the sink shouldn't be so deep that you or your kids are uncomfortable using it.

If you can't decide on a depth, then choose two. You'll find sinks with different depth bowls in stock at most home centers, or you can special order just about any combination. A popular design is one bowl at 9 inches deep with a second bowl between 6 and 7 inches deep (that way one of the bowls is deep enough to allow you to rinse or wash your largest pots and pans). You can place the different depths on either side, but more on that in a minute.

Be aware that bowls with different depths usually require some adjustments when hooking up the drain assembly. You must know the height of the existing drain line where it comes out of the wall when ordering your sink. If you order a sink with bowls that are deeper than the drain height, the sink won't drain properly! Although this situation is fairly rare, I've seen it a few times.

Lefty or righty? Choosing the multiple-bowl setup that works best for you

Which hand you want your sink to be isn't too difficult to figure out, after you figure out what a hand is in regard to sinks. The *hand* is the direction you work in that feels most comfortable. So, for example, if you wash dishes in the left sink bowl and rinse them in the right bowl, then your sink is considered left-handed because you work from left to right. Knowing which direction you work in helps you decide which bowl size you want on which side. For example, if you wash dishes left-handed (from left to right), you'd most likely want the larger bowl on the left for washing and the smaller bowl on the right for rinsing.

Unfortunately, most people don't think about selecting the correct hand, but they should. Think about how you use your existing sink, and then answer these questions:

✔ **Who uses the sink most, and which hand does that person favor?** The primary user of the sink should be the one who determines which hand setup works best.

✔ **How much counter space (in inches) is available on each side of the sink?** Sometimes the existing counter space area dictates which side a specific type of bowl must go on. For example, if you like to wash dishes from left to right but have only about 14 inches of counter space on the left side, you don't really have enough area to stack even a small amount of dirty dishes.

✔ **Do you prefer a certain side for preparing food?** Some people can absolutely only work in one direction when preparing food. If you must prepare from a specific side, select the appropriate bowl setup accordingly. This is also important to consider if you go to a three-bowl model, especially when determining the salad-prep sink position because the smaller salad-prep sink can be positioned in the center or on either side.

If you find that, when you think about it, you're not crazy about the current hand setup of your existing sink, now's the time to change it to the way you really want it. You can find sinks in just about every combination of depths and bowl sizes, so if you don't see the combination that you want on display, ask the salesperson if you can special order the design you *really* want.

Recognizing the Many Facets of Faucets

If you thought you had an overabundant choice in sinks, wait until you start trying to select the right faucet. Lucky for you, the advice in the following sections makes your options as clear as the water that will soon be streaming from your new faucet.

Considering the faucet and sprayer setup

Until recently, everyone's faucet setup was basically the same: A faucet was positioned in the middle of the sink's back lip with a separate pullout spray hose positioned on the right. Although many people still want and like the traditional faucet and sprayer setup, you have some other options. For example, some of the newer sink designs have the faucet position slightly offset, giving your sink an attractive yet different appearance and design element.

Consider your setup options carefully because they directly affect the number of factory-drilled holes you'll be working with and the plumbing design of the faucet assembly.

Is two better than one? Deciding on a faucet handle design

Faucets come in two handle setups or designs: A single, lever-style or a two-handled version. Both do the same thing — allow you to turn the water on and off and control the flow as it's running. So, if they do the same thing, how can there be such a divided camp of people when it comes to design? Let's look at what makes each one unique to help you decide which design is right for you.

A *lever-style faucet* (which controls both the hot and cold water flow with one handle) has the hot- and cold-water supply lines attached underneath where the spout is connected to the faucet housing. A *two-handled faucet* (which has a separate handle for turning on both the hot and cold water) has a separate supply feed (tailpiece) for each water handle.

Both single- and two-handle faucets are popular, but for different reasons:

- A single-handle faucet is usually easier to use, especially for people with arthritis or anyone who has trouble gripping objects.

- A single-handle faucet is a good choice for families with young children. The single handle eliminates the chance that a child will turn on only the hot water and scald himself.

- The single-handle design helps you get your desired water temperature more quickly with fewer adjustments.

- Single-handle models with longer, paddle-shaped handles allow you to turn the water on or off with your elbow or wrist. This is handy when your hands are full or covered with food.

- Because a single-handle faucet doesn't have a handle on either side of the spout, the spout has a greater swing radius.

- A single-handle faucet with a base that doesn't cover the adjacent holes is ideal if you plan to add a soap dispenser or hot water dispenser in the extra holes (see the "Adding Extras" section later in this chapter).

Two-handle faucets are popular for the following reasons:

- ✔ They give people a more traditional look for their kitchen. (Homeowners remember the two separate handles on the faucets of the house they grew up in and want to replicate that look and feel.)

- ✔ Most two-handle faucets also feature interchangeable handles so you can change the appearance of the faucet whenever you want — without doing any plumbing!

- ✔ Dedicated hot- and cold-water handles give you only hot or cold water from the respective handle.

- ✔ You can adjust the water temperature by adding or taking away from the flow of either the hot or cold water without changing the other's water flow.

Prices for single- and two-handle faucets are wide ranging. The low-end units start at under $30, but you get what you pay for, which could be a faulty faucet or one you'll need to replace in a year. Realistically, you should plan to spend at least $100, and don't be surprised if the faucet you really like is $200 or more. Some of the brands you're likely to see on display include Delta, Moen, Price-Pfister, and American Standard.

What's new in faucet colors and finishes

Cruise down the faucet aisle of your local home center and you'll see mostly good old chrome finished faucets on display. Why? Because chrome is still the most popular finish, even if it does look like the one in the kitchen of the house you grew up in. Besides being traditional, it works well color-wise with just about any sink color. And it's pretty easy to keep clean. Just wipe it down with a damp rag and dry it off. Look a little closer, however, and you'll see colors and finish combinations that your parents could never imagine. Today's faucet colors range from white to biscuit to bronze to black. And some elegant brass-finish faucets come with a lifetime warranty. (More on warranties later in this chapter.)

Faucet designers have come up with finish and color combinations that add elegant, unique touches to kitchen faucets. Polished and brushed metal finishes are paired together, or nickel and brass are combined for a classy, rich look. Color combinations are as subtle as a small trim strip around the end of the spout, and colors are as bold as cobalt blue. If you don't see the color or color combination that you're looking for on display, be sure to ask to see a manufacturer's catalog. Specific colors and color combinations can be special-ordered, giving you the exact look you desire.

Filtering faucets

Tired of holding your nose every time you take a drink of water because you can't stand the smell or taste? Then a filtering faucet may be a good choice for you. Filtering faucets typically contain a built-in, replaceable filter with activated carbon that removes organic contaminants and cleanses the water as it comes out the spout. See Figure 12-4 for a look at a filtering faucet. With the push of a button, the water is routed through a replaceable filter housed in the body of the faucet, which removes the most common contaminants found in municipal water supplies such as lead and cysts (micro-organisms that are in most water supplies). They eliminate odors and reduce chlorine taste too. If you want unfiltered water, you operate the faucet like any other.

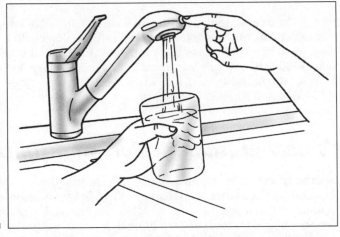

Figure 12-4: A filtering faucet gives you filtered water at the push of a button.

Filtering faucets are priced from around $150 to $300. Replacement filters run about $15. How long a filter lasts depends on how much water your family uses. Most filters last between 6 and 12 months. The filter is housed inside the faucet body and is easy to change, and many faucets also monitor the efficiency of the filter and indicate when you need to change the filter.

A separate drinking water faucet

Many homeowners now have water-purifying equipment for their water supply, which means a dedicated drinking water faucet (tap) at the sink (see an example in the color insert). So instead of filtering water *in* the faucet (as you do with a filtering faucet) you filter the water *before* it comes out and have a separate faucet dedicated to dispensing that water. Sometimes the tap is installed in the "extra" hole in the sink normally used for the pullout spray hose or soap dispenser. If, however, you've filled up the sink's factory-drilled holes and you want a drinking water tap, you'll need to either drill an additional hole in the sink or drill a hole in the countertop right next to the sink. Most filtering units mount under the cabinet and don't take up much room.

Prices range from around $140 to $160, which includes a lead-free water faucet. Replacement filters sell for $40 to $60, depending on what they're engineered to do. How often you need to replace the filter depends, primarily, on your family's water consumption habits. Under-sink water filters can have one, two, or even three separate filters, depending on their filtering capabilities. Take a look at Figure 12-5 for a glimpse of an under-sink water filter.

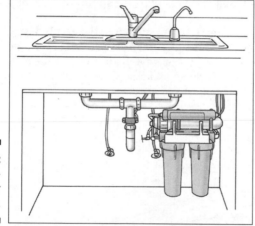

Figure 12-5:
An under-sink water filter.

Filtered water versus conditioned water: What's the difference?

Too many people think that if you have a water softener your water is filtered and has had all of the contaminants removed. Wrong, wrong, wrong! The easiest way to explain the difference between these two types of treated water is to remember that filtered water goes *in* you and conditioned water goes *on* you. To make your home's water as contaminant free as possible, filter either through a filtering faucet or a separate water filtering system.

Unlike the different kinds of water filtering systems, a water softener removes hardness from the water, thus "conditioning" it. Basically it "washes" the hard water by exchanging hard minerals (magnesium and calcium) for potassium and salt, thus softening the water. Your water softener's only goal is to make your water smell and look better; it doesn't remove contaminants or make water more suitable for cooking or drinking. See the "Filtering faucets" and "A separate drinking water faucet" sections for more on water filtering.

Spouting off

You've chosen the faucet setup, the number of handles, and even the color. But there's one more thing to consider — the spout. The spout is that long curved tube that the water actually comes out of.

The trend toward bigger sinks has lead to the demand for taller and slightly longer spouts. Large- or multi-bowl sinks are best served by a faucet with a 12- or 14-inch long spout. If your sink is average sized (around 25 x 22 inches), the standard 8- or 10-inch long spout should be adequate. And you don't have to stick with the traditional spout design; high-rise or goose-neck-shaped spouts are gaining popularity. If you frequently fill large kettles with water, for example when cooking pasta or boiling lobster, a high-rise spout may be for you.

A few years ago, the faucet manufacturers introduced a combination pullout spout/sprayer (see Figure 12-6). This popular design is great for when you want the convenience of a spray hose without having another device installed on your sink. The all-in-one unit's design also leaves one of the predrilled holes open for other accessories. This type of faucet is usually available in the same finishes and styles as regular single- or two-handle faucets. Prices range from around $170 to over $450 with finish, style, and overall design as the determining factors for the price.

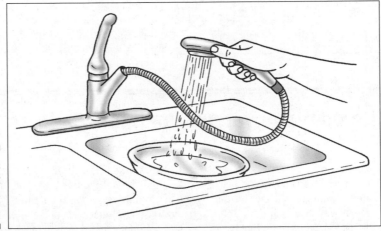

Figure 12-6:
A pullout spout offers versatility.

Adding Extras

When you buy a car, half the fun is in the extras; the same is true of the kitchen sink. From soap dispensers to hot water dispensers to garbage disposer, the options are many. Here's a look at the most popular ones.

Soap dispenser, anyone?

A lot of families want and enjoy the convenience of a built-in (or under-cabinet) soap dispenser because it keeps an ample supply of soap on hand, without having a separate soap container or bar of soap cluttering up the sink. These soap dispensers, which are installed under the sink with a line running to the dispenser next to the faucet, sell for around $25 to $30 and are displayed in most home centers near the kitchen faucets.

When you install the soap dispenser, plan to use the hole in the sink that's normally designated for a pullout sprayer. However, if you want a traditional (or two-handled) faucet configuration plus the soap dispenser, you'll need to drill an additional hole (or two) in either the sink or the countertop.

Hot water NOW! A point-of-use hot-water dispenser

Another great add on is an instant hot-water dispenser. These heating tanks mount under the sink inside the cabinet (you need an electrical outlet under the sink to power the unit) and have a separate dispenser spout mounted on or next to the sink. The tank can hold anywhere from ⅓ to 1 gallon of water, depending on the model, and the supply line is connected to the cold water supply. The water in the tank is kept near boiling, which is ideal for making instant coffee, tea, and soups. Prices range from around $90 to $160, depending on capacity and finish. In-Sink-Erator (made by the same folks who manufacturer In-Sink-Erator garbage disposers) is one popular brand.

Is a garbage disposer in your future?

Having a garbage disposer in your home is great because you can get rid of food waste quickly and eliminate the odors from foods that otherwise linger in your garbage can. But even though a disposer is a handy piece of equipment, it does mean you'll be running food waste through the drain lines. And if the inside of the drainpipe isn't as clean as it can be, you could be in for a plugged drain in very short order. I know this for a fact because it happened to me in the first house we owned. And, wouldn't you know it? The tragedy happened on Thanksgiving Day — when we were hosting our first family dinner in our new home!

Selecting the right garbage disposer isn't too difficult. Most manufacturers offer a few horsepower choices, ranging from ¼ to 1-horsepower. A ¼- or ⅓-horsepower unit is powerful enough for the average household. Installing one is also a manageable DIY project if you have moderate plumbing skills. See Chapter 15 for basic installation instructions.

Checking Out Those Warranties!

In my twenty-plus years of home ownership, I've never replaced a faucet under the manufacturer's warranty. I've always replaced faucets because we were ready for a cosmetic change in the kitchen, and not because they were worn out. A quality, brand name faucet should give you years of trouble-free service. Nonetheless, you could have a problem that falls under a warranty. Many of the major manufacturers feature a limited lifetime warranty for as long as *you* own the faucet. (A limited lifetime warranty usually only covers the cost of replacement parts. But, hey, it's better than nothing, right?) Less expensive or off-brand faucets will have a warranty, but it will probably only be good for one year. So, send in the warranty registration card to make sure you're covered should you ever have a problem.

That warranty isn't worth anything without documentation. You'll need to have proof-of-purchase, so keep the receipt in a safe place. I attach my receipt to the item's installation instructions. By doing this I keep my date-of-purchase information and everything else I need to know all in one place. The instructions also have contact information for the manufacturer.

Chapter 13

No Runs, Drips, or Leaks: The Right Way to Install Your New Sink and Faucet

. . . .

In This Chapter
▶ Getting the tools together
▶ Assembling the faucet and sink
▶ Finishing the installation

. . . .

*I*nstalling a sink and faucet in your kitchen is easy whether you're doing a complete kitchen remodel or simply upgrading the look of your kitchen. The information in this chapter, coupled with the manufacturer's instructions for both the sink and the faucet, will help you through the steps. And when you're done installing, you have a leak-free kitchen sink and faucet.

Gathering the Right Tools

The fewer trips you make to get tools and materials, the less time you waste and the faster you finish your project. Here are the tools you need to gather for installing your sink and faucet:

- Groove-joint pliers
- Adjustable wrench
- No. 2 Phillips screwdriver
- Medium-sized slotted (straight tip) screwdriver
- Caulk gun
- A tube of silicone caulk/adhesive

✔ A small container of plumber's putty

✔ Spud wrench

✔ Bucket and rags

Of these tools, the spud wrench is the one you are least likely to own, but it's one that will make the job easier. The spud wrench is engineered to fit the locknut that is used to secure the sink basket to the sink. A spud wrench costs under $10 and is available wherever plumbing tools are sold.

Setting the Stage: Preparing to Install Your Sink

Much of the work of sink installation actually takes place before you set the sink into the countertop. Taking your time with the preliminary work ensures a smooth installation.

If you don't install your sink and faucet according to the instructions, you'll have to foot the bill for the replacement even if the product is defective. If the manufacturer sees signs of abuse or misuse or an improper installation, they're off the hook. And I know from my years in the home center business that the first thing a manufacturer checks is how a product was used or installed.

Taking the measurements

In most cases, the old plumbing configuration will work with your new sink. But if you're making a major change in the design of the new sink, be sure that the old plumbing fits the new sinks requirements. So, before you buy or order a sink, take a few measurements.

Establishing the drain height

Make sure to measure the distance from the underside of the countertop to the center of the drain line that comes out of the wall. This distance is usually between 16 and 18 inches, which allows adequate space for the water to drop into the trap and still leaves enough space below the trap for storing items underneath the sink in the cabinet.

The drain height is usually not an issue unless you're going from a very shallow sink to one that has very deep bowls (9 to 12 inches deep). Even if you do switch to deeper bowls, it may only be a problem if your old setup had a shallow bowl coupled with a high drain exit position. This may sound like a less than likely setup but it does happen.

If you do find that you only have a few inches of space between the bottom of the bowl and the center of the drainpipe, contact a licensed plumber to assess the situation and determine if the drainpipe needs to be lowered.

Determining the shut-off valve heights

You should also measure the height of the shut-off valves. Measure from the floor of the sink base cabinet to the center of the valve.

Remember, though, that houses built before roughly 1980 were not required to have shut-offs on every sink supply line, so you may not have any at all. If your sink doesn't have shut-off valves, install them now while you're working on the system. (I tell you how to install shut-off valves in Chapter 7.) If your kitchen didn't have shut-offs when you tore out the old sink and faucet and you've been working on the sink installation for a few days, you better have installed individual shut-off valves by now or your family won't be speaking with you. Where there are no shut-off valves and there are open pipes or lines, the only way to keep the water from running out is to shut down the entire water supply. Not a good idea when your daughter is getting ready for a big date.

Making sure to attach the faucet before installing the sink

Yes, the heading is correct. The easiest and best way to install a faucet is before the sink is in place. If you install the faucet before installing the sink, you won't have to strain or reach because everything is completely open.

Getting to know your sink

Most sinks come with factory-drilled holes along the back edge or lip. The number of holes should be equivalent to the number of holes needed for your faucet, so pay close attention when buying your faucet and sink. If you have a single-lever faucet, you'll want a single- or two-hole sink, depending on if your faucet needs a separate sprayer hose hole or if you want a soap dispenser on the sink. (I discuss sink and faucet options in Chapter 12.)

Many sink and faucet combinations use four holes. In most cases, the first three holes from the left (as you face the front of the sink) are for the faucet. The hole furthest to the right is for a spray hose, separate water dispenser tap, or soap dispenser. Some newer sink designs have the holes positioned so that the dispenser hole is the one on the left, but this would be clearly marked on the carton or explained in the instructions. The first hole from the left and the third hole from the left are spaced 8-inches-on-center, which is commonly shown as 8-inches o.c.

Help is available

One of the great features offered by most of the brand-name plumbing fixture companies is the toll-free phone number listed near the end of the installation instructions. These ten digits give you access to the company's technical experts, who are there to help you with your product installation. Don't be afraid or embarrassed to call them, either. The goal of most companies is to make sure that their products are installed properly and give you years of trouble-free service.

Got a question? Give 'em a call!

Securing the faucet to the sink

Before you begin, create a stable workspace where you can safely position the sink. You can simply set the sink on a solid work surface, such as a workbench. Just remember to clean off the surface or put down some cardboard to prevent accidentally scratching the sink surface when it's time to flip the sink over to tighten the faucet nuts. Or, if you want to avoid flipping your sink over, place it on a set of sawhorses. Just rest the side ends on the horses and you're ready to have at it. Make sure that the sawhorses are stable and can't slip or move. If a sawhorse moves, chances are good that the sink will fall.

Well, it's time to begin the assembly process.

1. **Place the faucet over the three holes on the left with the faucet's water supply *tailpieces* (threaded pieces located directly beneath the faucet handles) going into the two outside holes.**

2. **Screw the plastic nuts onto the threaded tailpieces (which will later connect to the supply lines) and hand-tighten until snug.**

3. **Use groove-joint pliers to finish tightening the nuts.**

   Be careful not to over tighten the nuts. Plastic nuts are easy to strip or ruin with pliers.

4. **Seal the area where the faucet meets the sink, according to the manufacturer's instructions.**

   Some faucets come with a rubber gasket that goes on the bottom of the faucet body between it and the sink. Other faucet manufacturers recommend applying a bead of silicone tub-and-tile caulk on the bottom of the faucet body before positioning the faucet on the sink. Both methods keep water from getting underneath the faucet where it could run down the factory-drilled holes and drip onto the sink base cabinet floor.

At this point, you may want to install the sink *baskets* in the sink, but don't do it just yet. (The baskets are the stainless steel strainer-like baskets used in kitchen sinks to let water run out but catch food scraps and other sink debris.) Leaving the baskets out keeps the holes open and these holes are the perfect handholds for lifting and lowering the sink. Having these holes available also reduces the chance that you'll grab the neck of the faucet and lift the sink. I know of several folks who ruined a brand new faucet because they used it as the holding point to lift a cast-iron sink! One of the faucet necks simply snapped off, not only ruining the faucet but also causing a huge ding in the countertop when the sink dropped well before it was in position.

Attaching water supply lines to the faucet

After the faucet is secured to the sink, you can attach the water supply lines that will eventually be connected to the shut-off valves on the main water supply pipes. Regardless of what your supply line is made of, it probably uses a coupling nut to secure it to the faucet tailpiece. Simply screw the coupling nut onto the tailpiece until it's snug and then give it a couple of final snugs with groove-joint pliers.

Don't rush when attaching the supply lines. Faucet tailpieces are usually either brass or plastic, depending on the quality and the manufacturer. But no matter which material is used, the threads can be easily stripped if the coupling nut is started unevenly. Finger-tightening the nut onto the tailpiece helps ensure that it's going on straight. Eyeball it to make sure it looks straight; if it doesn't, back off the nut and start over.

Dealing with factory-attached tubes

Some faucets come with factory-attached soft-copper supply lines on both the hot- and cold-water tailpieces, which means the only attaching will be directly to the shut-off valves. You should, however, do a little preshaping of the soft-copper before setting the sink into position in the countertop.

Measure the distance between the water supplies under the sink and then gently bend the soft-copper supply tubes until they're about the same distance apart as the water supply. They don't have to be exact, just close.

Be very, very careful when shaping the soft copper. Notice I said *shaping* and not *bending* the pipe. When people hear or read the work "bend" they think they need to be forceful with the copper. But soft copper is very fragile and kinks relatively easily. And after it's kinked, you won't be able to get rid of the kink, which restricts water flow and will eventually begin to leak.

The best way to shape the copper into position is to gently slide it through your hands as you gradually move it into position. Don't try to shape it in one shot. Make two or three passes through your hands for best results.

Installing flexible copper supply tubes

Flexible copper supply tubes are similar to, if not the same as, the factory-attached soft-copper supply tubes found on some faucets. The same care is needed to bend and shape the copper tubes that you install. Try to shape the tube into position before attaching it to the sink's tailpieces. After the tube has been shaped, secure it to the tailpiece with the coupling nut.

Although these copper supply tubes are somewhat flexible, they can't be looped or twisted around if they're too long for your supply setup. You need to cut them to length to fit into the open end of the shut-off valve. Determining how much to cut off is easy:

1. **Position the tube between the tailpiece and the shut-off valve and mark the tube so that it will fit down into the valve after it has been cut.**

2. **Use a tubing cutter to cut off the excess.**

3. **Attach the tube to the tailpiece with a coupling nut and use the compression nut and ring to secure the other end of the tube to the shut-off valve.**

Installing the newest tubes — Braided!

One of the best new plumbing products to come along is the line of braided steel supply lines. They're constructed of a rubber supply (like a hose) wrapped in a steel-braided outer jacket. And what's really great about them is their flexibility. You can take the excess length and simply put a loop in it and then connect it to the shut-off valve as shown in Figure 13-1.

Because this product is fairly new, you should check with your plumbing inspector to make sure that they meet your local plumbing code. They're not accepted in all regions — yet!

After you've attached the supply tubes, attach the spray hose if you have one. Slide the coupling nut end of the hose through the mounting ring and hole in the sink. The sprayer head rests in the mounting ring when not in use. Attach the coupling nut on the sprayer hose to the threaded outlet on the underside of the faucet, usually located under the center of the faucet body.

Other sink extras, such as a soap dispenser or hot water spigot, should be installed now. Follow the manufacturer's installation instructions.

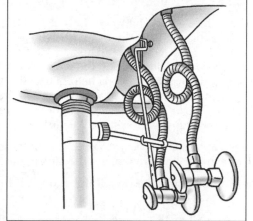

Figure 13-1: Braided steel supply tubes can be looped and then attached to the shut-off valve.

Putting Things in Position: Finishing Your Installation

Now that the plumbing supply stuff is in place, it's finally time to put the sink in place and see how it looks. After the sink is in place, you can make the supply line and drain line connections that will transform the gaping hole in your countertop into a working sink.

Setting in your sink

If you're installing a stainless steel sink, you can probably handle the lifting and positioning yourself. However, if your new sink is cast iron or cast enamel, get a helper. These sinks weigh 80 pounds or more and are awkward to handle.

1. **First, dry-fit the sink to determine exactly the right spot.**

   Set the sink into the opening in the countertop. Remember to use the basket holes to grip the sink, not the faucet. Center the sink in the opening and then draw a light pencil line on both sides and along the front edge of the sink.

2. **Lift out the sink and flip it over.**

   You don't need to take the sink back to your shop to do this, either. Lay a piece of cardboard on the countertop to protect it (and the sink) from scratching and then flip the sink over so that the faucet handles and neck hang over the edge of the countertop.

3. **Apply a bead of silicone caulk (about ¼-inch wide) around the edge.**

   The caulk prevents water from getting between the sink and the counter, and it also holds the sink in place. Use a silicone-based tub-and-tile caulk, which usually contain mildew killers and stand up against the dirt, soap scum, and crud that you're sure to find around the kitchen sink. Silicone caulks also remain somewhat flexible, which is helpful because the sink will actually drop very slightly when it's filled with water and then lift when the water is drained. The movement is very slight, but over time this movement would cause a regular latex-based caulk to crack.

   After the caulk has been applied, you need to keep the installation moving so the caulk doesn't dry before you get the sink in place.

4. **Lower the sink into position using the pencil lines to get it in the same location.**

5. **Let the sink rest for about 30 to 45 minutes before you install the sink baskets so that the caulk has time to set up or** *cure.*

Installing the sink baskets

After the caulk has cured, install the sink baskets (the stainless steel catcher/strainers I mentioned earlier).

1. **Start by applying a ¼-inch thick rope of plumber's putty around the entire underside lip of the basket.**

   The putty seals the gap between the lip and the groove of the sink basket hole. Don't put the putty on the groove — it's too easy for it to get shifted out of position and then the basket will leak.

2. **Now fit the baskets into the holes in the sink bowls and secure them to the sink using the rubber washer, cardboard gasket, and metal locknut that are supplied with the basket.**

   Make sure you install the rubber washer first, the cardboard gasket second, and the locknut last. If you don't, water will leak under the basket lip.

3. **After you've hand-tightened the locknut, use the spud wrench to finish securing the locknuts.**

4. **Finally, remove the excess putty that is forced out between the sink basket and the sink and beneath the sink.**

Always follow the manufacturer's instructions and use the right materials. Don't substitute a bead of silicone caulk for the rope of plumber's putty when installing the baskets. The caulk will be very difficult to remove if you need to remove the basket. Plus, it won't fill the gap as evenly as the plumber's putty. This putty has been used by professionals for decades and is the only way to go.

Connecting the supply lines

No matter what type of material you use for your water supply lines, you want leak-free connections. The fastest connection to use is the screw-on nut and washer that's on the ends of a steel-braided supply line. Simply tighten the nut onto the threaded outlet on the faucet tailpiece and the shut-off valve and you're set to go.

Another commonly used type of connection is called a *compression fitting.* It consists of a *coupling nut,* which secures the fitting to the faucet tailpiece and the shut-off valve, and a brass *compression ring,* which forms the sealed connection between the supply line and the fitting it's attached to. Compression fittings are a tighter connection than a screw-on nut and washer fitting. Here's how to properly install a compression fitting:

1. **Start by sliding the compression nut onto the supply line with the nut threads facing the valve.**

2. **Now slide the compression ring onto the supply line.**

3. **Place the end of the supply tube into the appropriate valve, making sure that it fits squarely in the valve opening.**

   If the supply line end doesn't go in straight, the connection will leak, because the angle of the end of the supply line won't allow the compression ring to sit or "seat" properly between the supply line and the valve fitting.

4. **Reshape the tube until it fits squarely.**

5. **Once the tube is in place, pull the compression ring and nut onto the valve and screw it tight.**

6. **Open the shut-off valve to check the connection for leaks.**

   Keep some rags handy, just in case.

Hooking up the drain line

Drain kits come in different materials and configurations, but installing them is a snap. Choose the kit with the configuration for your sink type, and you're halfway home!

Choosing the right kit

You have a couple of choices for drain kits: chromed metal kits and PVC drain kits. Both work well and are about equally easy to use. The main factor on deciding which one to use is cosmetic — will the drain line be visible? If it will be visible, you'll want to use the chromed kit. If it's out of sight in the sink base cabinet, which most kitchen drains are, then the good-old white plastic PVC kit is the way to go; PVC is cheaper.

Kitchen sink drain kits, whether they're chromed or PVC, use nut and washer screw-together connections. Besides being easy to install, they also let you easily disconnect the assembly when it's time to unclog a drain or quickly rescue that wedding ring that fell down the drain. A basic, single-bowl kit includes

- ✔ A **tailpiece,** which connects to the bottom of the sink strainer
- ✔ A **trap bend** (or P-trap), which forms a water-filled block to prevent sewer gas from coming up through the sink drain
- ✔ A **trap arm,** which is connected to the downstream end of the P-trap and then to the drain line that leads to the main drainage line

A double-bowl drain kit will have everything the single-bowl kit has along with a waste-Tee connection and additional length of drain line to connect both bowls to a single P-trap. Double-bowl kits come in two different configurations, but both use a single P-trap. Figure 13-2 shows the trap centered between the two bowls with a connecting Tee and two separate horizontal drain lengths. Figure 13-2 also shows the trap aligned beneath one of the drains with a vertical Tee and single horizontal drain length connecting the second bowl to the Tee.

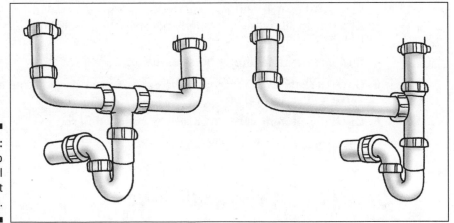

Figure 13-2:
The two double-bowl drain kit setups.

If your sink has a garbage disposer, you need an additional longer section of drainpipe to connect the disposer's drain line to the bowl drain line. The crosspiece that comes in the kit may or may not be long enough to make the connection between the disposer and other sink bowl drain pieces. You have to check yours out to be sure. Follow your disposer's installation instructions.

If your sink is a triple-bowl, you need a third set of pieces for the third bowl. Individual traps, bends, tailpieces, and pipe sections, as well as slip nuts and washers, are sold separately, so finding the extra pieces is no problem. Availability of individual parts is also especially nice for occasions when, for example, you accidentally cut off too much of the tailpiece and it doesn't reach the connecting waste-Tee. (Gee, does it sound like I may have some personal experience here?)

You probably won't find glue-together drain kits, but if you do, replace it with a nut and washer setup. (A glue-together kit uses liquid adhesive to secure the pieces of drain line pipe instead of a slip nut and washer, making it impossible to take apart and clean.)

Making the connection

Assembling and connecting the drain kit is fairly simple.

The great thing about drain line kits is that the pieces are really quite easy to move and maneuver, so you can adjust them to fit almost any setup. Don't expect the horizontal pieces to be in super-straight alignment with the tailpieces or the drainpipe. The only thing that matters is that they all eventually get connected together. Take a look at your old sink drain setup and you'll see what I mean.

1. **Start by attaching the tailpiece to the sink drain and tightening the slip nut and washer by hand.**

   If you have a multiple bowl sink, all of the drain tailpieces should be the same length for an easier installation.

2. **Next, slip the trap onto the tailpiece and then position the trap's horizontal piece next to the drain line coming out of the wall.**

   The horizontal piece must fit inside the end of the drain line. Remove the trap and cut the horizontal section to fit.

3. **Reattach the trap to the tailpiece and into the drain line and tighten the slip nuts and washers.**

Checking for leaks (Put on your raincoat first)

Before you do anything else, get the bucket and rags ready. Lay some rags directly below each connection so that, if there is a leak, the towels will immediately soak up the water. And leave the rags there for a couple of days, just in case a leak develops over time. I've had a slow leak develop a couple of times, and I was glad that the rags where still in place to soak up the water!

Have your helper turn on the water while you begin inspecting for leaks. Don't open up the shut-off valve just yet. Let the water pressure build up to the shut-off valve so that there's time for any slow-leak drips to occur. Leaving the valves closed for a few minutes should be long enough to know whether any water is leaking. Once you know the shut-off valve connection isn't leaking, open the valve so that the water goes into the supply lines. Again, let the water pressure build in the supply lines for a few minutes and then inspect the supply connections at the faucet tailpieces.

Don't be alarmed (or upset) if you have a joint that leaks. I've done a lot of plumbing projects and I still get the occasional leaky joint. Just shut off the water, take a deep breath, disassemble and reassemble the connection, and check again for leaks. No sense crying over spilled milk — or, in this case, a drippy plumbing joint.

Are two sinks better than one? Adding a second sink and work area

New kitchens in many of today's homes have two separate sink and work areas because many households have more than one person who enjoys cooking and entertaining. And just because your old kitchen layout had only one sink, that doesn't mean your redesigned space couldn't accommodate two. With two sinks, though, come some additional plumbing concerns.

Installing that second sink involves more than simply dropping in another sink and faucet near the old location. Most two-sink kitchens locate the sinks opposite each other or at least in a different section of counter space. Placing a second sink in a center island unit is quite popular (as shown in the color insert). But no matter where your new sink is located, you're looking at adding drain lines and getting water supply lines to the new spot — a major project that may mean cutting into or removing sections of the subfloor to run pipes between or through the floor joists. These changes are best handled when the rough carpentry is being done.

Once again, when you get into dealing with this type of modification to the drain line layout, you probably need to hire a plumber.

Chapter 14

Appliance Appreciation: Choosing the Right Ones

In This Chapter

▶ Considering your budget

▶ Checking out refrigerators

▶ Researching ranges and ovens

▶ Discussing dishwashers

▶ Disposing of food and garbage

▶ Wondering about warranties

*N*ot all kitchen remodels need to include the purchase of new appliances. However, new appliances do help make life easier in the kitchen, and they're more energy-efficient, which means cheaper utility bills. But new appliances are a major expense and they do use up a good chunk of your budget.

Buying new appliances isn't as simple as driving to the local department store and pointing to the white refrigerator and white range. In addition to colors, you need to consider brands, sizes, and configurations. Plus, today's kitchens incorporate more appliances than in the past, so your shopping will take a bit longer.

A good way to start shopping for appliances is to eliminate the ones that you don't want or need or that won't work in your kitchen. Eliminating some choices helps you to better focus your shopping attention on the things that matter. Start checking out things like which refrigerator and freezer setup you prefer: side-by-side or over-and-under. You may find that you absolutely hate the way one works versus the other. After you know that, you can eliminate one option. See what I mean?

Before purchasing any appliance, consult *Consumer Reports* magazine, which does a fabulous job at testing and evaluating all categories and brands of appliances. Check your local library for back issues of *Consumer Reports* or log onto their Web site (www.consumerreports.org) and review their advice for a fee.

Now, with these hints in hand and an open mind for styles and designs, take a look at your appliance options.

Making Money-Related Decisions First

Shopping for new appliances may seem a bit like shopping for a new vehicle. Beyond deciding which brand you want, you need to weed through the various features of the individual models. But, take heart. If you do your homework and take your time when you're checking out appliances, you should be able to find close to if not exactly what you want without breaking your appliance budget.

Considering a fuel source change

When shopping for new appliances, consider the type of fuel source you currently use in your home and what type of appliance you now own. If your home has all electric appliances and you're set on owning a gas-fired range, then be ready to pay for running a gas line into the house or the kitchen, depending on your setup. Yes, some homes have only electric-powered appliances, including the furnace. On the other hand, if you want to install an electric-powered appliance where you currently have a gas-fired counterpart, you'll need to run a new circuit to the appliance, and you may even need to upgrade your home's electric service to accommodate the increase in electric power requirements.

The cost between gas-fired and electric appliances can be significant. Gas appliances usually cost more, however, they generally last longer because they have fewer parts that wear out, for example heating coils or heating elements on an electric oven or range. They're also less expensive to operate because gas prices are lower than electric prices, generally speaking. You need to do the math to calculate how much you'll save in operating costs versus the price difference between the two types of appliances. Also factor in the time you plan to own the appliance to determine the length of time for pay-back if you do have to pay to convert the fuel source.

If you decide to make a fuel-source change, consider budgeting for a professional to come in and make the changes. Working inside your home's electric service panel can be very dangerous and potentially deadly if you don't know what you're doing. When in doubt, hire a licensed electrician. And running gas into the house or tapping into an existing gas line requires using the right type of fittings and making leak-free connections — the first time! A licensed plumbing contractor will be able to install code-approved gas lines and connections. Chapter 15 explains what's involved when installing either new electrical service or a gas line.

Deciding between commercial-grade and residential appliances

Most folks opt for residential appliances — the standard sized, reasonably priced, efficient models sold at all home-improvement stores. But some folks want the ultimate in kitchen quality, which requires taking the plunge into commercial-grade appliances. This upgrade will really take a chunk out of your budget. Commercial-grade units are generally at least twice as expensive as residential-grade appliances, and sometimes more. In addition, commercial-grade appliances have larger motors that use more energy, so they're more expensive to operate.

So, why go commercial? Well commercial-grade appliances are designed for harder use and longer use than residential appliances are. Not that your everyday brand appliances can't handle a normal home's workload. But commercial-grade units are built to last for many years more than their residential counterparts. They have longer warranties that often cover both parts and labor. Many residential-grade appliances only cover parts for a few years, usually around five. In addition, commercial-grade appliances are larger with more storage capacity and cooking space. For example, the typical residential range has four burners, whereas a commercial range will have at least six and sometimes eight burners and a separate griddle or grill area. But not just the capacity increases; the dimensions on these items are also larger. So, make sure your kitchen design has room *before* you opt for the bigger commercial units.

Some brand names you'll see when shopping for commercial-grade appliances are Sub-Zero, Viking, DCA, Dacor, Asko, and Wolf. You should be able to get product information from the appliance dealer. All of these companies have Web sites, too. Just plug the brand name into your search engine of choice and you'll get to their respective Web site. Commercial-grade appliances are usually sold through appliance dealers that sell to contractors. However, most dealers will be happy to sell to you, the general public buyer.

If residential-grade appliances suit you just fine, then look for the usual array of the popular brands such as Frigidaire, Whirlpool, Amana, and Kenmore.

Analyzing your exterior options

I'll bet we can all remember the color of the appliances in our folks's house. In my parent's house, everything was white, which was the most affordable color for the average American homeowner. And although white has been and continues to be a popular — and affordable — choice, you have more options today. Take a look at the world of color choices.

Sticking with standard colors

White was always a good, standard color choice. Then came the avocado green and harvest gold years. Today, you still see white, but you also see black, almond, and, yes, even some harvest gold and avocado appliances. The biggest difference in picking one color over the other, aside from personal preference, is that colors cost more and you may have to wait for delivery. White and black appliances are usually kept in stock at most appliance stores and home centers. Keep in mind that lighter color appliances lighten and brighten up the room, which makes the room look and feel larger.

Stainless steel: Tough and usually fingerprint free!

One of the newer finishes in major appliances is stainless steel. Stainless steel is often used on commercial-grade appliances, but only in the last 10 or 12 years has stainless steel made inroads into residential kitchens. Some of this can be attributed to the influx of commercial-grade appliances into the home. Another influence is that people want to bring the look of a professional kitchen into the home. Besides looking cool, stainless steel appliances are tough. And the new designs and technology even give you virtually fingerprint-free steel!

The downside: If you want stainless steel, be ready to pay more. Stainless steel appliances can be anywhere from 25 to 50 percent more expensive than their enamel-finished counterpart.

Designer patterns: Yep! They have 'em

Nowadays, you can even match your appliances to your cabinets. Some refrigerators, ovens, dishwashers, and even trash compactors have a matching or interchangeable faceplate or panel designed to match your cabinet color and style. Of course, you'll pay more for appliances with this feature. But, if you want all the vertical surfaces to match, this is your only option. The interchangeable panels also allow you to change one or more of the appliance faces if you think you'd like a bit of a break in the uniform look of your kitchen.

Chillin' Out: Exploring Refrigerator Options

The refrigerator is the most-used appliance in the kitchen. Its doors are opened and closed dozens of times a day, especially if you have kids. Selecting a style and design that works best for your family is critical. Choose the wrong type and you'll fuss and fume every time you open the door.

When it is fridge-shopping time, consider your family size, how often you entertain, and your food-buying habits. If, for example, you like to buy frozen foods or meats in bulk, consider a unit with a large freezer compartment. Or, consider purchasing a separate freezer unit to store bulk purchases.

Selecting a setup

Choices in refrigerator setups are actually quite narrow. The two units are either stacked on each other or they're side by side. But, there are advantages and disadvantages to either style. Let's take a look at your choices so you get the setup that's best for you and your family.

Over-under or under-over

A refrigerator with the freezer compartment on top and the refrigerator on the bottom is the most common design. This over-under design allows for easy access to the refrigerator. And easy access to the fridge is important for kids and elderly folks. Your other option in a stacked configuration is to have the freezer on the bottom and the fridge on top. The under-over design is easier on the back (no more bending over and reaching way in the back for that jar of pickle relish that always seems to "walk" to the rear), plus this design reduces the chance of damaging the floor — or your toes! — if you drop a frozen item from the freezer.

Both of these designs are less expensive than side-by-side units, which I discuss shortly. Over-under units are less expensive than under-over and both are more energy efficient than side-by-sides. The major drawback to the stacked styles is that their doors are the width of the unit and you need adequate clearance and space for the doors to swing completely open.

Don't forget, too, to get your doors to swing in the correct direction for your kitchen. If you set bags of groceries on the countertop to the right of the refrigerator, then you want the door to be hinged on the left (when you face the fridge) so you don't have to move around the door when loading items into the fridge. If there's more counter space on the left, you'll want the door hinged on the right.

Side-by-sides

When you think of an upscale kitchen, you probably imagine a side-by-side refrigerator. Why? Probably because most professional kitchens have this style. The side-by-side design can also accommodate an in-door ice and water dispenser, a very popular option. And the doors on side-by-sides are considerably narrower than those of a stacked setup, which means you need less space for opening the doors.

The drawback to a side-by-side unit is that each compartment (the refrigerated section and the freezer section) is much narrower, so storing wider items, for example party trays or even a large frozen pizza, can be a problem. Remember, too, that these units cost more to buy because of the way the motor and cooling units have to be positioned to accommodate the side-by-side design. Still, the elegant look of a side-by-side refrigerator/freezer really dresses up a kitchen.

Sizing up your choices: Freestanding or built-in

Refrigerators come in two basic categories: built-in or freestanding. The biggest difference between the two types is how the cabinet is designed to accommodate the motor and cooling/refrigeration coils. But, no matter which style you choose, you must identify the space and the size of the space where the refrigerator will be positioned. Unless you're tearing out and allowing for new or additional refrigerator space, you need to size the fridge to the space.

Built-in refrigerators house the motor and coils either over or under the food compartments, which reduces the depth dimension and increases the height. Built-in units are typically 36 inches wide, only 24 inches deep, and 84 inches tall (to accommodate the motor). The shallower depth makes it much easier to see your food — especially the stuff at the back of the compartment.

A freestanding unit has the motor and coils located below and behind the two food compartments. This design makes it deeper than its built-in counterpart. The typical dimensions of a freestanding unit are 36 inches wide, 30 inches deep, and 66 inches tall. These units are also deeper than most base cabinets (usually 24 inches deep).

If you want the style and look of a built-in refrigerator, you'll have to pay extra. Built-in units cost about twice what a freestanding refrigerator costs. If you upgrade to the professional-grade level, you'll pay even more.

Paying a little more for the extras

Today's refrigerators come with several optional bells and whistles. Not all of the extras are things that only the rich and famous would have (or want). Some are handy extras that make using the fridge easier and, in some cases, safer for everyone. Of course, each extra costs you more money, and buying a more basic or bare-bones model will help you stick to your budget if you haven't or can't allow a lot of money for fancy appliances. The following list names a few of the extras:

- Adjustable door bins allow you to adjust the distance between door bins to accommodate various height bottles and containers.

- A refreshment center built into the refrigerator door gives you access to drinks and snacks without having to open the main refrigerator door.

- Sliding shelves allow you to move shelves from side to side to stagger the storage space on the bottom shelf and to stagger spacing between other shelves.

- In-door ice and water dispensers give you the convenience of ice and water at your fingertips, without having to open the refrigerator or freezer doors. A built-in water filter keeps dispensed water tasting fresh with each glass.

- Spill proof shelves designed with catch-edges and raised front and rear lips prevent spills from spreading to other shelves.

- Child lock-out systems keep young kids (and hungry teens, too!) out of the fridge when you're not around or when they shouldn't be ruining their dinner.

- Beepers let you know when a door is left ajar, and lights turn on when it's time to change the water filter.

- Temperature controls allow you to adjust the humidity in the crisper drawers and the temperature for the ice and water dispenser.

Do you need a second fridge?

Before you run out and get a second fridge, you need to decide where to put it. Remember, refrigerators take up at least 2 to 3 feet of width, so if you're thinking of fitting another one into the kitchen, you'll lose at least one base cabinet, and possibly two — not the amount of storage space that most people are willing to sacrifice. But if you do a lot of entertaining or have a big family that needs a lot of room for refrigerated or frozen food storage, a second fridge/freezer may be a logical choice.

Remember, you don't have to put it in the kitchen. My family of four has a second refrigerator in the basement. We use it for storing a couple of extra gallons of milk (that way we really never run out), butter, juices, pop, and other beverages of choice. We can also use it when we stock up on refrigerated sale items. The best use we get out of the second fridge,

however, is when we're entertaining and need extra cold storage space. We can prepare food ahead of time and know that it will be stored at a safe temperature. A second fridge is also a great place for keeping leftovers. Just don't forget about them!

Another popular second fridge is the wine refrigerator. These units are the size of a standard drawer-width base cabinet (about 18 inches) and take the place of one of your base cabinets. They have several racks for laying the wine bottles and a glass door for easy viewing of what wines you have on hand. The unit runs on a standard 120-volt circuit, but does not need to be on its own circuit. You can pick up one of these handy wine refrigerators for roughly $400. Most stores need to special order a wine fridge, but you'll be able to get it in a couple of weeks.

Warming Up to Cooktops, Ranges, and Ovens

Cooktops with built-in woks, ovens built into the wall — you have more options today than ever before. If you want to keep things simple, you can stick with an all-in-one cooking top and oven appliance (called a *range*). But if you want to spice up the look and flow of your kitchen, consider some of the modern advances I describe in the following sections. When incorporated properly into the kitchen layout, they make the kitchen much easier to use and work in.

Be sure to assess your cooking style and use needs before shopping. For example, do you like to bake? Do you do a lot of entertaining? Do you cook big meals because you have a large family? The answers to these questions should help you determine which unit is right for you.

Keeping with tradition: Slide-in, drop-in, and freestanding ranges

Aside from how they're installed, the functions of the three different types of ranges are the same. A slide-in range fits between two base cabinets and has unfinished sides. A drop-in range actually rests on part of a cabinet base between two base cabinets. It, too, has unfinished sides. A freestanding range can fit between two cabinets or can be placed at the end of a cabinet. Freestanding units have finished sides.

Ain't nothing like a grilled steak in the wintertime: Downdraft cooktops

The real joy of owning one of these babies is when the weather's bitterly cold and you're dying for a grilled steak. With a downdraft cooktop or range, you can have your steak and eat it, too, regardless of the weather. Downdraft units are engineered to pull the smoke and fumes down into the range as you're cooking and then vent them outside. The ductwork is an additional installation and can substantially drive up the cost of having a downdraft range. Make sure that the ductwork is vented to the outside, too, and not into a crawlspace or interior area. One of the most popular brands, and the originator of the design concept, is Jenn-Air, although many of the major range and oven manufacturers now offer downdraft units.

All three range styles come in gas-fired or electric-powered styles and typically have a four-burner cooking top. Some upgrade models may have a grill in the center of the cooking surface (more on cooking surface options in the "Getting creative with additional cooking surfaces" section).

Many of the styles still have knobs for operating the individual burners and oven settings. However, newer models also offer electronic controls — some even come with one-touch controls preset to commonly used cooking temperatures.

24- or 30-inch-wide ranges are the two most common sizes, however, you can find other sizes. Make sure you measure your existing range/oven space before you buy the new unit.

Getting creative with additional cooking surfaces

Many new kitchen designs are set up for using a cooking surface unit that has separate burners or heating elements (depending on the fuel source) and are not part of an oven combination. These units are commonly called "cooktops." Why? Because they're so versatile. Today's cooktops have options such as griddles, down-drafting grills (described in the "Ain't nothing like a grilled steak in the wintertime: Down-draft cooktops" sidebar), rotisseries, and woks. Don't be surprised to see a cooktop used in an island, either, as a second cooking surface. Another neat feature when using a cooktop is that the space that normally is occupied below the unit by the oven is open for storage drawers, making it a very convenient spot to store your pots and pans.

Installing an additional cooktop involves getting power and ductwork to the location. These steps are best left to a pro to ensure proper operation and, just as important, proper ventilation.

Some units even come in dual-fuel combinations (say that three times fast), so that you can harness both gas and electric heating sources. Who would want that, you ask? Well, some people only like to cook with gas and others only like using electricity. And if you happen to have one each of these people using the same kitchen, well, a combination fuel-source appliance can make both parties happy.

Electric cooktops are less expensive than their gas-fired counterpart, however, they're more expensive to operate. Controlling the heat on an electric unit is more difficult than with a gas-fired cooktop and electric coils take much longer to cool down. On the flip side, however, an electric-coil burner actually heats water faster than a gas-burner unit.

Ogling your oven options

I remember learning how to bake from my mother. We'd turn on the gas to preheat the oven. While it was heating up, we'd mix up the batter for whatever we were making, pour it into pans, and put them in the oven. Oh, how times have changed. It's no longer gas or electric, there's convection, microwaves, or combination units. And lots more.

The key to selecting the right sized oven is to look at its interior dimensions — the actual amount of cooking area. The amount of interior space can differ greatly even in ovens with the same external dimensions. If you choose a 24-inch-wide unit, be prepared for problems. An oven of that width can usually accommodate a standard cookie sheet, but not a roasting pan. A 27-inch-wide oven will handle just about any size roasting pan, even a large turkey roaster, and a 30-inch oven can even handle two cookie sheets side-by-side.

- ✔ **Conventional ovens:** Conventional ovens are the most common type of oven. They cook food by using radiant energy from their fuel source and natural convection from the heated air inside the oven. They can be either gas-fired or electric. Gas ovens bake moister; however electric ovens bake more evenly. I know of several people who have a combination fuel-source with a gas range (for better heat control), coupled with an electric range (for more even roasting).

- ✔ **Convection ovens:** Originally developed in the 1950s to help commercial bakers save time and bake things more evenly, the convection oven is not particularly popular, especially as the only oven in a kitchen. They cook with an electric heat source and use a fan to circulate hot air within the oven. Because the unit uses moving air to cook the food, the oven tends to dry food out. Recipe cooking times must also be modified because a convection oven cooks much more quickly than a conventional oven. Many folks go through a period of trial-and-error to get cooking times adjusted and ruin a fair amount of food in the process.

- ✔ **Combination units:** A combination convection/conventional oven uses a heating element inside the oven (conventional) and a fan to circulate the heated air (convection). The drawback to this design is that this oven doesn't heat as evenly as a true convection oven, so you really need to watch the food you're cooking to avoid burning it.

- ✔ **Wall ovens:** As the name implies, this type of oven is a unit unto itself and is installed in the wall and not as part of the range. Wall ovens are usually placed higher than the ovens in ranges, often around chest height, which makes them very accessible. And you can locate them just about anywhere in the kitchen that makes sense. And, because it's a separate unit, adding a second wall oven is a popular option and upgrade, especially if you do a lot of baking. Wall ovens come in 24-, 27-, and 30-inch wide styles and can be either gas or electric powered.

Most folks ask a pro to install a wall oven because running the electrical cable or gas line to the oven and making the hook ups can be tricky.

Sizing up your range hood

Simply opening a door or window to provide ventilation in the kitchen doesn't cut it these days. (Chapters 7 and 15 discuss ventilation requirements and how to evaluate your existing ventilation system.) With the amount of smoke, grease, and especially moisture released into the air while cooking, you must remove as much as possible to reduce possible damage to your home. Also, as you peruse your options, keep in mind the fact that the range hood should be considered as a key element in the look of your kitchen, because it's a fairly large appliance that is prominently positioned over a very busy area — the cooking area.

An over-the-stove range hood offers the best form of ventilation because it captures the most heat and the steam that goes along with it, especially if you cook with tall pots. Downdraft ventilation systems (which use a special fan to pull smoke, steam, and moisture down into ductwork rather than pulling the same contaminants up, like with an over-the-stove hood) do work, however they're better suited for use with low pots and pans.

If your kitchen has a center island cooking area and it has an exhaust hood over it, make sure that the exhaust hood's fan is powerful enough to draw the smoke and steam up and out. This also applies to all exhaust hoods. They must be powerful enough to draw the steam and smoke out.

If you install a commercial-grade range hood, be sure to check its air movement capacity (CFMs — cubic feet per minute) rating. Most residential range hoods have a rating of between 50 and 100 CFMs. Commercial units are designed to move two and three times that much, which can create a serious back-drafting situation for any gas-fired appliance. Back drafting is caused when carbon monoxide or CO (the colorless, odorless byproduct of a gas-fired appliance) is pulled back into the house instead of being pushed out through an appliance's venting and ductwork. This happens because enough make-up air isn't being drawn into the room to take the place of the contaminated, CO filled air, so you could be overcome by carbon monoxide fumes, which can kill!

When shopping for a new exhaust fan, bring along the dimensions of your kitchen (square footage). Then, be sure to check the information from the manufacturer so that you purchase the right size fan for your kitchen — one that's strong enough to remove the contaminated air without causing a back-drafting situation.

No-hassle cleanup options

One oven option that makes life in the kitchen easier is a self-cleaning feature. Most ovens, except for the least expensive models, are self-cleaning. The continuous-cleaning feature, however, is even nicer because the oven does what the name implies: It continually cleans the oven box whenever spills and splatters occur so you can say good-bye to spray-on oven cleaners, scrub brushes, rubber gloves, and nasty fumes from the cleaner.

Moving in on microwave ovens

When the microwave oven was first introduced, it was billed as the do-it-all oven of the future. Well, it never quite achieved that high status, but it did become and still is a handy appliance to have in the kitchen. Most folks use their microwave ovens for thawing or defrosting frozen foods, and to quickly reheat leftovers. But finding the best place for a microwave oven can be a perplexing dilemma. Just think through your family's needs and capabilities when deciding where to install a microwave oven.

Placing a microwave oven on the counter creates a problem because you're using valuable countertop space. However, this placement is a safe one. Even though you often see a microwave oven installed over the range or stove, this placement isn't entirely safe. Removing hot foods from an over-the-stove unit can be a real problem, especially for children or people with physical impairments. On the other hand, if your family members are older and all physically able, an over-the-range unit is a popular choice and takes away less space than a countertop unit or one mounted under the countertop in a base cabinet.

If your budget allows and you have the space, a second microwave oven is a good choice. Because microwave ovens have limited capacity, they can't heat, thaw, or cook too many things at one time. But a second microwave oven allows you to do more cooking faster and helps make meals come together more quickly. A second microwave oven is nice, too, for making snacks, for example popping twice as much popcorn when your kid's friends descend on your house to watch movies.

Getting the Dish on Dishwashers

Okay, if you have kids you have ready-made dishwashers, right? Well, you'd like to think so. But most kitchens today include a dishwasher as one of the must-have appliances. Built-in units take the place of a base cabinet, so you do lose storage space. But the time you save by not washing dishes by hand is worth the storage space you sacrifice.

One of the major selling points of a good-quality dishwasher is how quietly it runs. The first built-in unit we ever owned was about 10-years old and came with the house we purchased. And although it cleaned the dishes well enough, you couldn't carry on a conversation in the kitchen if the unit was running. When I replaced that old unit, I found out why it was so noisy. Our new dishwasher had insulation all the way around the outside of the washer tub body, to deaden the sound and reduce the noise. The old dishwasher had no insulation. Better quality units will have insulation or be engineered with a body that reduces noise. Most of the major brand name dishwashers, such as Whirlpool, Maytag, Amana, and Bosch, are fairly quiet. If you want the maximum in dishwasher-quiet, however, you'll have to spend twice as much to get the high-end or commercial-grade units. Personally, I'd rather spend that money somewhere else in the kitchen, because the major brands do a very good job at a very reasonable price.

Other dishwasher features and design issues to consider include

- ✔ How the dishwasher loads: Most have plates and large items on the bottom rack with glasses on the upper rack, however, some models load just the opposite.

- ✔ How many cycles the unit has: Some have just a few basic cycles (soak, wash, rinse, and dry) while high-end units have many. Ask yourself if you really need the delicate or china cycles.

- ✔ What type of controls the unit has — electronic or manual: Tests have shown that electronic controls are more durable and last longer than knob-style controls.

- ✔ Tub material and construction: Stainless steel and porcelain tubs are more durable than a plastic version.

- ✔ Capacity: If you have a large family that uses a lot of dinnerware, silverware, and pans at each meal, buy a unit that is large enough to accommodate your family's dining habits.

Taking Out the Garbage: Disposers and Compactors

Garbage disposers are found in most kitchens today. They come in a range of sizes, based on the horsepower of the motor. For most families, a disposer with a ½– or ⅝–horsepower motor performs well and should last for years. One-quarter-horsepower units are also available, but because they're not as powerful as the slightly larger units, they don't last as long. And spending the money for a 1-horsepower unit is, in my option, a waste of money, unless you throw away an awful lot of food waste every day.

Another appliance growing in popularity every year is the trash compactor. They've been around for several decades, but used to be considered pretty fancy and up-scale. Well, not anymore. Trash compactors fit neatly beneath the counter and reduce the bulk size of trash that leaves your house. A trash compactor doesn't reduce the *amount* of trash; it takes your trash and compresses it down into smaller packages.

Both of these appliances can be installed by DIYers. Check out Chapter 15 for the basic steps on how to install either of these appliances.

Working with Warranties

All major appliances come with some sort of manufacturer's warranty. Most extend for several years on both parts and labor. The exact length of the warranty varies among manufacturers. Be wary, however, if a major appliance has a warranty only good for one or two years. Remember, a manufacturer usually issues a warranty for as long as they know a product will last. The more moving parts, the more likely the warranty will be shorter. With so few moving parts to break, refrigerators usually have the longest warranty time period. Refrigerators last for 15 to 20 years, easily. A dishwasher, on the other hand, with all of its moving parts, pumps, motors, and valves, usually carries a much shorter warranty — sometimes only a few years. But whatever your choice, if you go with a known, brand-name manufacturer, you'll probably be happy with product performance. And if you ever have to use their warranty should a problem arise, the major players know how to provide good customer service. That's why they've been in business for so many years.

Chapter 15

Fridges, Ranges, Disposers, and More: Installing Appliances

. . . .

In This Chapter

▶ Putting in a range, cooktop, or oven

▶ Figuring out how to install your fridge

▶ Looking into installing a few other appliances

. . . .

*I*f you've decided that new appliances are part of your kitchen remodel, I hope you did your homework to make sure that the new units will fit properly in your remodeled kitchen. If you're simply replacing your old range with a new one, chances are good that the new one will fit in the old space. But, if you're replacing the old range with one that is larger or uses a different fuel source, you need to make some adjustments. You're in luck! This chapter explains how to handle the situation should you need to make adjustments in order for your new appliances to fit in your remodeled kitchen. It also covers how to convert from gas-fired appliances to electric and vice versa.

I'm not going to go into great detail with regard to running a gas line to the kitchen for a new gas range or running a new circuit to the kitchen for an electric range. Both of these tasks involve making some tricky connections that are probably better left to a licensed plumber and electrician (see Chapter 4 for advice on hiring a pro). I will, however, give a broad explanation of each process, so you'll have an understanding of how they work. After reading this chapter, you'll be a smarter shopper and homeowner when it's time to get bids on the work.

Installing Ranges, Ovens, and Cooktops

The two major questions to answer for this part of the remodel are

- ✔ What is the fuel source: gas or electric?
- ✔ Where is the appliance going to be installed? In the row of base cabinets, in an island, or freestanding?

This section takes a look at installing a new cooking unit as well as converting your fuel source from gas to electric (which is most common), including the basic installation steps for ranges, cooktops, and ovens. You don't need many tools, because this job is best left for a pro.

Changing the power/fuel source

The most common fuel-source change is going from gas to electric. However, the last house I purchased came set up for an electric range and clothes dryer. I was raised using gas-fired appliances and, in my opinion, once a gas appliance user, always a gas appliance user. So, I decided to run gas lines to both.

Running a new power or fuel source to the kitchen isn't as messy as you might think, especially if you (or the pro you hire) do the work before the cabinets and new floor are installed. Doing the work when the kitchen is torn apart means walls and floor areas are easier to access, which is important if you have to pull a new circuit through the wall for an electric range/oven.

Wiring ID — It's all in the numbers!

Understanding electric wire numbers isn't difficult. For example, a 6/3 cable means that the wire thickness of all the individual wires is a #6 wire and that there are three individual wires (not including the ground wire) within the cable's sheathing. Therefore, a 6/3 cable will use #6 wire and have one black, one white, and one red wire, plus a bare or green wire for the ground. Some regions may only require 8/3 cable for an electric range. The only difference is that the wires used are slightly thinner than the #6 cable, but there are still three individual wires plus the ground wire.

Just remember, as the first number of the wire designation gets bigger, the wire thickness or gauge gets smaller; and the second number indicates the number of individual wires within the cable, excluding the ground wire.

Gaining space in your electric service panel before converting to electrical appliances

Just because you want electric-powered appliances doesn't always mean your home's electrical service can handle it. The best way to figure out whether your system can handle adding electric-powered appliances is to have an electrician or your electric service provider come out and inspect your main panel.

If your home has fuses, either the screw-in plug type or fuse blocks, you probably won't be able to add electric appliances without upgrading to circuit breakers. If your home has circuit breakers, you might be able to add electric appliances without increasing the amperage to the house. However, just because the service panel has unused slots, it doesn't mean you can simply knock them out and add a few breakers. Homes with circuit breaker panels have at least 100 amps of power *(100-amp service)*, which is considered the minimum standard for a medium-sized home with no more than three major electric appliances, including central air conditioning. So, for example, if your home has 100-amp service and it has central air, an electric water heater, and an electric clothes dryer, you probably wouldn't be able to add an electric range without upgrading your system. Many new homes have 150- or 200-amp service or more.

Upgrading an electrical system should be left to a licensed electrician. Cities are (rightly) very picky when it comes to who can make what changes to a home's electrical system and will be almost overly picky if you attempt a complete service upgrade as a DIYer. A complete system upgrade should cost between $1,500 and $3,000, depending on material and labor costs. Just remember to build the costs of a system upgrade into your budget if you're considering electric appliances. You don't want a three-grand surprise just because you fell in love with an electric cooktop and you didn't budget for it!

Making the move from gas to electric

A first-time electric range installation needs a 240-volt circuit that is dedicated for the range and oven. This involves installing and attaching the correct size cable to your home's main electrical service panel. And unless you're skilled at working with electricity, you should hire an electrician to handle this job.

Electric codes require an electric range and/or oven to be on a dedicated 40- or 50-amp circuit. Check with your electrical inspector as to which is required in your area. To do this job, you (or your contractor) need(s)

- Enough 6/3 cable to run from the service panel to the new receptacle in the kitchen. (See the "Wiring ID — It's all in the numbers" sidebar for more on wire numbers.)

- A 240-volt appliance receptacle, which has three plug prong holes and a ground prong hole. The orientation of the prong holes is different than on a standard 120-volt receptacle (see Figure 15-1).

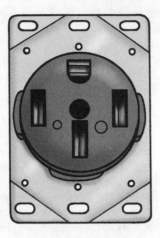

Figure 15-1:
A 240-volt receptacle has three prong holes and one ground prong hole.

✔ A double-pole, 40- or 50-amp breaker. A *double-pole breaker* consists of two individual breakers joined together to form a single unit and used on 240-volt circuits.

Make sure the new breaker is the same brand as your service panel. In most cases, brands are not interchangeable, and you could create a fire hazard by installing the wrong brand.

After the new circuit cable is run to the kitchen, it needs to be connected to the receptacle. And new ranges don't come with plugs, so you'll need to install one. Make sure you buy a four-wire appliance plug. Most ranges or the plug packaging will have instructions for making the right connections.

If you're replacing an existing electric range, it may have a three-wire setup, however, the current electrical code requires a four-wire setup. You cannot use a four-wire plug with a three-wire receptacle, so the old setup must be replaced.

Converting from electric to gas: Running a new gas line

If your home has one gas-fired appliance, then you can add as many as you desire. The only thing you need is a gas line to each of the new gas appliances. For this job you need:

✔ A roll (coil) of ½-inch outside diameter (O.D.) soft copper pipe (tubing). The beauty of running a gas line from an existing line is that most codes allow the use of soft copper from the main gas line pipe (which is usually black threaded pipe) to the appliance.

✔ Assorted short lengths of threaded black pipe, usually from 3- to 8-inches long (in 1-inch increments). These short lengths are called *nipples*.

- *Union fittings,* which connect the nipple to the main pipe.

- A Tee fitting for the nipple that will have the flexible copper line attached to it.

- A separate shut-off valve for the range gas line supply. You must have this so that you can shut off the gas to the range without having to shut off the gas to other appliances.

- Pipe joint compound, often called *pipe dope*, for coating all threaded connections (required by code).

Flexible copper pipe uses flare-fittings to connect to the gas pipe. What makes this type of fitting so good is that it's easy to disassemble if you need to move the range out for service or any other reason. You will need a flaring tool kit to hold and form the flared end on the copper. The pipe is secured in the flaring tool base while you use a flaring tool to form the small lip or flare on the copper. If you work with flare fittings and don't form the lip properly the first time, don't try to reuse or reshape the lip. Cut off the flared lip using a copper tube cutter and start over. Once a lip is out of shape, it's not safe to use. The lip must be round to seal properly inside the flare nut and against the flare union.

After reading all that's required for tapping into a gas line, you'll probably want to hire a professional to handle the job. Most plumbers can do this.

If you do install a gas line yourself, be sure to check it for gas leaks. Here's what to do:

1. **Apply a soap-and-water solution to each connection and look for bubbles.**

2. **Turn on the gas.**

3. **If bubbles form, tighten the fitting slightly with a pipe wrench and recheck.**

   Be sure to wipe off the old solution and apply a new round of the mixture.

4. **If you still see leaks, disassemble the fitting and check the flare shape.**

   You may need to redo the flare end of the copper pipe.

If you smell any gas odor, immediately shut off the gas! Open a window to help move the gas fumes out of the room. Don't turn on a light switch or start an electric fan, either. This has been known to cause a spark and ignite the gas fumes, causing a devastating and sometimes fatal explosion.

When working with flexible copper, be sure to leave two or three extra loops of copper behind the range before you attach it to the range and shut-off valve. The loops allow you to move the range in and out without putting stress on the connections. Repeated movement on the connections can cause them to leak. I've seen too many gas-fired ranges and clothes dryers with a straight line of soft copper pipe leading directly to the connection. And the first time the appliance is moved, it puts a kink in the pipe, which then needs to be replaced.

If you kink soft copper pipe, cut off the kinked section and redo the fitting. This may mean replacing the entire length of pipe. Kinked soft copper pipe will usually have a split in the sidewall that is sometimes almost invisible. When you have a split, you also have a gas leak and a dangerous and possibly life-threatening situation.

Wranglin' with a range

Assuming you purchased a *range* (a cooktop and oven combination unit) that uses the same fuel source as your old range, installing the new appliance should be as easy as sliding in or dropping in the unit. (You could also choose a free-standing range, but it's the same as a slide in model — only not surrounded by cabinets.)

The slide-in range is the easiest to install regardless of the fuel source. After the fuel source connection is made, you simply push or slide the range into position. Hence the name, slide-in.

The main thing to avoid in this installation is damaging the floor. Plastic appliance mover strips that you position under the legs of the range allow you to easily slide the range into place without scratching, or even contacting, the floor. You can also use part of the cardboard carton that the appliance was shipped in; however, be careful not to rip the cardboard while sliding the range. I've seen floors get damaged and it really sours the mood of the project and its participants when it happens.

Electrically-powered slide-in ranges use either a heavy cord that's plugged into a dedicated 240-volt/50-amp circuit or a length of flexible metal cable with individual wires inside, which is connected to an electrical box located behind the range. Gas-fired slide-in ranges use a flexible gas line that's attached to the gas supply line's shut-off valve, or *gas cock,* on one end and to the range's gas connection on the other. Gas connections use *flare nut fittings* to attach the gas supply line to the main gas line. When installed properly, they provide the best seal for preventing gas leaks and they can be taken apart easily if, for example, you need to move the range out to work on the area behind it.

Making a gas connection to an appliance isn't difficult, but it must be done correctly to prevent a gas leak. Flare nut fittings are used on both ends of the flexible gas line. After the connections are made, check for leaks as I explain in the "Converting from electric to gas: Running a new gas line" section earlier in this chapter. If you detect a gas leak after testing and refitting the connection a couple times, you may want to call a plumber to handle the hookup. Yes, plumbers know how to do gas hookups.

Both electric and gas ranges usually have a clock and other cooking accessories that run off of electrical power, but only 120 volts or a standard circuit is required. The ranges will have a standard 120-volt power cord that's plugged into a 120-volt receptacle located on the wall behind the range. An electric range needs two outlets behind it — a 240-volt for powering the cooking components and a 120-volt for the clock and timer(s).

A drop-in range requires a cutout cabinet and countertop area so that the range drops into the cabinet. This type of range often has a flange around the edge of what is the cooktop surface. The flange rests on the countertop and supports the entire range. Then the range itself is screwed to the cabinet. The fuel-source hookups are the same for a drop-in range as they are for a slide-in type.

Installing a cooktop

Cooktops come in either gas or electric models and are installed in a cutout area of the countertop or in an island. Fuel-source connections are the same as for a range. The main difference is in how each type is installed in the countertop.

Electric models typically have a flange around the cooktop (similar to a drop-in range) that supports the unit in the countertop. The weight of the cooktop is enough to keep it from shifting position.

Gas-fueled units are installed a little differently than their electric-powered counterpart. Electric units have a flange around the edge for supporting the unit, the same as for a drop-in range. Gas cooktops do not have a flange. Instead, they need to fit into a cutout or *dropped* section of the countertop and actually sit on the top of the cabinet frame. You (or your cabinet and countertop designer) should have figured this drop section into the plans (see Chapter 8) so that the correct cabinets and countertop are ordered.

Built-in baking — Installing a built-in oven

A built-in oven is installed in a similar manner to a slide-in range except that it slides into a cabinet or, in some up-scale installations, an opening in the wall. Built-in ovens come in gas or electric versions, so hookups are the same as for slide-in units.

If your built-in oven is going into a cabinet, be sure that the oven dimensions will work in the cabinet opening. Most use industry standard dimensions, but double-check when ordering your cabinets to be sure that the new oven will fit the cabinet opening.

Installing a New Fridge Complete with Dispenser Unit

The refrigerator is the easiest of all appliances to install. In many cases, when there's no in-the-door water and ice dispenser, it's as easy as sliding it into its designated space and plugging it in.

However, fridges today often come with popular extras that require more from you in the way of installation. The most popular of these extras is the in-the-door icemaker/water dispenser unit. For this, you need to run a water supply line to the back of the fridge. Fortunately, even the greenest of DIYers can handle this easy job.

You need the following tools:

- Two adjustable wrenches
- A ⅜-inch power drill (electric or cordless)
- A ½- to ¾-inch diameter spade bit
- An icemaker water supply kit (which usually includes a saddle Tee for tapping into the cold water supply line)
- A compression-fitting Tee kit (if a saddle Tee is not code-approved in your area)

Take a look at how the installation is done:

1. **Determine which of the water supply pipes is the cold.**

   To find the cold water supply pipe, simply follow the two pipes that supply water to your kitchen sink. They should run parallel and be fairly close together. If the hookup is done correctly, the pipe on the right (as you're looking at them and as they're going to the sink) should be the cold. Believe it or not, I've been in a few houses where the hookups are backwards from the standard — hot on the left and cold on the right. If you're still not sure which is which, turn on the hot water tap at the kitchen sink and grab the pipes. Whichever pipe turns warm is the warm water supply pipe, so you know the other pipe supplies cold water.

If you have a basement, tap into the cold water pipe down there. This gives you easy access to the pipe and doesn't take up space under the sink with another valve and the necessary supply pipe to the refrigerator. If your home doesn't have a basement, tap into the cold water supply line that goes to the faucet.

2. **Determine whether you can use a saddle valve in your area of the country. Most icemaker kits come with a length of copper tubing and a saddle valve; however, in many areas a saddle valve doesn't meet code. If you can't use a saddle valve, you need to install a compression-fitting connected valve (see Figure 15-2).**

    1. **If you can use a saddle valve, attach the two straps (saddles) over the cold water pipe and secure them with the supplied bolts and nuts.**

        The shaft or spike of the valve is hollow and pointed so that when you tighten or close the handle of the valve completely, the tip of the shaft pierces the copper pipe and water then flows through the hollow center.

    2. **Then just open the valve completely to allow water to flow through the tubing to the fridge.**

        The copper tubing uses a compression fitting to connect it to the tapping valve's threaded end. Use an adjustable wrench to tighten the nut to the fitting.

    3. **If you can't use a saddle valve and need to install a compression-fitting valve, simply cut out a short section of copper and install the compression-fitting valve as explained in Chapter 7.**

        Turn off the water before cutting into the water supply pipe!

        Don't reopen the saddle valve or the compression-fitting valve until you've attached the tubing to the refrigerator or you'll have a big, wet mess!

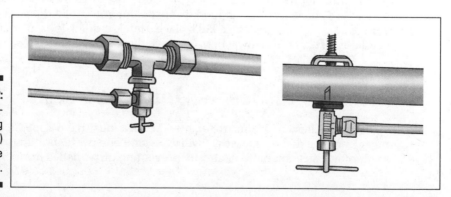

Figure 15-2: Compression-fitting valve (left) and saddle valve (right).

4. **Next, drill a hole through the floor (if you're coming up from the basement) so that you can feed the copper tubing up to the refrigerator.**

   Use a spade bit to drill up through the flooring. Remember to wear eye protection as you'll be drilling overhead and it's easy to have something fall in your eye.

   If you're working in your basement, a quick way to be able to spot the hole location from below is to drive a nail through the kitchen floor from above. Then, simply go in the basement and look for the tip of the nail — that's where you drill the hole.

5. **After the hole is drilled, feed the tubing up into the kitchen.**

   Don't cut off any extra tubing; instead, leave it coiled behind the fridge so that you can move the fridge in and out for cleaning without putting any stress on the tubing or the connections.

6. **Use a compression fitting to connect the kitchen-end of the tubing to the back of the refrigerator's water fill valve, usually located in the lower left corner.**

7. **After all the connections are made, open the water supply and check for leaks.**

You shouldn't have a leak at the refrigerator unless you didn't connect the threaded fitting on the water inlet valve properly. If it leaks there, carefully remove the fitting and reconnect it keeping the fitting straight with the threads. If the compression-fitting valve leaks, turn off the water and redo the compression fittings.

Installing Other Popular Appliances

If your house is like mine and you have a teenager or two, then you already have natural appliances in the house. My kids *looove* to wash dishes and my teenage son is our human food disposer. But you can find actual appliances that conveniently take a kid's place. Here's a quick look at the basic installation steps for dishwashers, garbage disposers, and trash compactors.

Doin' the dishes — Automatic style

For most families, an automatic dishwasher is a must-have appliance. It not only cleans the dishes, glasses, silverware, and cookware, but it also keeps your counters cleaner and neater by preventing dirty dishes from piling up.

Try to install a dishwasher next to the kitchen sink, because then the connections and drain lines are shorter. Shorter connections ensure that you get hotter water to the dishwasher and that dirty water gets into the drain lines sooner. Plus, loading dishes is easier when the dishwasher is right next to the sink.

Gathering the right tools

Installing a dishwasher is pretty straightforward, and you don't need a lot of fancy tools and equipment. Simply gather the following common tools:

- ✔ A power drill
- ✔ A bit for drilling a hole in the cabinet side wall (correct size bit will be listed in your dishwasher's installation instructions)
- ✔ A straight-tip screwdriver
- ✔ A 6-inch adjustable wrench

You'll also need a hot water supply connection (which you get by tapping into the hot water supply line of your kitchen sink faucet), a drain connection, and a 120-volt receptacle or electrical box. Check with your city's electrical inspector to find out which type of power hookup is allowed in your area. A dishwasher can drain directly into the sink's drain line or into a food (garbage) disposer.

Some cities require that an air gap be installed if you drain the dishwasher directly into the disposer. The air gap prevents a clogged drain from backing up into the dishwasher by actually causing a break in the direction of the water flow. An *air gap* is a piece of plastic pipe with a V-shaped split at one end; the split ends are called *nipples*. This setup allows you to attach the dishwasher drain hose to the smaller straight nipple and a second, shorter length of pipe to the other air gap nipple and to the nipple on the disposer. Check with your city plumbing inspector to see what's required for your installation.

If you do drain your dishwasher through your food disposer, be sure to remove the plug or knockout in the dishwasher nipple on the disposer before attaching the drain hose from the dishwasher or air gap, depending on your situation. If you don't remove the plug, the dishwasher won't drain and you'll be bathed in dirty, soapy water when you open the dishwasher door!

Installing the unit

Here are the basic steps for installing a dishwasher. Be sure to follow your manufacturer's instructions as some steps may vary slightly among brands.

1. **If an air gap is required, mount it in one of your sink's predrilled openings.**

   If you don't have enough openings in your sink, drill a hole in the sink or in the countertop next to the sink.

2. **Cut a hole in the side of the sink base cabinet right next to where the dishwasher will be installed.**

   This hole is for the dishwasher drain hose and the water supply line. Consult your instructions for size and exact location of the hole.

3. **Slide the dishwasher into place and feed the drain line hose through the hole in the cabinet.**

4. **Level the dishwasher by following your installation instructions.**

   Most dishwashers have adjustable front feet that are threaded for easy adjustment. This is one time when it's okay to eyeball the unit for level.

5. **If your system has an air gap, attach the dishwasher drain hose to the smaller of the air gap nipples.**

6. **Attach a second hose to the other air gap nipple and then to the dishwasher nipple.**

7. **Secure all hose connections with screw hose clamps (often referred to as "radiator hose clamps").**

   If your unit didn't supply the clamps, you'll find them at home centers or auto parts stores. Buy a 2- or 3-inch size clamp.

8. **Connect the dishwasher water supply tube to the hot water shut-off valve.**

   Get a supply tube that has a braided steel or nylon shell. This type of tube is very flexible, it doesn't have to be cut to the exact length, and it can last for years! You need a shut-off valve that has two outlets — one for the dishwasher and one for the faucet — which means you have to replace the shut-off valve if there's only one outlet for the faucet. See Chapter 7 for instructions on how to install a shut-off valve.

9. **Now move to the front of the dishwasher and remove the lower access panel.**

   This is where you'll make the water and electrical connections to the dishwasher.

10. **Attach a brass L-fitting to the water inlet valve.**

    This fitting is threaded and is simply screwed on. Apply some pipe dope on the threads of the fitting that go into the inlet valve to make a leak-free connection. Consult your installation instructions for the location of the water inlet valve. It varies between manufacturers.

Again, your machine may or may not come supplied with a brass L-fitting. Check this out before you start the installation so that you can keep moving. L-fittings are sold at home centers and hardware stores.

11. **Attach the other end of the water supply tube to the other threads on the L-fitting.**

12. **Open the water supply valves and check for leaks.**

13. **If no leaks are found, make the electric connections so that the unit will run.**

    Consult your owner's manual for step-by-step instructions for this process because the steps vary between brands. But one rule applies to all units: Turn off the power before making any electrical connections!

Takin' out the trash — Sink style

A food (garbage) disposer's main job is to grind food waste so it can be flushed down the drain. This cuts down on the amount of bagged garbage that goes into the local landfill. Yes, it does create more waste water to be treated, but at least it can be treated and reused.

A food disposer takes the place of a sink basket and drain piece on one of the kitchen sink bowls. To install this appliance, you must consult the installation instructions that come with the unit, because the steps vary among brands.

Here are the basic installation steps for any food disposer:

1. **Remove the sink basket (if one was installed).**

2. **Send the *sink sleeve* (which replaces the sink basket and secures the disposer to the sink bowl) through the hole in the sink bottom and secure the sleeve to the bowl using the gasket and mounting rings, following your installation instructions.**

   The gaskets and mounting rings keep the sink sleeve from leaking when you run water. There are two mounting rings: the upper mounting ring and a backup mounting ring. There's also a snap ring that goes into the groove on the backup mounting ring as extra security for keeping the unit in place.

3. **Lift the disposer and align the *mounting lugs* (small, rolled curls of metal attached to the mounting ring) and *mounting ears* (90-degree angled metal clip-like pieces also attached to the mounting ring near the lugs) with the mounting screws located between the upper and backup mounting rings.**

The mounting screws are threaded. The lugs and ears are located on the lower mounting ring, which is attached to the *disposer housing* (the main body of the unit).

Turn the disposer clockwise until it's supported on the mounting assembly (sleeve and mounting rings).

4. **Attach the *discharge tube* (a short approximately 90-degree plastic elbow where the waste and water is discharged) to the *discharge opening* (the larger hole in the side of the housing) in the side of the disposer housing.**

The tube uses a rubber gasket and metal flange to secure it and keep it from leaking.

5. **If you're draining your dishwasher through the disposer, remove the plug in the smaller dishwasher nipple and attach the dishwasher drain hose to the nipple with a hose clamp.**

If you don't have a dishwasher, *do not* remove the plug! If you remove the plug but don't have a hose to connect to the nipple, the water will spew out the hole.

6. **Connect the drain line pipe from the sink drain setup to the disposer's discharge tube with a slip nut and washer.**

You may need to cut either the discharge tube or the drain line pipe to fit.

7. **Lock the disposer in place by using the disposer wrench (included with the unit).**

Insert the wrench into one of the mounting lugs on the lower mounting ring and turn it clockwise until it locks.

8. **Finally, make the electrical connection.**

The electrical power connection for most disposers is made using a standard plug-end cord. But you do need to connect the cord to the motor wires — here's how:

   1. **Start by removing the disposer's bottom plate.**

   2. **Strip off about ½ inch of insulation from each wire of the power cord.**

   3. **Connect like color wires using wire connectors.**

   4. **To ground the unit, attach the green ground wire from the power supply to the green ground screw that will be on the disposer housing.**

      The screw's easy to spot because it actually is painted green.

   5. **Gently push all the wires in and reinstall the bottom plate.**

   6. **Plug in the cord and you're good to go!**

All disposers need a dedicated electrical circuit with an on-off switch on the wall near the sink. If you're replacing an existing disposer, use the existing circuit, as long as it meets current electrical codes. If you need to install the on-off switch, have an electrician install the circuit. Working with the combination of electricity and plumbing can be dangerous — let a pro do it!

Mashin' the trash

One other popular kitchen appliance is the trash compactor. Having one of these little beauties allows you to put more trash in a smaller container. Installing a trash compactor isn't difficult, either. They're often installed inside a base cabinet or put inside one of the storage areas in an island. The cabinet door hides the actual appliance so there's no visual distraction.

The only step involved with installation, other than getting the unit itself inside and secure to the cabinet, is to plug it in to a standard 120-volt receptacle. You need an outlet on the wall behind the base cabinet section that houses the compactor or an outlet in the island, if that's where your trash compactor is going.

Make your icemaker work better and last longer

For pure, clean ice and better tasting water, install an in-line water filter on the icemaker's water supply tube. Adding a filter increases your icemaker's life because it removes particles and sediment from the water that would otherwise end up on the moving components of the icemaker and water dispenser. These hot dog–shaped filters get rid of particles and contaminants that can eventually clog the water inlet valve, the dispensing spout of the water dispenser, and the fill spout for the ice cube maker. Install the filter unit where you can access it easily. I've seen them installed behind the refrigerator in the coiled tube section and in the basement, too, before the tubing goes up to the kitchen. Either place works fine. You will need to change the filter about every six months (actual length of time depends on your family's water usage habits), so be sure to install it in an accessible location so you won't be discouraged from changing it because it's a hassle to reach. Adding a water filter costs less than $20, including the fittings. Replacement filters cost between $10 and $15, depending on whether you replace just the filtering material or the entire cartridge. All of the materials are sold at appliance parts stores and most home centers.

Part V

Adding the Final Touches: Walls, Windows, Floors, and More

The 5th Wave   By Rich Tennant

"You said you wanted me to add space to the kitchen."

In this part . . .

Want to make your kitchen the talk of the neighborhood? Then follow my advice and add a few (maybe all?) of the final touches I suggest in this part to really jazz up your new kitchen. Bright lights, colorful walls, and elegant window treatments add to the splendor of your new kitchen.

Don't forget what's under your feet, too. The most used and abused floor in the house deserves top-grade, tough flooring. From wood to tile, I show you what's new, what works best, and how to install it all.

Chapter 16

Illuminating Your Kitchen Lighting Options

. . . .

In This Chapter

▶ Looking into electrical light

▶ Taking advantage of natural light

. . . .

Your new kitchen probably has new cabinets, countertops, and appliances. But if you can't see, you can't use all your new stuff. Sufficient lighting is essential for a safe kitchen, plus it shows off your new kitchen the best, too.

Lighting a kitchen is a little more complicated than just sticking a fixture on the ceiling and one more over the sink. This chapter explores your lighting options, first electrical and then natural, and may just be the beacon of light you need to guide you on your journey to a lighter, brighter kitchen.

Making Thomas Edison Proud: Getting the Most Out of Interior Lighting

Ah, if only good-old Thomas E. could see what his little invention has created. You have options from lights that hang from metal framework to recessed metal (or can) units, all of which provide light for working and general use in the kitchen. With inadequate lighting, your new kitchen will lack the pizzazz that gives it that extra special edge. Plus, low or insufficient lighting actually makes a kitchen more dangerous because you can't see well. So, how do you know what type of lighting you need? Read on!

Determining your needs

Three major factors influence the number of lights you need in your kitchen:

✔ **The size of the kitchen:** Obviously, the larger the kitchen, the more lights you need.

✔ **How much natural or ambient light is available:** *Ambient* light refers to a combination of natural daylight and high overhead light fixtures.

✔ **How many different work stations you have:** Each work station and surface should be well lit.

Take these three factors and add in your personal wants (such as fixture styles) and you can see that there's more to illuminating a kitchen than simply flipping on a light switch.

Deciding what changes you want — and can do — is part of the planning process. In the following sections, I try to shed some light on this subject.

Matching your lights to your task

Lighting falls into three categories: ambient lighting, task lighting, and accent lighting (see Figure 16-1). Today's kitchens use a variety of lighting types to illuminate and accent. Most folks don't realize it, but their current kitchen has probably one, two, or maybe even three different types of lighting already in it. And in lighting, different it good. In fact, you could say it's critical to having a smooth running kitchen.

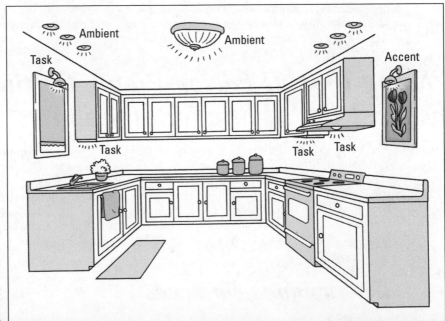

Figure 16-1: Ambient, task, and accent lighting.

Visit a lighting store showroom or a kitchen design center to get an overview of the different types of lighting. The design center usually has display kitchens as examples of how the lighting types work. A lighting showroom will have fixtures to show you but probably won't have them in a display kitchen. Plan on visiting both places to gain the best perspective on what you want in your kitchen. And price shop, too. Light fixtures always seem to be on sale, so shop around to get the most for your buck.

Bring along a snapshot of your current kitchen as well as the dimensions of your kitchen when shopping for lighting. This info will help the sales associate suggest the right lights for your kitchen.

Even though there are three types of lighting, that doesn't mean that a single light fixture will fall into only one of the categories. Many fixtures can perform two or even all three lighting functions. It just depends on where it's installed. In the next section, I take a closer look at each type of lighting to give you a better understanding of how lights function in certain settings.

Ambient lighting

Ambient lighting is a combination of natural light (daylight) and high overhead light fixtures, such as ceiling-mounted, track, or recessed (can) lights. Ambient lighting provides illumination so that you can perform everyday tasks and see and walk safely.

In a larger kitchen, you may be able to get by with one large, centrally positioned ceiling fixture, which provides much of the overhead light for the entire kitchen. Combine that light with a few smaller lights near the wall and ceiling and your overhead lighting needs should be adequately met. If you have a smaller kitchen, you may find that two or three smaller ceiling fixtures provide adequate light.

If you use incandescent light, 2 to 2.5 watts of incandescent lighting per square foot is a good amount; use 1 to 2 watts of fluorescent lighting per square foot. You can do the math before you head out to the light shop. Then all you'll need to do is add up the wattage from all the fixtures you've chosen to see whether you're providing adequate illumination.

Indirect lighting is another useful form of ambient lighting that hides the light source from view but still spreads the light itself in the room. Bouncing light off the walls and ceilings is another form of ambient lighting. (Chapter 18 talks about using the right type of paint to help bounce light and provide more ambient light.) Even accent lighting contributes to your ambient lighting. Unless you're using a very narrow, almost pinpoint type of light for an accent, you will have some light spill and thus more ambient light.

Task lighting

Task lighting provides extra light where you're working. For instance, task lighting might be used over the sink, around the range, along countertops, and in eating areas. Several types of light fixtures provide task lighting:

- Under-cabinet lights are great for illuminating countertops.

- Small wall- or ceiling-mounted fixtures can provide task lighting over the sink, eating areas, or an island.

  For areas without cabinets mounted directly above, a wall fixture mounted about 24 inches above the surface works well. Just be sure that the fixture has a shielding glass or the light will be too bright and actually distract you.

- A range hood or microwave oven light provides task lighting over the range.

- Hanging or pendant lights are most often used over an eating space or table, or over a center island.

  The great thing about a hanging light is that you can adjust the height of the light to the area it's illuminating. Just remember to keep it high enough that you don't hit your head. The recommended bulb wattage for a pendant light is one 100-watt bulb, two 60-watt bulbs, or three 40-watt bulbs.

- Recessed can lights can be positioned directly above a work area. You can use spotlight bulbs that have a tightly focused beam for more pinpoint lighting. Use one 60- or 75-watt bulb for every 20 inches of countertop.

Accent lighting

Accent lighting is more decorative than functional, because you use it to spotlight or accent a specific item. You don't have to use accent lighting all the time, only when you want the item to be illuminated. If you do have accent light in the kitchen, however, it will provide additional ambient light when it's on.

If an accent light is needed, then you want the brightest light available. The beam of an accent light should be three to four times more powerful than general lighting. Low-voltage halogen lights work well for this, because their beam is very intense. Another option is to use what's called an "eyeball" lens recessed light. This type of light fixture has baffles that allow you to focus and direct the light beam on a very specific area or item.

Most accent lights are either wall-mounted (usually directly over the area to be highlighted) or on a track light system. Track lighting allows almost unlimited positions on the track. I discuss track lights in just a bit.

Bulb wars: Incandescent versus fluorescent

Incandescent bulbs are the old, familiar pear-shaped bulbs with the screw-type base. They're easy to install, relatively inexpensive, and are used in a variety of fixture types. They produce a warm light that provides a comfortable, cozy feeling in a room. However, incandescent bulbs produce light by heating a filament with electricity, which can actually raise the temperature in a room if enough incandescent bulbs are operating at the same time. And they also use more electricity than fluorescent bulbs, so they do cost more to operate over time. The lifespan of an incandescent bulb is considerably shorter than a fluorescent bulb and the amount of light it produces decreases as the bulb gets closer to burning out. However, a new generation of tougher, more efficient, longer living incandescent bulb is available. They still produce the small warm, cozy light but last a lot longer than a regular incandescent bulb. Some are guaranteed to last for years! All incandescent fixtures can be used with a dimmer switch.

Fluorescent bulbs are more expensive than incandescent bulbs; however, they're more energy efficient and last up to 20 times longer. The traditional tubes are the long, round ones that come in either 4- or 2-foot lengths, but today, fluorescent bulbs come in a variety of sizes and shapes. All fluorescent bulbs produce light that is brighter and whiter than any incandescent bulb. And up until a few years ago, it was difficult to use fluorescent lights and incandescent lights together. The intensity and colors just weren't compatible. Early generations of fluorescent bulbs appeared to change your skin tones and the color of your walls. Some people had to repaint rooms to adjust for the fluorescent bulbs. Today's fluorescent lights, however, emit warmer tones and you can even find color-corrected fluorescent tubes. To better understand what color producing bulb you're getting, you need to check the bulb's color rendition index (CRI). A fluorescent bulb's CRI should be at least 80 for light that will be pleasing to use. Incandescent bulbs have a CRI of between 98 and 100. The more closely you can match the fluorescent CRI to the incandescent's CRI, the more compatible and pleasing the color production will be. The light emitted from a fluorescent bulb can't be focused so you can't use it as an accent or task light. Finally, some fluorescent fixtures cannot be used with a dimmer switch.

If you decide to go fluorescent, don't buy a really cheap fluorescent unit. They tend to flicker a lot, which is really annoying and you'll eventually quit using the light leaving your kitchen or part of it under illuminated. Most stores have all of the fixtures they sell on display and wired for use. Try to see how the unit actually performs before purchasing it.

Fancy's fine, but function is foremost: Shedding light on fixture options

Too often a homeowner absolutely falls in love with a fixture because of its look, shape, color, or what have you and never fully understands or realizes what type of light it will provide. When it comes to choosing the fixtures, don't let decorating decisions overshadow what the light fixture can and will do. I know that the only way to really know whether a light will work for your situation is to install it and see how it fits in your kitchen's layout. This, however, can be a very expensive way of doing things.

Try to work with your lighting consultant so that you can return the fixture if it just doesn't work out in your kitchen. Keep all the boxes, packaging, instructions, and anything else that came with the fixture. Remember, too, that you probably have only a limited amount of time to return the light.

On the subject of overhead fixtures

The following list overviews many of the overhead light fixture options:

- **Ceiling-mounted fixtures:** These fixtures are mounted on the ceiling (hence the name) and provide most of the ambient light in kitchens. You can find ceiling-mounted fixtures in styles ranging from one- and two-bulb incandescent round lights to 4-foot-long, four tube fluorescent fixtures. Pendant lights are also considered ceiling-mounted units even though the actual light is not flush to the ceiling after the unit is installed. Recessed can lights are another form of ceiling-mounted lights. Although they're not actually mounted on the ceiling, they're often used along with ceiling-mounted fixtures to fill all of a kitchen's ambient lighting requirements, so I included them in the ceiling-mounted category.

- **Suspended ceiling lights:** If your kitchen has a suspended ceiling, the light fixtures will be a part of the ceiling system. The most commonly used fixture is the 4-foot long fluorescent fixture that takes the place of one of the suspended ceiling tiles. Another popular type of light in a suspended ceiling is a recessed unit. Recessed lights can be placed wherever they'll do the most good. I've seen kitchens with as many as a dozen recessed lights in a suspended ceiling. Some provided ambient light, and others were in the perfect position for providing task lighting.

- **Track lights:** Track lighting is my favorite type of lighting. You can position the individual fixtures anywhere along the track. Plus, the fixtures swivel, so you can direct them to an almost unlimited number of positions. Add in that you can use either a flood-type bulb for a wider light beam or a spot-type bulb for a more directed or focused beam and you can see why I love this system. Installation is easy, too, and I discuss that in detail in Chapter 17. If you do want to use track lighting, be aware of the total wattage of the bulbs being used. I've seen situations where folks added two track light units, consisting of nine fixtures per system for a total of 18 additional lights. They were both on the same circuit and couldn't be turned on at the same time without tripping the circuit breaker. They loved the lights and weren't about to get rid of them, so they fixed the problem, though not inexpensively, by having an electrician come in and split the circuit.

- **Ceiling fans:** Okay, I hear you, "A fan's not a light, buddy!" But just about all ceiling fans come with a light kit. So besides getting the light from the bulbs, you'll also get the comfort of circulating air from the fan. Before you buy a ceiling fan for your kitchen, consider what size fan you need. If you're interested in adding a ceiling fan in your kitchen, read the "Choosing a ceiling fan" sidebar in this chapter and skip ahead to Chapter 17, where I explain how to install the fan.

Incorporating under cabinet illumination

Under cabinet lighting provides illumination for both safety and ambience. There are two ways under cabinet lighting is installed:

- **Hard-wired:** This is the best looking of the under cabinet systems because there are no exposed wires or cables. The electrical wires are in the wall and ceiling and come out only at the electrical boxes where the operating devices are used. The wiring for the under cabinet lights can be run in or on the underside of the cabinets, too, which keeps the wiring as invisible as possible.

  The biggest drawback to this type of system is getting the power cable where you need it. You can tap into an existing circuit that's located near the cabinets, but you still need to pull some new wiring to the lighting. You also need to install an electrical box for the switch(es) for the under cabinet lights. Chapter 17 tells you how. But, if you're unsure about taking on this installation, hire an electrician to do the work.

- **Strip-wired:** This system is the easiest to install and hook up, because it simply plugs into a nearby, existing receptacle. The units themselves are secured to the bottom of the wall cabinets and then you run the power cord to the outlet. You can secure the power cord to the underside of the cabinet with electrical staples, which makes the cord as discreet as possible.

Under cabinet lighting uses one of three types of lights:

- **Fluorescents** are the most commonly used under-cabinet lighting option because they're the least expensive to buy and the cheapest to run. They light evenly because of their length. You can also install different types of fluorescent bulbs ranging from warm to outside light.

- **Halogen** bulbs come in either a disc or linear design. Both provide bright, high-color-quality light. The linear style is very slim in design and easy to hide under the cabinet. The lights are powered by a transformer; however, you can hide the transformer by installing it inside one of the cabinets. You have to wait for halogens to cool before you can touch them or you get severely burned. Prices range from very inexpensive to outrageous. I'd recommend a mid-priced (around $25) system if you're going with halogen.

✔ **Xenon** lights are relatively new to the residential market. What makes them so great is that they provide equal or better light than a halogen bulb but with much less heat. Xenon bulbs come in both disc and linear designs (both powered by a transformer) and are installed much the same way as halogens. Just be ready to spend more money.

Deciding whether you need major changes

Most kitchen lights are powered on a single 15-amp circuit. This takes care of the ceiling fixture (remember, you often only need one) and the one or two other lights in the kitchen. If you plan to add lights for the countertops, over the stove, and maybe even some in-cabinet lights, consider running an additional lighting circuit to the kitchen. Adding a new circuit and getting it to the specific lights can be tricky, especially if the wall and ceiling surfaces are finished. To be honest, calling in an electrician is best. Besides pulling the cable for the new circuit, the electrician can help make the best decisions about which lights should go on which circuit.

If your kitchen has only one ceiling fixture and you want to add another, then you'll have to add electrical boxes for the fixtures. This means cutting holes in the ceiling for the boxes and pulling electrical cable from the existing box to the new ones to power the light. Someone with moderate to advanced DIY skills can handle this task, but I wouldn't make it my first electrical remodeling project.

On the other hand, adding track lights is easy for almost anyone. You need to install the track's main box where the old ceiling fixture was mounted. The track box is attached to the electrical box in the ceiling so you don't need to

---

Choosing a ceiling fan

Ceiling fans come in a wide range of sizes that are defined by the blade size. You can find fans in sizes from 24 inches wide to units up to 54 inches wide

The size of your kitchen and the location of the power source are key factors in choosing the right fan. Choose a 24- to 29-inch fan for kitchens up to 50-square feet; a 36-inch fan for kitchens up to 75 square feet; a 42-inch fan for kitchens up to 100 square feet; and a 50-, 52- or 54-inch fan for kitchens up to 400 square feet. There must be at least 24 inches between the fan's blade tips and the nearest wall. The bottom of the fan (including a light, if your fan has one) must be at least 7 feet from the floor to allow people to walk under it safely. Many models are mounted on an extension piece located between the mounting box and the fan itself. If you think that 7 feet won't be enough clearance, you can still install a ceiling fan. Look for a model that mounts flush to the ceiling. Head to Chapter 17 for advice on installing the ceiling fan of your choice.

install anything new. After the track box is in place, you follow the manufacturer's instructions on attaching the track sections and securing them to the ceiling. I provide detailed installation instructions in Chapter 17.

What you can do if you can't make major changes

Take a look at this list of things you can do to lighten and brighten up your kitchen, even if major lighting changes aren't an option:

- ✔ **Go with a glossy surface.** Semi gloss paint reflects light better than flat or satin paints. And the reflected light helps brighten up the room. Glossy paint surfaces are easier to clean, too. For more on paint, check out Chapter 18.

- ✔ **Install dimmer switches.** Ambient lighting wired to a dimmer switch allows you to adjust the light level and create the appearance of more or less light as needed. You don't change the actual amount of available light, but you are able to adjust it. Also consider installing a dimmer on the eating area fixture.

  Most electrical boxes can handle the additional size of the dimmer's body, so fitting it into an existing box shouldn't be a problem. The thing to remember with dimmers is that not all light types can use them. Check the manufacturer's instructions before installing a dimmer. (See Chapter 17 for advice on installing a dimmer switch.)

- ✔ **Under-cabinet lights.** Under-cabinet lights are great for task lighting. They also provide additional ambient light when they're on. For more on under-cabinet lights, check out the "Incorporating under cabinet illumination" section earlier in this chapter. Installation of under-cabinet lights is explained in Chapter 17.

Letting the Light Shine In: Natural Lighting Options

Like interior light fixtures, your kitchen windows are important sources of light. This section gets you thinking about the benefits of new energy-efficient windows, and it also tells you how to make your existing windows aesthetically pleasing with a fresh coat of paint and blinds if new windows aren't in your budget.

In most cases, it's best to let a professional carpenter install your windows. They're used to making the openings in the walls, lifting the windows (which can be a real chore, especially with a larger window unit), sealing around the windows so that moisture doesn't get between the windows and your home's siding, as well as making sure there's no air leakage or drafts around the windows.

You need a building permit to add windows and, in some cases, to replace existing windows. Your city inspector will want to inspect the new framing or rough opening for any new window(s) to make sure that they're properly supported and installed.

Boldly going where no window has gone before: Adding new windows

If your kitchen has a blank exterior wall, then you have the perfect opportunity to add windows. And why would you want to do that? For two good reasons: 1) More windows mean more natural light, which makes any kitchen brighter and more inviting and 2) Adding windows provides more or better ventilation, especially if the new window allows for cross ventilation.

Adding new windows, however, isn't as simple as punching a hole in the wall and slapping in a window. If there's an exterior wall that doesn't have a window, there's probably a good reason why a window wasn't installed when the house was built. So it's important to consult a designer to see where new windows might work in your kitchen. They can help you select the window size and type that will provide the most light and ventilation.

It's also a good idea to hire a pro to cut the openings in the wall. And if you plan to use any non-traditional shaped windows, leave the installation to the pros. Installing a round or oval window is tricky to say the least, and professional carpenters are more accustomed to dealing with unusual construction situations and usually have a trick or two to accomplish this.

In days gone by, the main shapes for windows were square or rectangular with an occasional round window over a doorway. But designers and architects have pushed the window manufacturers into creating many new sizes and shapes for windows. If you do decide to add new windows to your kitchen, take a look around at what's available before you decide. You can choose from so many shapes and sizes. (I discuss quality and maintenance issues in the following section.) For example, you can install very small 1 foot by 1 foot stationary units or large, sliding patio door type windows. I've even seen a wall of windows that was 12-feet wide and the same height as a standard doorway (6 feet 8 inches) that overlooked a wetlands area located out the back of a friend's home. They used windows rather than patio doors,

CALL A PRO

Setting your sights on a skylight

A skylight can add beautiful, natural overhead light to a kitchen all year 'round. (Check out the skylight photo in the color insert.) Remember that you need to have direct access to the roof of the house to install a skylight. If your kitchen is on the main level, located directly under a couple of bedrooms, you're out of luck.

Installing a skylight is not something a novice DIYer should even consider. There are framing issues to deal with, including possibly having to cut into existing structural roof components and then reframe the opening to not only house the skylight but also support the roof. But, the money spent for a professional's experience and "touch" will make the end result well worth the expense.

Keep the following ideas in mind when considering a skylight:

✔ Determining where to position a skylight is critical. If you live in a very warm climate, don't place a skylight on south- or west-facing roof, unless the skylight comes with a powered shade between panes of insulated glass. Otherwise, the intense sun and heat is too much for most people. (Don't worry, most skylights that come with shades also come with a remote control, so you can open and close the blinds without having to use a ladder or turn a crank.)

Also, a skylight placed at the edge of a room provides more light than one that only shines in the center of the kitchen because the incoming light bounces off of the wall.

✔ Rectangular skylights fit relatively easily in the joist space (cavity) between the roof rafters or trusses.

✔ The most commonly used skylight design has a relatively flush-mounted appearance against the ceiling. Even when a skylight is used in a light-shaft design, the interior framing of the unit does not extend beyond the ceiling surface.

✔ Skylights come either with an operating sash or a fixed sash. An operating sash allows for ventilation, which is a great addition in a kitchen, especially because a skylight is mounted in the roof, which means that some of the hot, moisture-laden air will naturally rise and exit out of an opened skylight window. Operating units come in either manual or electric-powered versions. The electric units also come either hard-wired (you use a wall-mounted switch to operate the sash) or with a remote control that allows for operation virtually anywhere in the room.

because there was no deck or access on that side of the house, but they wanted the full view of the outside area. It worked fabulously!

You can also purchase custom-built windows to fit your new kitchen design. For example, the use of a trapezoid window above a traditional rectangular window unit in a kitchen with a vaulted or sloped ceiling makes the entire wall look like a sloping surface, creating a smoother visual effect between the wall and the ceiling. Granted, you may have to pay more for a custom-built

Great ways to gather design options

Want to see examples of new and creative ways to use windows both in overall design as well as function? Then

✔ Visit the "Parade of Homes" when it's advertised in your area. Most major cities or regions have some sort of home showcase period, either in the spring or fall or sometimes both. Around this part of the Midwest, the Spring Home Show is the best time to see the newest trends and options being used by today's home builders. (It's also a great way to stay on top of the current decorating trends.) A walk through these homes, especially one's that are in the upper-bracket price range, usually provides fascinating, interesting or call it whatever you like ways of using windows.

✔ Keep an eye out, too, for a remodeler's home tour. Though not as prevalent as a

builder's show parade, remodeling home tours feature smaller projects that are often just what the DIY homeowner is looking to uncover. If you're not sure when these events take place in your area, contact your local Builder's Association office. Check the yellow pages under "Home Builders". You can also check with your city's inspection office.

✔ Drive through new home construction developments. Although you may not be able to or want to get out and trudge around on a construction site for safety reasons, a slow drive around the development will give you a good look at what size, styles and shapes of windows are being used. Visit the development's display home and/or office. The real estate agents are generally very cordial and willing to answer any of your questions.

window, but if it provides the look you want, it's worth the cost to complete the design.

Replacing existing windows

Too often, homeowners don't include or even consider new windows as part of a remodel, but they should. New windows are energy efficient and save money on monthly energy bills. Plus, you can choose exterior finishes that are almost, if not completely, maintenance-free. New windows are also easier to operate.

Installation of replacement windows into the same size openings is a job that many folks can and do tackle themselves. However, it's critical that the new windows be installed properly so that no moisture leaks around or on the top of the window frame. I wouldn't recommend this as your first attempt at a DIY project.

When shopping for new windows keep the following tips in mind:

- Leaky, drafty windows waste energy and money. Look for a window brand that carries stickers or information about how good their *fenestration rating* is. Fenestration rating testing of a window is done to see how much heat is lost (the *U-factor*) through the window (both the glass and the frame), as well as how much air leakage there is around the *sash* (the wood framed area that holds the glass) and the frame components. The lower the U-factor, the better thermal insulating value of the window. Most of the major window companies have comparable ratings numbers, so you should be pretty confident buying any of the major brands.

- If you want low maintenance windows in terms of painting, look for a window that is wrapped or *clad* in vinyl or aluminum, which needs no painting or staining. Non-clad, wood windows are still readily available and are primarily bought to match the style or color of the existing window; however, they do require ongoing care in terms of scraping and painting.

- Buy double or triple pane windows. Old windows (pre-1960s) used a single pane of glass. The next generation used two panes, separated by an air space, forming an insulated sash. Today's windows can use as many as three panes (called a triple-glaze) in a one sash unit.

- Opt for windows coated on the inside of the glass with various light and UV-reflective coatings to reduce energy loss and ultra-violet ray intrusion. A low-E coating is quite common and provides added energy savings. (I discuss low-E coating later in the "Protecting your interior with window film" section.)

- Follow the guidelines for what's being installed in your area. For example, if you live in the desert southwest, heat and ultra-violet ray protection is critical, so go with what the retailers have to offer in your region. Just because your cousin in Vermont ordered a certain type, that doesn't mean you need the same type if you live in New Mexico.

Sprucing up the windows you have

Even if you can't afford to include new windows in your kitchen remodel, rejuvenate your existing windows to let in more light and do away with the old, worn look. Now's the time to sand and re-stain the wood frame and *mull centers* (the wood strips separating windows) so that your old windows don't stick out like sore thumbs.

Sanding, staining, and painting

Most window interiors require a light sanding to remove old varnish and to even out the color of the wood. Kitchen windows often have black streaks and stains from mildew. You need to remove or lighten the mildew color with

Tips and tricks to installing window film

Applying window film isn't rocket science, but you must follow the manufacturer's instructions carefully and be patient! Here are a few tips that will hopefully make the installation process go smoothly:

✔ Make sure the window is clean, clean, clean, especially along the edges and in the corners. Otherwise, the film will not bond securely. Use a razor scraper to remove any paint or other stuff on the glass. Wipe the glass with a lint-free cloth when finished to avoid leaving any small bits of debris that will cause bumps in the film.

✔ Cut the film to size, but make the dimensions 1-inch wider and longer than the dimensions of the glass. Doing this allows you some give and play when positioning the film and still allows you to cut the film to an exact fit on the glass.

✔ The directions tell you to spray the window with a wetting solution. Film manufacturers sell their own solution, but you can make your own. Just mix 1 quart of water with ½ ounce of clear liquid dishwashing soap, for example Ivory or Joy.

✔ All window film has backing that needs to be removed before you apply the film to the window. The easiest way to separate the film from the backing is to put short strips of masking tape at a corner with one piece on the backing and the other on the film. Gently pull the two pieces of tape away from each other to separate the film and backing. Also, have a helper spray a light coating of the wetting solution onto the back of the film while you're separating the film and backing. Don't let the adhesive side of the film touch itself or you'll never get it apart without ripping and ruining the film.

✔ When positioning the wet film on the wet glass, try to avoid wrinkles and creases, but also make sure the film overlaps onto the window sash on all sides to provide the best protection.

✔ When you're ready to trim off the excess film along the edges, use a razor knife and leave a ¹⁄₁₆-inch gap around the edges. A good way to create this gap is to use a credit card as your guide for the knife. It's about the right thickness. After the edges are trimmed, rewet the edges and squeegee them for best adhesion. If you get bubbles, gently pull back the film to release the bubbles, rewet with the solution, and squeegee the bubbles out.

a wood-bleach solution, which you can find in the paint department of home centers and hardware stores. Just follow the directions on the container. Then, stain and varnish the wood to bring the appearance back to life.

Treating windows to new treatments

Adding a splash of color or changing the appearance of a window area can be accomplished by choosing the right window treatment. Select drapes and curtains that let natural light shine in — big and puffy treatments only block out natural light.

✔ **Shades:** Don't think of shades as the old, white rollup type that your grandmother (and maybe your mother, too) used on every window. Shades come in different colors and different shapes of shading material (when viewing their profile) and they can really spruce up a window while providing privacy and light control. You'll also find shades that are insulated to help control drafts and heat-loss around the window area. This feature is especially nice if you have a table or dining area located directly below the window.

Most paint and wallpaper stores, as well as home centers, have a wide selection of shade designs to choose from. What makes them really adaptable is that you order-to-size to fit your window. Shades can be mounted either on the inside edge of the window frame or on the face of the window trim, depending on your window's design.

✔ **Blinds:** Pull-up blinds are still popular because they provide the traditional look and feel of blinds but with colors and sizes that work for today's windows. Mini-blinds are especially popular. Their narrow slats are not intrusive looking, yet they function well at letting in and keeping out sunlight whenever you want. Blinds are available in dozens of colors, so you can match or accent your kitchen's color scheme. And blinds are also affordable. They come in sizes that fit today's most common window widths, and they're also available in custom-made sizes if you can't find a pre-cut size to fit your windows. Blinds, like shades, are available at wallpaper stores, home centers, and most window stores.

✔ **Shutters:** Want to give your kitchen the charm and feel of a country house or a cozy café? A pair of shutters on each window can help. Their moveable slats, their hinged center joints, and the fact they're wood add charm and warmth to any kitchen design. Shutters come in set widths, but you should be able to find a width or combination of widths to fit any size window.

Most interior shutters are wood, so you have the option of leaving them natural and only applying a couple of coats of varnish to seal them, staining the wood to match the kitchen's trim, or painting them to add color.

✔ **Drapes and valances:** A colorful fabric valance or a set of thin, colorful drapes around a kitchen window can add that finishing touch on a kitchen remodel that takes it from ordinary to extraordinary.

A valance will work over almost any window in a kitchen and is a beautiful way to add color and texture to a small area or to help break up an otherwise flat, dull wall surface. Drapes work well around windows that are over tables or around eating areas. However, I don't recommend hanging drapes around windows that are near the sink and countertop because both surfaces make your drapes an easy target for splashes and spills.

Protecting your interior with window film

If you're not upgrading your kitchen windows, you can still upgrade the protection capabilities of your old windows by applying window film to the interior side of the window glass. The advantages of applying window-tinting film include blocking visible light rays (the ones that heat up a room) and screening the invisible or ultra-violet rays (the ones that cause furniture, drapes, and other items to fade). Filtering out sun rays also reduces glare in the room, putting less strain on your eyes. *Note:* All types of interior window films sold in most home centers are compatible with residential windows and should not effect a window's warranty.

There are three basic types of window-tinting films: low-E; reflective, and non-reflective. The type of film you should choose depends on where you live (region), what you want the window to look like, and what you want the film to do — protection-wise. Take a look at each type of film more closely:

- **Low-E film** blocks almost as much incoming summer heat as a reflective window film. But in the winter, low-E films reradiate as much as 50 percent of the original incoming heat back into the room instead of allowing it to be lost out the window. Low-E films are expensive; however, they can be expected to last for 10 years.

- **Reflective film** comes in silver and other tinted shades, such as smoke and bronze. Their primary function is to block heat gain. Their silver or tinted appearance also offers the most in the way of daytime privacy, although some people don't like the reflective appearance. These are the least expensive of the three types, but they also offer the least amount of protection.

- **Non-reflective film** started in the automobile industry and made its way into the residential window market. This film doesn't do much to reduce heat loss or gain, but it's excellent at blocking out glare and ultra-violet light.

Hanging window film is a bit like hanging wallpaper: Just take your time, be patient, and you'll be happy with the work you've done. If you decide to install window film on your new or existing windows, read the "Tips and tricks to installing window film" sidebar in this chapter for insider advice to consider before you begin.

Chapter 17

Lighting the Way: Installing Lights and Windows

In This Chapter

▶ Figuring out what you need

▶ Installing an incandescent ceiling fixture

▶ Putting in a ceiling fan

▶ Tackling track lights

▶ Putting in some canned lights

▶ Taking on a dimmer switch

▶ Understanding under cabinet lights

▶ Letting in more natural light

*1*n Chapter 16, I explain the various types of lighting, both electrical and natural, and indicate where you might want to use each one. In this chapter, I show you how to install these illumination wonders. You may find that you can tackle this part of the project.

This chapter covers the basic steps for installing an incandescent ceiling fixture, a ceiling fan with a light, track lighting, a dimmer switch, and under cabinet lights. I also discuss installing new windows, which should probably be tackled by a professional in most situations, because you may need to make structural changes, but you'll play a big part in measuring your kitchen and deciding where the windows will be installed.

Gathering the Right Tools

Here's a list of the basic electrical tools you need to install light fixtures and switches. You may need a specialized tool or two, but I'll point those out and explain what they are and what they're used for. Remember, get all the tools together before you begin a project and you'll complete the job faster and with less frustration.

Here's a list of the tools you need to get together:

- ✔ No. 2 Phillips screwdriver
- ✔ Medium-sized slotted (straight-tip) screwdriver
- ✔ Wire cutter/stripper
- ✔ Needle-nosed pliers
- ✔ Multi-tester or voltmeter
- ✔ Power drill with a ⅜-inch drill bit (needed to install the track lighting hardware)
- ✔ Extra twist-on wire connectors (sometimes called by the trademark name Wire Nuts)

The screwdrivers and needle-nosed pliers should have insulated handles. The rubber coating breaks the circuit between you and an electrical wire that may still have power to it, called a hot wire. Breaking the circuit prevents you from receiving a shock.

Installing a Bright New Ceiling Fixture

This task is one of the easiest to perform and is perfect for folks who are uncomfortable working with electrical stuff because, in most situations, the wiring is very straightforward. Things can get a little tricky if you have a single fixture that can be operated with two or three different switches, only because you have more than the two wires to the light fixture in the electrical box. However, if you examine the existing light's connections and either sketch them out or take an instant picture, you should be able to handle those scenarios, too.

Removing the old fixture

Taking down the old fixture is fairly easy, if you use the following steps. Don't be in a big hurry to get the old one out. Pulling and tugging on existing wires and electrical boxes may only damage them, which means spending extra time and money to get things back to a useable state. Follow these steps to remove the old fixture:

1. **Turn off the power at the main electrical service panel to the fixture or box you'll be working on.**

   Verify that the power is off by turning on the light and then flipping off the circuit breaker. Older homes may still have fuses in the service panel. In that case, instead of flipping off a breaker, you need to unscrew and remove the fuse from the box.

   Never simply back the fuse out until the circuit is dead. My electrician friends all tell stories about how a fuse mysteriously tightened itself back into place and made the circuit hot. Don't ask me how it happens, because they can't explain it. But it does happen.

2. **Remove the fixture glass or globe to expose the bulbs and the screws that hold the fixture to the electrical box.**

3. **Remove the bulbs.**

   Always remove the bulbs before you unscrew the fixture from the box. Leaving the bulbs in place only increases the chance of breaking one of them, plus the bulbs add weight to the fixture.

4. **Remove the screws that secure the fixture to the electrical box.**

5. **Pull the old fixture down so that the wires are pulled out of the electrical box.**

   In most cases, you'll see two wires (one white and one black) connected to the old fixture. The white wire is neutral and the black wire is hot. You should also see a ground wire in the box, which will either be bare copper or have a green sheathing.

6. **Test each wire to make sure that the circuit you turned off is the only one going to that particular electrical box.**

   Multiple cables and wires running into an electrical box may not all be on the same circuit. To test the wires, use a multi-tester or voltmeter. Touch one of the multi-tester probes to the green ground screw in the box; insert the other probe into each of the wire connectors. If the needle on the tester moves or jumps, power's still running to one of the cables or wires. Leave the probes in place and have a helper turn off each breaker until the needle drops back to zero.

   If you don't own a multi-tester, you can still check the wires for voltage with an inexpensive tool (around $3) called a neon circuit tester. This tester has a neon bulb in the handle that glows if voltage is detected after the probes are touched to the ground screw and inside the wire connectors. If the bulb glows, then you haven't found the correct circuit or all of the hot circuits running into the box.

7. **Disconnect the wires (including the ground wire, if there is one) from the old fixture by loosening the screws, often referred to as** *screw terminals.*

Some fixtures may have stranded wire leads connected to the fixture sockets and then connected to the wires in the box with wire connectors. If this is what your old light has, simply remove the wire connectors and disconnect the wire leads from the electrical wires.

If you discover you have multiple circuits to one electrical box when you test the wire, note which breakers supply power to the box by making a rough sketch of the box and wires coming in and noting on each wire which number breaker controls its power supply. Breakers should be number 1, 2, 3, 4, and so on, starting with the upper left breaker, then the upper right breaker, then the second breaker on the left, then the second breaker on the right, and so on. Numbering the breakers and sketching the power source for each wire saves you time the next time you need to turn off a particular breaker. Keep the sketch in your home files or wherever you keep information on your home's systems.

Hanging the new fixture

Now you need to consult and follow the installation instructions included with the new fixture. Here I walk you through the basic steps that work for all ceiling fixture installations:

1. **Attach the mounting strap included with the new fixture to the electrical box.**

   Attach the fixture to the strap, rather than attaching it directly to the box. Mounting straps also come with a preinstalled grounding screw for easier attachment of the ground wire.

2. **Attach the ground wire in the box to the ground screw on the strap.**

   This way, the fixture will be grounded after you attach the fixture body to the mounting strap.

3. **Attach the fixture's white lead to the white wire from the box with a wire connector.**

4. **Do the same for the black lead and black wire.**

Most new fixtures have wire leads rather than terminal screws for the connections. Fixture leads are usually made of stranded wire whereas the wires in electrical cable are solid wire. To ensure a good connection, twist the lead's stranded wire around the cable's solid wire in a clockwise rotation. The clockwise rotation keeps the two types of wire together as you twist on the wire connector.

5. **Carefully push all of the wires up into the electrical box.**

Be sure that all of the wires go up behind the mounting strap and not over it. A wire going over the strap could be pinched or cut after the fixture housing is secured, which would result in a short in the wire. This can lead to the breaker constantly tripping or even to the fixture overheating and potentially catching fire. Also, be careful not to force things too much or you could loosen a connection.

6. **Install one bulb of the correct wattage in the fixture and have your helper turn on the breaker to check whether the connections are good.**

If the connections are good, turn off the breaker, remove the bulb and continue with the installation.

If the light doesn't work, turn off the breaker and remove the bulb. Then, check each connection with your multi-tester or neon tester. Touch one probe to the ground screw and the other to the wires inside each connector. The connection that doesn't move the needle or make the neon bulb glow is the one to redo. Turn off the power and remove the wire connector. Twist the wires together once more, twist the wire connector back on, turn on the circuit, and retest. If the light works, turn off the power and push the wires up into the box.

7. **After the wires are tucked in the box, position the fixture housing over the strap so that the mounting screw holes align with the screw holes in the mounting strap.**

8. **Install the glass or globe.**

Be sure to check the installation instructions or look for a label on the fixture indicating the maximum wattage bulb(s) to use. Using a bulb with wattage greater than the fixture rating will cause overheating and possibly a fire.

Circulating in Style: Adding a Ceiling Fan

Keeping air moving in the kitchen, even when you're not cooking, adds to the overall comfort of the room. A good way to move the air with little disruption is by using a ceiling fan. In fact, most units are so quiet when they're running that you won't even know they're there. Most kitchen ceilings are at least 8 feet high, so overhead clearance won't be a problem. If your ceiling is vaulted (sloped), you can still install a ceiling fan using extension rods and a pivoting connector or knuckle where the fan is attached at the ceiling. Be sure to follow your fan's installation instructions for a solid and wobble-free installation.

Supporting a fan

The National Electrical Code (NEC) is very specific on how a ceiling fan must be installed. You cannot hang a ceiling fan from an existing electrical box, even a metal box. Ceiling fan-rated metal boxes have been available for the last couple of years. But if your kitchen is more than four or five years old, your metal electrical boxes are probably not rated to support a ceiling fan. You have two options for supporting a fan.

✔ **Replace the existing box with a rated box.** This can be difficult, however, if you can't get access from above or if you don't want to dig into your finished ceiling.

✔ **Install a fan-support brace kit.** These kits are available at home centers and hardware stores and are fairly easy to install. The brace is positioned between two adjacent ceiling joists and screwed tightly between them. The electrical box is then attached to the brace with a metal bracket to ensure that the box is fully supported and can handle the weight of the fan and light. Figure 17-1 shows a fan-support brace and box with a ceiling fan and light kit installed.

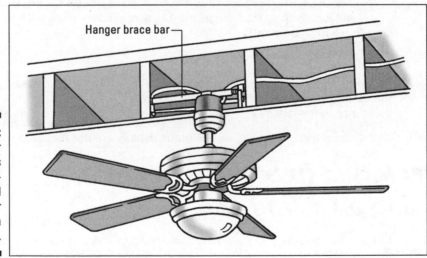

Hanger brace bar

Figure 17-1:
A hanger brace bar is a code-approved method for supporting a ceiling fan.

Wiring a fan

In many cases, when a ceiling fan and light are installed the old single electrical switch won't allow you to operate both the light and fan from the same switch. If you have this wiring setup, you may find it easier to operate the fan with a pull chain. Most, if not all, ceiling fans come with a pull chain option, although all can be operated by a switch when wired properly.

If you want to operate both the fan and light from one electrical box but you're at all uncomfortable or unsure about working with this type of setup or doing electrical work, hire a licensed electrician to install your ceiling fan.

Or you can purchase a fan that's operated by remote control, which allows you to turn both the fan and light on and off as well as set the fan at its various speeds without flipping a switch or pulling a chain. Remote-control fans usually cost about 20 to 30 percent more than regular ceiling fans, but the added expense is cheaper than hiring an electrician to do the wiring work!

Getting on Track with Track Lighting

I love track lighting because of its versatility. You can use it as ambient light and you can direct individual fixtures to be used as either accent or task lights. Plus, track lighting is easy to install.

The best way to purchase track lighting is in a kit. You'll get the track, several lamps (actual number depends on the system's wattage rating), the canopy and mounting plate, and a bag of mounting hardware. Most kits contain enough track to do a couple of straight runs or one right angle set up. Track sections typically come in 2-, 4-, 6-, and 8-foot lengths. If one of these sizes doesn't fit your needs, you can cut the track with a hacksaw or a jigsaw with a fine-toothed metal-cutting blade. Secure the track in a vise or clamp it down before you start cutting. The track bends very easily, so take your time. You should not use a track if it's been bent.

If you buy a kit, you may need to buy a few parts separately to fill your layout needs. Go over your plan with the salesperson to make sure you get all the parts in one trip. For example, the bulbs usually are not included with the lamps, so you want to choose the right type of bulb as well as the correct wattage. Use flood-type bulbs for a broader light beam and spot-type bulbs for a more focused or directly light beam. You'll also need to purchase connectors if you want to join multiple runs of track and end caps to finish the end of the last section of track.

Attaching the mounting plate

You install track lights the same way you install an incandescent ceiling fixture: using an existing ceiling electrical box and lighting circuit. Follow the steps in the "Removing the old fixture" and "Hanging the new fixture" sections earlier in this chapter, with a few additional steps that are specific to installing track lighting: 1) Be sure that the live-end connector hangs outside of the mounting plate or you won't be able to power the track. 2) The wires must be pushed into the box and the mounting plate screwed to the electrical box. 3) The mounting plate should be snug against the ceiling so that the canopy (cover) fits correctly.

1. **Use the mounting plate as your reference point and measure and mark where you want to position the track.**

   Mark the ceiling in three spots so that the track will be parallel with the wall. If your track will have a right angle, use a framing square at the mounting plate to start the lines and keep the corner at 90 degrees.

2. **Attach the first section of track to the mounting plate, following the manufacturer's instructions.**

   Get a helper to hold the opposite end of the track, especially 4-, 6-, and 8-foot-long sections, to prevent unnecessary stress on the mounting plate while you're screwing the track to the plate.

3. **Use a stud finder to determine whether the track can be secured to the stud with a 2-inch drywall screw that you need to provide.**

   If you don't find a stud directly under the track's position, use a toggle bolt (usually provided in the mounting hardware) to secure the track to the ceiling.

4. **Secure the other end of the track to the ceiling.**

5. **Attach the live-end connector to the track by twisting it in the slot until it snaps into place.**

   Again, check your instructions for specifics.

6. **Cover the open ends of any track sections with end caps.**

Creating right angles and tees is simple. Just buy and connect the right kind of connector. Slide the desired connector into the end of the track that's attached to the ceiling and then attach sections of track to the other end of the connector. You need to secure the track to the ceiling the same way you secured the first section.

Positioning the lights

The lamp units typically twist into place. Place each lamp in the approximate location that you want it and then turn the power on. Turn on the wall switch (you can use the same one that controlled the old ceiling fixture) and swivel the lights until they're in the desired position. Remember that if you can't get the light into the right position by swiveling it, just move the entire lamp up or down the track!

Can It! Installing Recessed Lighting

Recessed or canned lights are ones that are actually installed in the ceiling, unlike track lighting, which is installed on the ceiling. Recessed lights are able to perform many of the same function as track lights, provided you buy units that allow you to swivel and adjust the direction of the bulb's light stream or that have moveable baffles to focus or direct the light stream. The biggest drawback to installing canned lights is the actual installation, especially when you don't have plans to remove or tear into the ceiling. These units can retro-fit into an existing ceiling, but it's a project that's best left to an electrician.

Lots of Light Levels at Your Fingertips: Installing a Dimmer Switch

A dimmer switch gives you unlimited control over the amount of light you get from a fixture. Any standard single-pole light switch can be replaced with a dimmer switch. *Single-pole* refers to a fixture that is controlled by only one switch. If the fixture is controlled by two switches (called a three-way switch set up), you can still install a dimmer, but it must be one designated for use in a three-way switch set up. If you have a three-way dimmer, it's the only switch that will be able to dim the lights. The other switch will only turn the lights on and off.

Once again, turn off the power to the switch at the main panel. Remove the switch cover plate and unscrew the switch from the electrical box. Carefully pull the switch out so that the wires and wire connectors are pulled out of the box, too. Check each terminal with your multi-tester or neon tester. Disconnect the wires from the old switch terminals. Most connections are made with screw terminals, although some connections use a slip-in or stab slot in the back of the switch. To disconnect a stab connection, slip the tip of a slotted screw-driver into the slot that's just above where the wire goes into the switch and pull out the wire.

If the old switch had screw terminals, you'll need to straighten the ends of the wires that are coming out of the box because you use a wire connector to connect the dimmer's leads to the circuit wires. Use your needle-nosed pliers to gently straighten the curved end.

Now install the dimmer:

1. **Connect the leads to the circuit wires using wire connectors.**

   If you have a single-pole two-wire switch, connect either of the leads (they're the same color and interchangeable) to either of the two circuit wires.

   A three-way dimmer will have three leads. Two are the same color and interchangeable and can be connected to either the black or white wires in the box. The third lead is red and must be connected to the red wire in the box. The red wire is the common wire that connects the two switches.

2. **Push the wires into the box, leaving the green ground wire exposed if your system has one.**

   If your dimmer has a green ground wire lead (some do, some don't) connect it to the box if it's metal or to the ground wire in the box.

3. **Secure the switch to the box with the screws that come with the switch.**

4. **Install a cover plate and you're all set.**

Ambiance and Function: Installing Under Cabinet Lighting

Under cabinet lighting is an excellent and attractive way to illuminate countertops and other work surfaces where cabinets are mounted overhead. These lights solve the problem of the shadows created by the cabinets, plus they provide beautiful ambiance even when you're not using the countertops.

Looking at two kinds of under cabinet lighting

You have two choices in under cabinet lighting: plug-in or hard-wired.

- Plug-in units are the easiest to install. Simply attach the fixture to the underside of the upper cabinet and plug the unit into a nearby outlet. You turn the units on and off with the switch that's built into the fixture. Plug-in units are a good choice if you only have a small area to illuminate.

- A hard-wired system is more attractive because there's usually no exposed wiring and a dedicated wall switch controls the unit. However, this system is also more difficult to install, because you need to tap into a nearby power source, or pull a new circuit to the kitchen. Either way, major electrical work is involved, so you may want to consider hiring a professional to install your hard-wired system.

Installing a hard-wired system

In this section, I show the very basic steps for installing a hard-wired system. A lot of electrical work is involved, and you may find that you don't want to attempt this project. Either way, you'll at least know what to expect when you hire an electrician.

Finding the power supply

The easiest way to get power for the hard-wired under cabinet system is to tap into the power in a nearby receptacle. This involves running a new cable to a new switch box that you need to install and then pulling cable from the switch to where each fixture will be located. Figure 17-2 shows a rough layout and how the cables will need to be positioned.

Figuring out where to run the cables to the fixtures can be tricky. You want to disturb the walls and backsplash as little as possible. If the backsplash is removable, remove it and cut a channel in the wallboard just above the back of the countertop. You also need to drill holes in the wall studs so that you can pull the cable. If you can't remove the backsplash, you still need to access the studs and drill holes for the cable. This means cutting into the walls, so add time for patching and drying (see Chapter 19).

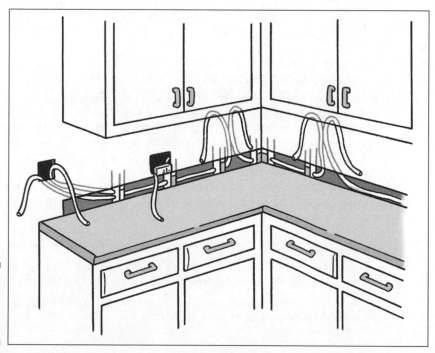

Figure 17-2:
A hard-
wired
system.

Pulling cable

Try to keep the cutting (for getting the cable out of the wall and to the fixtures) to a minimum. If possible, try to get the cable high enough that it could come out of the wall inside the cabinet rather than out of the wall directly below the cabinet. If your cable does have to come out beneath the cabinet, make the hole as tight as possible to the cabinet so that the fixture will cover it. Make sure you have about 16 to 18 inches of cable coming out of each opening so that you have enough extra cable to make connections. Strip off enough of the cable sheathing so that the individual wires are exposed about 8 inches.

You also need to cut a hole for the switch. Use a remodeler's box for this switch. These types of boxes have spring flanges, side clamps, or foldout ears that secure the box when you can't nail it to a wall stud. All three types are available at most home centers. After the box is installed, pull the cable for the switch, leaving 16 to 18 inches extra.

Installing the fixtures

Now you should start putting the lights in place. Follow the manufacturer's instructions and disassemble each fixture necessary for the installation. Pull the cable through the knockout holes in the fixture body and secure the cable with a cable clamp. Make sure that the sheathing is in the clamp and not the individual wires. Most hard-wired fixtures supply the cable clamps. If you don't have any, you can find them in any electrical department of a home center store. Next, position the fixture under the cabinet and screw it in place.

Wiring the fixtures and the switch

Connect the wires from the fixtures to the individual wires from the cable. Again, connect like colors to each other. Position the wires so that they lay flat in the base, being careful not to pinch them when you reattach the base to the main housing. Follow the manufacturer's instructions and finish assembling the fixture.

You're almost there! Now that the individual fixtures are connected, it's time to wrap things up by connecting the wires to the switch and then testing your beautiful new lights. Here's how:

1. **Begin by splicing the white wires together from both cables.**

   Remember there are two cables to the fixture: One that brings the power to the switch and the other that sends the power to the fixtures.

2. **Next, attach the black wires from each cable to the terminals on a single-pole switch.**

3. Connect the ground wire to the switch's ground screw (it will be green) and to the box if it's metal.

4. It's important to note that you've done nothing yet with the box or cable that supplies the power. Before you take the next step, turn off the power to the box that you'll be tapping into.

5. Now, splice the white wires together and the black wires together using the new cable and the existing power-supply cable. If you see a colored wire in the box, connect it to the black wires.

   Use wire connectors on all connections.

6. Restore power and test the system.

Drawing In Natural Light: Upgrading Your Windows

Don't forget you have a second lighting option — natural light. Windows work to your advantage by providing as much natural light as possible. (For more on window options, see Chapter 16.)

Measuring and sketching your plan

If new windows are in your budget (either same-size windows, bigger windows, or decorative, shaped windows), first you must measure, measure, measure. Grab a tape measure, paper, and a pencil. A 25- or 30-foot tape rule is best, because it allows you to measure most kitchen wall lengths in one shot. Plus, the longer-length tape rules have a wider blade (usually ¾-inch and sometimes 1-inch wide), which is stiffer and easier to use when the tape is fully or almost fully extended.

Start by measuring all exterior walls — from the interior side! Believe it or not, I know of a few people who took exterior wall measurements on the exterior of the house. You need to know the inside size of the walls, not the exterior height. Measure from corner to corner for the width and from floor to ceiling for the height. If your kitchen has a soffit, but sure to measure the height to the ceiling, not the bottom of the soffit.

After you measure the exterior walls, measure the existing windows. You can measure existing windows two ways to get useful dimensions:

✔ One way is to measure width and height from the outside edges of the trim molding. Although this measurement is larger than the actual size of the window, it gives a designer or a window sales consultant a good idea of the size of the existing windows.

✔ A better way to measure windows is to measure the width and height of the glass of each window panel. That's the amount of light-area that a particular window will allow. Glass size is also a good dimension to use if you're ordering replacement windows of the same size. Frame construction and size is very similar on all brands of windows, so knowing the glass size helps a salesperson provide you with a comparably sized window from any of the manufacturers that they deal with.

If you're replacing your existing windows with windows of the same size, take the measurements to the store and order your new windows. Skip ahead to the "Installing your new windows" section for advice on doing just that. If you plan to hire a pro to install your windows, either because you plan to install larger windows than those currently in the kitchen or you plan to add a window where there wasn't one before, draw a sketch of your current kitchen and window layout. This sketch will help a designer or contractor better understand your wants and needs, especially if they're not going to visit your kitchen before they install the windows.

Try to make a fairly detailed and accurate sketch of the old kitchen, including the width and height of the existing windows. It's okay to measure from the edges of the trim — this dimension only needs to be approximate. Be as accurate as possible when placing the window location on the walls. Your sketch doesn't have to be to-scale or even on graph paper, but try to indicate the window location accurately: If the window is in the middle of the wall, then draw it there, and so on. Also, be sure to note the direction each window is facing. Knowing whether you're looking at a south wall versus a north wall makes a big difference in determining the size window you have and/or may want to install.

Installing your new windows

Tearing out old windows and replacing them with identically sized replacements may seem like a fairly straightforward project — and it is. You should know, however, that it generally takes about a half a day to remove an old window and install a new one — replacing a lot of windows adds days of work to the length of the project.

There's a lot more to replacing windows than simply ripping out the old ones and slapping in new. You'll need to do finish trim work once the new windows are installed, and there's always the possibility that some of the existing framing could have rot and must be replaced before the new windows are installed.

Whether you decide to install same-size windows or change the window sizes — especially if you go larger — you must take certain structural issues into consideration. In either case, I suggest you hire a pro to install the new windows. That way, you can kick back and relax and let the contractor worry about getting the necessary permits and inspections and whether or not the new openings are structurally strong enough to support the windows — and the wall!

Adding natural light without a window— Is that possible?

Although windows are only installed on exterior walls, you can let more natural, ambient light into the kitchen by opening up a wall or part of a wall to an adjacent room. Creating a look-through, pass-through, or even a countertop/serving area allows light to spill from one room to another. Couple this type of light increase with new or additional fixtures and your kitchen can look like those kitchens you see in magazines and showrooms.

Chapter 18

Walls That Wow: Selecting Elements for Your Walls

In This Chapter

▶ Perusing the paint palette

▶ Weighing wallpaper options

▶ Adding extra touches

A fter the cabinets, the walls are the most noticeable feature of your kitchen, and they make up the largest surface area. Deciding on a color scheme that fits your taste and then adding a dash of texture can change average walls into surfaces that could be in a kitchen showroom. However, you should know about some do's and don'ts when selecting materials for use on kitchen walls and the ceiling. This chapter helps you figure out which materials to choose and which ones to stay away from.

Picking Paint for Your Kitchen

The number-one wall coating for kitchens is paint. Why? Well, first of all, almost every homeowner can paint, which saves money on labor costs. Second, paint is available in any color, letting you mix and match finishes, as well as textures. But with so many choices, how do you know which one (or ones) to choose? Hopefully, the following words of wisdom will help in your selection process.

Considering color: A rainbow of choices

Selecting the color scheme for your kitchen walls is probably the first thing you do when you're at the paint store. The use of color can make the difference between an average-looking room and one that has warmth, feeling and, yes, even a soul. Color choice can shrink or enlarge the look and feel of a room, and it can even accentuate or hide particular areas.

To understand how color affects the perceived size of a space, you need to understand a term called *color temperature*. Colors are divided into two classes or types: warm hues, such as reds, oranges, and yellows; and cool colors, such blues, greens, and violets. Warm colors tend to come out at you, whereas cool colors appear to be retreating. For example, a red wall makes a room feel smaller because the color (and the wall that it's on) appears to be coming toward you. A blue wall, on the other hand, makes the room feel larger and less constricting.

So, just how do you pick the right colors and color combination for your kitchen? Start by looking at the family of colors (the various shades and hues) around your favorite color. For example, if your favorite color is red, then start by focusing on colors that use red, orange, and yellow as the main tint tone. All paint stores have paint swatch samples on display that group similar colors together. If you're having trouble, ask the salespeople for their opinions. They work on a daily basis with homeowners like you, trying to find the right combination and color schemes to make every room attractive and inviting. Don't forget to coordinate your paint with the colors of your flooring, countertops, cabinets, and window treatments.

Don't forget about the ceiling!

An often overlooked surface is the one above your head — the ceiling. Handled properly, the ceiling can become an important part of the overall color scheme in the kitchen.

All paint stores sell a paint labeled "ceiling white," which makes many people think that all ceilings must be painted white. Ceiling paint is usually a bit thicker than regular paint to reduce dripping. However, in all my years of painting ceilings, I've found that wall paint works very well on the ceiling, too.

Color on a ceiling can alter your perception of the size and feel of the room. For example, if you want the ceiling to disappear, choose a color in the same family of colors as the walls but just slightly lighter, maybe one shade. If you want a ceiling to appear lower, use a dark color. If you want the room to seem open and airy, use a lighter color. Finally, you can increase ambient light by using a semi- or high-gloss paint on the ceiling. The hard surface will reflect light and help make the entire kitchen brighter.

Plan to work with three to six colors. Using fewer than three colors will give the room a monochromatic look. Using more than six colors will make the room look too busy. If you choose one bold color to use as an accent, use it sparingly. Overuse causes it to lose its accent quality.

Don't assume that paint is only for the walls, either. You can add color by painting the trim in a doorway or maybe by adding a small piece of painted trim at the ceiling. The ceiling can also be painted a color other than white (yes, it's true!) — find more on that in the "Don't forget about the ceiling!" sidebar in this chapter.

Paint prototypes: What's best for the kitchen?

After you select the colors for your kitchen, you need to select the right type of paint. If you don't pick the right kind of paint, the colors won't look how you expect them to, and performance (durability and washability) may be less than stellar.

Oil-based and water-based (or latex) are the two main types of paint for residential use. The main difference between the two is in the cleanup of paint tools and equipment. Oil-based paints are cleaned with solvents, such as mineral spirits or paint thinner. Water-based or latex paints clean up with soap and warm water. In addition, latex paints generally have less of an odor than oil-based paints when they're applied and as they dry.

Oil-based paint was at one time considered the best choice because of its durability. However, it contains toxic volatile organic compounds (VOCs) that are released into the air as the paint dries. Because of these VOCs (air pollutants), oil-based paints are no longer available in many parts of the country. Don't worry, however, about not having durable paints available. Today's generation of latex paints are as durable as previous generations of oil-based paints and without the VOCs and the messy solvent cleanup.

You also have choices in the finish. Most of today's paint manufacturers offer five different finishes: high-gloss, semi-gloss, satin, eggshell, and flat. All finishes are usually available in either oil- (if sold in your area) or water-based paint. Don't be surprised if you need to buy paints in more than one finish. Different areas and elements of a kitchen have different needs and may require different finishes.

- **High-gloss** paint is the most durable and is easiest to clean after it's dry, because its hard surface is very stain-resistant. On the downside, its high gloss shows flaws in the wall surface, plus the gloss fades over time. High-gloss is most often used on woodwork and trim, backsplash areas (the vertical surface at the back of the countertop around the sink), and cabinets.

✔ **Semi-gloss** paint is not quite as durable as high-gloss but is still a very popular choice in kitchens. Semi-gloss is fairly durable and easy to clean. It does show surface flaws but does not lose its gloss over time. It's also a good choice for doors, woodwork, trim, and cabinets.

✔ **Satin** finish has become very popular in the last dozen or so years. As its name implies, it has a softer-looking appearance and is not as glossy as either of the previous finishes mentioned. Even so, it's still relatively durable and easy to clean. One drawback is that its softer finish is less resistant to moisture, so it's not the best choice for high-moisture areas, such as a backsplash. Satin is still a good choice for most kitchen walls and woodwork.

✔ **Eggshell** is very similar in look and durability to satin. Its pros and cons are the same as satin, and many folks can't tell the difference between the two even when samples are placed side by side. (Quite frankly, I think the paint industry should do away with one or the other to make it easier for the average person to choose a finish.)

✔ **Flat** paint is a good choice if the wall surface has a lot of flaws that you just can't get rid of. However, you can't wash flat paint easily without damaging the paint surface. If your kitchen walls take a lot of abuse — for example, if you have little ones who love to run their hands along the walls as they walk — a flat finish should not be your first choice. Go with eggshell or satin.

So which finish should you use where? My recommendation for the kitchen is to use satin/eggshell or semi-gloss on the walls and semi- or high-gloss on the ceiling. Any of these will provide excellent protection and make cleaning dirt and grease as easy as possible. For really high-traffic areas where the walls are constantly getting bumped and rubbed, consider using flat or satin because they're more easily touched up than gloss or semi-gloss finishes.

Paint quality: Getting what you pay for

When I was managing a home center, I spent many a busy Saturday in the paint department. I used to tell customers that they were going to have to spend a certain amount of money for materials anyway, so why not spend the extra 20 to 25 percent and buy the better quality paint. The small difference in the price of the better-quality paint would make the job easier, and they'd be happier with the results, especially over time. Incidentally, I never had a single customer come back and complain that they were disappointed that they had spent the extra money for the better paint.

Expect to spend at least $20 per gallon and probably more like $25 to $40 a gallon for a good-quality, brand name paint, for example, Sherwin-Williams, Dutch Boy, and Pratt & Lambert. The type of finish you choose affects the price: The higher the gloss, the more you have to spend. Off-brand paints aren't a good choice. They may cost less, but they're not as durable and they don't cover as well. Buying cheap paint could result in your applying three or four coats to get decent coverage and an even look. Cheaper paints can also be rubbed away when you wash them, even after they dry!

Calculating your paint quantity needs

Now that you have a better overall understanding of paint, you need to figure out how much to buy. This process involves some math, but it's really quite simple. You need a tape measure, a calculator, and a pad and pencil to write down the square footage of the various surfaces. So with these tools in hand, go ahead and calculate!

A gallon of good quality, brand name paint covers approximately 300 to 325 square feet; a quart covers around 75 square feet. I know the numbers don't quite add up — four quarts times 75 square feet equals 350 square feet. But trust me on this one — use these approximate coverage numbers when calculating how much paint to buy.

1. **Measure the length of each wall in feet. (Most wall heights are 8 feet.)**

   Don't worry about subtracting for doors and windows. Err a little on the high side when calculating quantities, as coverage may vary. Don't forget to measure the backsplash areas between the wall and base cabinets, too, if they're going to be painted. You may be surprised by how much square footage these seemingly small areas add to the total.

2. **Take each wall's length and multiply it by the wall's height to calculate the square footage for each wall surface.**

   Most homes have 8-foot-high ceilings. If your house has taller ceilings, say 9 or 10 feet, then multiply by that figure.

3. **Add together the square footage for each wall and divide the number by 300 (the average coverage for one gallon of paint) to determine how many gallons of paint you'll need.**

Always round up and don't try to stretch the coverage. If, for example, you have to cover 1,000 square feet, don't try to get by with only three gallons. Buy that fourth gallon of paint and then you'll have some leftover paint to handle the inevitable touchups. Plus, all of the gallons will be tinted at the same time using the same batch of base paint. Different batches, even of the same color, can vary slightly, which makes matching more difficult. Also, if you're covering a dark color or a glossy surface, you may have to apply two coats, so plan on doubling the quantity. I deal with coverage problems in greater detail in Chapter 19.

When using multiple gallons of paint, always cross-mix or *box* the gallons to keep the colors consistent from gallon to gallon. To box paint, you need a clean, empty one-gallon container or bucket. Clean, unused paint cans are sold at paint stores and home centers. Empty about half of one gallon of paint into the empty container. Then, empty half of another gallon of the same color into the can you just emptied. Now, empty the paint from the extra container into the second half-full can. Work this rotation a couple of times and you're assured that the colors of the two gallons will be consistent. After you've used about half of the second boxed gallon of paint, box it with the third gallon of paint, and so on.

If one of your color choices is an off-white or a very light shade of another color, you may have to buy it in a gallon quantity even if you only need a quart, because tint formulas are calculated for a gallon of paint. The tint colors must be divisible by four to correctly mix only a quart, and some tinted colors use so little of one tint color that mixing a quart just isn't possible.

Finishing options for that extra-special look

Strolling through model homes is a great way to brush up on today's decorating trends. You can see the popular colors as well a variety of decorative finishes, styles, designs, textures, and techniques used in today's kitchens. Each of the following techniques is quite popular. Some involve building up layers of color and use various painting tools and equipment for applying each layer. Here's a brief overview of several of these techniques. Check with the paint sales professional for additional assistance.

Sponge painting

This technique is great for hiding a not-so-perfect wall surface. You can sponge paint in two ways: sponging paint on and sponging paint off.

To sponge on paint, you first apply a base color with a brush or roller. The base coat is often a lighter color. After the base coat is dry, take a natural sponge (light brown in color and not one of those colored kitchen sink sponges), dip it into the accent color, and then simply dab the paint onto the wall. Different amounts of pressure affect the look of the paint, so you may want to practice on a scrap piece of drywall or cardboard. Remember to apply the base coat to the practice piece so you get the same look that you want on your walls.

Sponging off paint is a little trickier, but it does create a more subtle effect. You apply the accent color over the dried base coat and then, while the accent color is still wet, lift the color off using a natural sponge. You can also use two different accent colors to create a more dramatic effect with either technique.

Rag painting

This technique is similar to sponge painting except that you use a soft, lint-free rag to add the accent color paint. An old T-shirt works well. The main difference between sponge and rag painting is that rag painting has a more textured appearance on the surface. Both techniques, however, are good choices for hiding imperfections and flaws on the wall surface.

Feather dusting

And you thought feather dusters were only for dusting! HA! My wife used this easy technique in the bathrooms, and the unique look is still getting compliments six years later. You start with a base coat, and then you use feather dusters to apply the top accent colors. Just dip the tips of the dusters into the paint, and then use the feather dusters as you would a paintbrush. The randomness of the strokes along with the varying degree of pressure with each stroke gives each wall a unique look.

If you do try this technique, plan to apply two accent colors. We found that using only one accent color left the surface looking flat and uninteresting. Applying the second accent color made the wall come alive and added a textured appearance.

Painting with stencils

Adding a stencil pattern to the wall is a great way to add a personal touch. You can buy stencil patterns, but many people enjoy coming up with their own unique pattern or design. Stencils can be applied near the ceiling, much like a wallpaper border. Or you can paint a stencil or border about a third of the way up the wall to help break the wall into two sections — use complementary colors above and below the break.

If you do want to try stenciling or painting a border, use latex paint or artist's acrylic paints for the best result. This, too, is a good technique to practice before you start on the walls in your kitchen.

Working with Wallpaper

Just as paint colors can accent a kitchen, so can wallpaper. And even though wallpaper isn't a hard, stain-resistant surface like paint, it is a viable design option in the kitchen. One important factor to keep in mind is that wallpaper prices range widely. The top-quality paper (which is what you'll want in a kitchen for durability) is very expensive — so much so that you may want to consider papering only one main wall and painting the rest.

Picking the right paper

The selection and options in wallpaper are greater today than ever before. Most types aren't actually made of paper anymore, either. Many styles come in vinyl (with a fabric back) or vinyl-coated paper, both of which are washable with a sponge, and some are even scrubbable. The package will say whether or not a wallpaper is scrubbable.

Vinyl and vinyl-coated wallpapers are pretty easy to hang and actually fairly forgiving during the hanging process. Plus, they're both nearly always strippable if the wall is prepped properly. Find out more about wall prep in Chapter 19. Vinyl and vinyl-coated wallpapers are both mildew resistant, which makes them good choices for kitchen walls.

Paper-faced, natural fiber, embossed, and flocked wallpaper are not good choices for the kitchen. They all look great when first applied; however, they absorb dirt, grease, and odors, and you won't be able to clean them because of the material's natural absorption properties. At best, you'll only be able to vacuum or dust them, which won't remove the grease and odors.

Many types of wallpaper come *prepasted* (the paste is already applied; all you need to do is wet or activate the paste). Better-quality prepasted wallpaper has the paste evenly applied at the factory and very rarely has bare spots. Even so, keep a small container (a quart should be plenty) of premixed wallpaper paste on hand to handle bubbles and other small trouble areas. See Chapter 19 for more information.

Don't ever start a wallpapering job without paste activator. You spread the activator on the prepasted side of the wallpaper instead of using water, let it rest for as long as the directions indicate, and then you're ready to hang the paper. Wallpaper activator is easy to use and a lot less messy than wetting the paste with water. Cleanup's easy, too — all you need is warm water and a little bit of liquid dish soap.

Borders: Small touches with big results

A wallpaper border is an easy way to add color and accent to any wall. Borders can divide a wall horizontally or can be used near the ceiling to add color and texture to a plain wall surface. They're also used to frame doorways and windows. Pattern and color choices in borders are wide ranging, so you should be able to find an in-stock border that you'll like.

Border paper usually comes *prepasted* (the paste is already applied; all you need to do is wet or activate the paste) and in various widths. You hang it the same way you hang wallpaper. Borders can be hung over a wallpapered or painted surface. Borders are sold by the roll, usually about 15 linear feet per roll. Calculating

how many rolls to buy is easy. Add the lengths of all the walls that you want to add a border to and then divide that figure by the roll's linear footage.

If you're hanging the border at the ceiling, consider positioning the top edge of the border a few inches down from where the wall and ceiling meet. This joint is often not straight, which makes hanging the border and making it look good almost impossible. By moving the top edge of the border down anywhere from one to several inches (the choice is up to you), you can make sure that the border's top edge is level and straight.

Knowing where wallpaper won't work

Don't use wallpaper on areas that you know will get wet regularly. For example, wallpapering the backsplash is an invitation to an unattractive look, as well as periodic repairs. Even vinyl wallpaper can't handle getting wet all the time. You can wallpaper around the stove, but make sure you use a vinyl paper so that grease and other cooking splashes are easier to clean.

Breaking up a flat surface

Large wall surfaces that are all the same color can be boring. Breaking the wall into two sections allows you to mix colors and even different decorating elements on the same wall surface. A good way to divide the wall is to install chair rail molding. It's called chair rail because it used to be installed at the height where a chair back would hit the wall. Now people install it at whatever height they think looks best, but it's still usually between 32 and 40 inches from the floor. You want it between these dimensions so that the two wall sections are not equal. Unequal sections provide a more interesting visual appearance. The two sections allow you to, for example, wallpaper one section and paint the other with an accent color.

Wallpaper math: Deciding how much to buy

Most better wallpaper stores carry a large number of patterns in stock. This means you'll probably be able to find a pattern and color scheme that fits your taste without having to wait for a special order. Figuring out how much wallpaper you need starts the same way as figuring out how much paint to buy. Measure the width of each wall to be wallpapered and then multiply that figure by the ceiling height. Don't forget to measure the width and height of smaller areas, too. Again, don't worry about allowing for door and window openings.

You need to add an extra 10 percent or so to allow for waste, trimming, and pattern match. Wallpaper rolls (*bolts*) vary in width; however, most cover approximately 56 square feet, regardless of their width.

If you do choose an in-stock wallpaper, make sure that all of the rolls you purchase are from the same dye-lot and have the same lot-number. Choosing paper with the same lot-number ensures that the rolls were printed with the same dye-lot and that the color is consistent for the entire lot. If you can't find enough of the same lot-number in stock, have the retailer order your entire roll quantity for you. You cannot order one or two rolls specifying a dye-lot number because after that dye-lot was finished the next dye-lots (even in the same pattern) will probably be slightly different.

Adding Final Touches

Walk through most model homes and you'll see artwork and personal photos in colored or designer-style picture frames and other items such as decorative plates on the walls adding a touch of color and personal style to the kitchen. These items used to be reserved only for the living room or dining room, but today's kitchens see a lot of traffic and a lot of your guests spend time in there, so don't be afraid to decorate — bring a little class into your kitchen!

Chapter 19

Preparation for Wall Transformation

In This Chapter

▶ Preparation is crucial

▶ Dealing with drywall repairs

▶ Preparing for painting

▶ Prepping for wallpapering

▶ Doing something with a doorway

*B*efore you can transform your walls into what you want them to be, you have to roll up your sleeves and get the room ready: You need to do some preparation and repairs. I don't know of any kitchen remodel where the walls didn't need at least *some* minor touchups and repairs before they were ready for the finishing touches.

Most of the tasks covered in this chapter, such as repairing drywall and prepping walls for painting or wallpapering, are perfect for the DIYer, which means you save money! Even if you've never fixed a bad tape joint on drywall or stripped wallpaper, this chapter shows you how to get it done. The only thing you need to invest is some of your time, and when you're done, you can beam with pride and proclaim to all those around you, "I did it myself!"

The Importance of Preparation

No matter what the job, preparation is a key component of successful projects, and getting your kitchen walls ready for their pending transformation is no exception. You want to fill in any nicks or gouges with drywall compound and make sure that they're sanded smooth. If you don't, each nick, gouge, or rough spot will be accentuated when you paint or wallpaper the surfaces. You also need to make sure the wall surfaces are clean before you paint. Dirty, greasy walls prevent paint from adhering properly. You should apply sizing to the walls before hanging wallpaper. Sizing is a chemical solution that helps the wallpaper and paste bond to the wall surface yet leaves the wallpaper relatively easy to remove when you decide it's time for a change.

Repairing Drywall

If your house is like mine, then your drywall exhibits small nicks, scratches, and maybe even a gouge or two. One of your walls may even display that nasty doorknob hole caused by an overzealous teenager in a hurry to open a door. But no matter whether the damage is tiny or terrible, you can make your wall look good again by following the tips and instructions in this section.

Fixing holes

When fixing small holes in drywall, you're basically bridging a gap with drywall tape and joint compound. When fixing larger holes, however, you need to replace the missing drywall with a new piece that fits inside the hole.

Small holes

If the hole is less than 4 inches in diameter, you can just patch it with tape and joint compound. First, gather the following materials:

- A mesh peel-and-stick patch (usually sold in a pack of three or four)
- A utility knife with a new blade
- A 6-inch taping (broad) knife
- 200-grit sandpaper
- Premixed drywall joint compound

When you've gathered what you need, follow these directions:

1. **Use a sharp utility knife to trim off any loose pieces of drywall or to trim off any loose ends of the drywall's *facing paper* (the paper surface that faces the room).**

2. **Peel off the backing paper on the patch to expose the adhesive. Center the patch over the hole and use your hand or a 6-inch taping knife to press the patch into place (see Figure 19-1).**

3. **Apply a thin layer of joint compound over the entire patch. Allow the compound to dry according to the manufacturer's instructions.**

   Make sure the edges are smooth and free of rough spots to reduce the amount of sanding.

4. **Apply a second thin layer of joint compound. Allow it to dry thoroughly.**

5. **After the second coat is dry, lightly sand the patch with 200-grit sandpaper, blending the edges into the surface of the wall.**

6. **Prime and paint the patch when you paint the rest of the room.**

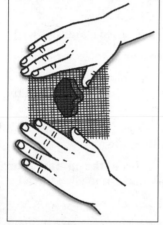

Figure 19-1:
Apply a patch over the small hole.

Large holes

Large holes require a replacement piece of drywall. Basically, when you fix a large hole, you use the replacement piece of drywall as a template to cut away the damaged area, and then you fit the replacement piece into the hole you've made. To make this repair, you need the following materials:

✔ A scrap piece of drywall

   Use ½-inch thick drywall for walls and ⅝-inch thick drywall for ceiling patches

✔ A utility knife with a new blade (buy some extras, too!)

✔ A metal straight edge for guiding the knife when cutting the patch

✔ Drywall clips

✔ A screwdriver for installing the clips

- A 6-inch taping knife
- Drywall joint tape (either paper or self-stick)
- A drywall saw
- Fine-grit sandpaper
- Premixed joint compound

Follow these steps, illustrated in Figure 19-2, to repair a large hole:

1. **Use a piece of scrap drywall and cut a patch that will completely cover the hole in the wall.**

   Make the patch a square or rectangle, even if the hole is round or oblong. Straight tapelines are easier to deal with.

2. **Place the patch over the hole and then trace around it with a pencil.**

3. **Cut out the damaged area of the drywall.**

   If the lines aren't too long (say, less than 6 inches), use a straight edge as a guide and cut out the damaged area with a utility knife. If the damaged area is fairly large, cut along the lines with a drywall saw.

4. **Trim any protruding facing paper or drywall chunks from around the edge of the patch area, using a utility knife.**

5. **Install the drywall clips on all four sides of the cutout area. Secure the clips to the drywall with the screws that come with the clips.**

   Note: Clips should be no more than 12 inches apart.

6. **Insert the drywall patch into the hole. Drive screws through the patch into each of the repair clips.**

7. **Snap off the temporary tabs on each clip.**

8. **Apply a layer of joint compound along each seam.**

9. **While the compound is still wet, lay a strip of drywall tape over the compound and run the 6-inch knife over the tape to set it into the mud.**

10. **Apply a second layer of mud over the tape. (You don't need to wait for the first coat of mud to dry.)**

    Make the second coat as smooth as possible. Let the compound dry completely.

11. **Use fine-grit sandpaper to smooth and blend the patch into the surrounding wall surface.**

12. **Prime and paint as usual.**

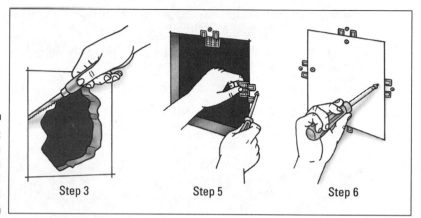

Figure 19-2:
Fix large
holes as
easy as
A, B, C.

Step 3   Step 5   Step 6

Nail pops

As houses shift and settle, the drywall often pulls away from the wall studs in spots. When this happens, you get a *nail pop* where the facing paper of the drywall is torn and the drywall actually pops over the nail head. Fixing nail pops isn't difficult; just gather the listed materials and follow the instructions.

To fix nail pops, you need the following materials:

✔ A hammer

✔ A nail set

✔ Some 1⅝- or 2-inch drywall screws

✔ A drill/driver (with Philips-tip bit)

✔ A 6-inch taping knife

✔ Fine-grit sandpaper

✔ Premixed joint compound

Now, follow these simple instructions illustrated in Figure 19-3:

1. **Drive drywall screws into the drywall 2 inches above and below the nail pop.**

   The screws will pull the drywall tight against the wall studs. Drive the screws just deep enough so that the head of the screw slightly dimples the drywall facing paper.

2. **Use a hammer and nail set to drive the old nail completely through the drywall and tight against the stud.**

3. Use a 6-inch taping knife and apply a coat of joint compound over the heads of both the new and the old fasteners.

4. When the mud is dry, sand the spots smooth with 200-grit sandpaper. Feather the edges to blend into the wall surface.

5. Apply a thin second coat and then sand it smooth.

6. Prime and paint to finish the repair.

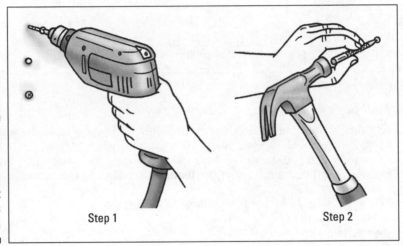

Figure 19-3: A nail-pop-free household is just minutes away.

Step 1   Step 2

Dealing with cracks

There are two types of cracks found in drywall: hairline and structural. *Hairline cracks* are caused by poor workmanship, usually bad taping techniques. *Structural cracks* are caused by the house shifting and settling. You'll usually see these cracks become larger and smaller as the weather (humidity) changes. The drier the air, the larger the cracks. So you see these cracks clearly in the winter, but they seem to get smaller during the humid summer months.

Cracks in the corner

A crack at a joint in a corner means that the joint compound was applied too thick. These cracks, however, are in the top layer of mud and don't go all the way down and through the drywall tape. To get rid of this type of crack, grab some 200-grit sandpaper and a 6-inch taping knife and follow these instructions:

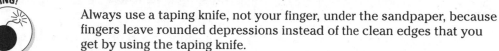

1. **Fold a piece of 200-grit sandpaper over the end of a 6-inch taping knife and carefully sand away the excess material.**

   Be careful not to gouge or nick the joint with corner of the blade.

   Always use a taping knife, not your finger, under the sandpaper, because fingers leave rounded depressions instead of the clean edges that you get by using the taping knife.

   Sand only enough to remove the crack, and don't sand into or through the drywall tape.

2. **After you've finished sanding, use a small paint brush to touch up the area.**

   Or prime and paint when you finish the rest of the wall.

Deep cracks or cracks in the wall

If the crack is deep or in the flat wall surface, you need to do a bit more. First gather these materials:

- A 6-inch taping knife
- A 10- or 12-inch taping knife (needed to make smooth or "feathered" edges)
- Premixed drywall compound
- 200-grit sandpaper
- Drywall joint tape

Now, follow these steps, illustrated in Figure 19-4, to make the repair:

1. **Clean out the interior of the crack to remove any loose material using the corner of a 6-inch taping knife.**

2. **Apply a thin coat of mud over the crack using the 6-inch knife.**

   Use enough to fill the crack but not so much that it leaves a ridge or mound.

3. **Embed the drywall tape into the mud with the taping knife.**

   Make sure the tape isn't wrinkled. If you see wrinkles, pull the tape out of the mud and reset it. If the wrinkles won't come out, remove that piece of tape and use a new one.

4. **Apply a thin coat of mud over the tape using the 10- or 12-inch taping knife to feather out the mud and reduce sanding.**

   Let the mud dry overnight or longer.

You'll know the drywall mud is dry when it changes color. It goes on gray and turns very light or white when completely dry. It should also feel dry to the touch. If the wall feels even the least bit damp, has darker spots, or you can leave a fingerprint in the mud, leave it alone. It's not dry. Allow another 12 to 24 hours of drying.

5. **After the first coats are dry, apply another coat of mud using the wider-blade taping knife.**

6. **Allow this coat to dry completely.**

It shouldn't take as long as the first two coats because this is a single thinner coat.

7. **Apply a final coat and allow it to dry.**

8. **Sand the taped areas smooth.**

9. **Prime and paint.**

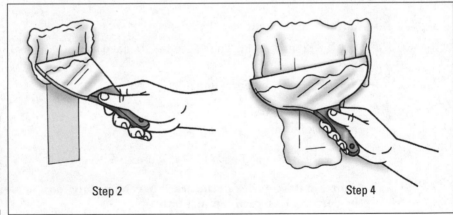

Figure 19-4: Take a crack at repairing cracks.

Step 2

Step 4

Repairing bad tape joints

Ugly, wrinkled, or damaged tape joints ruin the look of a wall and stick out like a sore thumb. The best way to handle them is to remove the old mud and tape and remud and retape the joints. The steps for retaping are the same as for repairing a crack, except that you need to remove the old tape and mud.

To remove the old stuff, follow these instructions:

1. **Slip the corner of a 6-inch taping knife under and through the taped joint to break the dried mud and old tape away from the drywall.**

2. **Slowly slide the knife up behind the old tape, pulling the tape and mud as you go.**

   Don't go too fast or you could damage the wall area around the joint by pulling the drywall's facing paper off.

To repair the joint, follow the steps listed previously in the "Deep cracks or cracks in the wall" section.

Fixin' to Paint

The key to a good-looking paint job is preparation, preparation, preparation. If you cut corners here or try to rush through the cleaning and prep, you'll pay for it later. A poorly prepped surface will allow the paint to show every little flaw. And worse yet, the paint may not stick and you'll find yourself repainting in very short order.

A wall that's ready for paint is smooth, non-shiny, and clean. If you notice any flaws or problems in your drywall or have old wallpaper bits stuck here and there, you need to take care of these things before you do anything else. Refer to the "Repairing Drywall" and "Removing wallpaper" sections in this chapter for details. After those chores are done, you're ready to prep your walls for paint. The following sections tell you how.

For paint preparation you need:

- A bucket, sponge, and rags
- A small box of *tri-sodium phosphate* (TSP) cleaner or other wall washing cleaner
- Fine-grit sandpaper
- A paint pan and roller
- Brushes:
  - A 1-inch tapered sand brush
  - A 2-inch tapered sash brush
  - A 2½-inch straight sash brush
- Drop cloths
- 1½- or 2-inch-wide blue painter's tape
- A 6-foot stepladder

Smoothing the rough spots

Fix any damage or smooth out rough spots on the walls and ceilings before scrubbing down the walls. A smooth wall means you can run the palm of your hand over the entire surface and not feel any high, low, or rough spots. If you clean the walls and then go back to make repairs, you will have to clean the walls again. Making the type of repairs we just described will cause some light dust, so you might as well wash that away when you're getting rid of the other dirt.

Dulling shiny surfaces

Paint does not adhere well to glossy or shiny surfaces. Deglossers, available at most home centers and paint stores, knock down the gloss. They contain strong solvents that cut through the shiny surface but stop working after a short period of time and only etch the surface of the paint. Typically, you only need to wipe on the solvent, let it work, and then wipe it and the etched paint off. However, check the container for specific instructions. The solvent is strong, too, so wear rubber gloves and provide adequate ventilation — preferably by opening the windows.

Cleaning the surface

Getting the walls and ceilings of a kitchen clean for painting is crucial and takes longer than in most other rooms of the house. Why? Years of dirt, grease, food splatters, and other crud that you probably never noticed collect on the walls, especially near the stove and sink and around the old range hood.

The best way to clean the surfaces is to wash them with a heavy-duty detergent, such as a solution of *tri-sodium phosphate* (TSP).

Some areas of the country have banned the use of TSP or any cleaners containing phosphate because of its potential for polluting water. If you live in such an area, just use a heavy-duty kitchen cleaner, such as Ajax or Spic-and-Span. You may need to wash the walls twice using either of the cleaners, but they will eventually get the walls clean and ready for painting.

Check out the following cleaning tips to get the best results:

- Wash the walls from the bottom to the top to avoid the cleaner running down the wall causing streaks.

✔ Work in small areas, maybe no more than 10 square feet at a time, to keep the solution from drying on the wall.

✔ Use two buckets — one with the cleaning solution and the other with clean water. Don't use the same sponge for both, either.

✔ After you've rinsed the area, dry it with a towel.

✔ Make sure that there are no streaks of dirt or grease anywhere on the wall. A clean wall not only looks clean, but feels clean as well.

Getting Ready for Wallpaper

Wallpaper was — and still is — a popular way to add color, texture, and life to the walls of a kitchen. Whether you cover an entire wall or simply add a border along the ceiling, wallpaper livens up the room. Unfortunately, the wallpaper that was put up, say, in the 1980s probably isn't what you want today. Getting rid of the old paper can be relatively easy — or it can be a real pain in the butt — depending on what prep work was done to the walls before the paper was hung. The following sections show you how to get rid of even the toughest wallpaper and then prepare the walls for new wallpaper.

Removing wallpaper

Fact: Removing wallpaper isn't fun. Fact: Removing wallpaper is something that almost any do-it-yourselfer can handle. Fact: Doing-it-yourself saves you money!

If you're lucky, your walls will have only one layer of old wallpaper. If not, be ready for a job that requires patience and plenty of time to be done right. Ideally, we'd all love to be able to grab a corner of the wallpaper and simply pull it off of the wall. Unfortunately, what usually happens is that the top layer of the wallpaper peels off, leaving the glued-on backing paper stuck to the wall surface.

So, instead of trying the old grab-and-pull method, follow the steps for getting all of the wallpaper off of the wall.

You'll need these items to remove your wallpaper:

✔ Drop cloths

✔ 1½- or 2-inch-wide painter's tape

✔ A wallpaper perforating or scoring tool

✔ Wallpaper remover solution

✔ A 1- or 2-gallon pump sprayer or a rented wallpaper steamer unit

✔ Rubber gloves

✔ A 4-inch-wide putty knife (your 6-inch-wide taping knife can also work)

✔ A sponge and bucket (and plenty of clean water)

Soak and scrape method

If you have a single layer of wallpaper and it's not a foil-faced or vinyl wallpaper, this method (illustrated in Figure 19-5) should work just fine. Here's what to do:

1. **Spread drop cloths to protect the base molding and the floor.**

   Use blue painter's tape to secure the drop cloths along the top of the molding.

2. **Score the wallpaper with a perforating wallpaper tool.**

   These tools have tiny teeth on circular blades that cut through only the wallpaper. They don't penetrate deep enough to score the drywall's facing paper. Run the tool around the entire wall surface. You should be able to see the tiny cuts or teeth-marks in the wallpaper surface.

3. **Mix a wallpaper-removing solution in a 1- or 2-gallon pump sprayer.**

   If you don't own a pump sprayer, mix the solution in a bucket and then apply it with a paint roller.

4. **Apply the solution to the entire wallpapered surface.**

   Be sure to saturate the entire surface or you'll be left with dry spots where the paper may not come off.

5. **Use a broad-knife (a 6-inch blade works well) to gently work the wallpaper off of the wall.**

   Start with a seam, if possible. Otherwise, pick a spot that is bubbled or already loose. After you get started, the rest will come off.

   If the paper doesn't come loose easily, resoak the area and let the remover solution work for a few minutes. (Check the package for the recommended soaking time.) Then, try removing that section again.

6. **Clean off the excess glue while it's still wet.**

   If the old glue dries on the wall, you'll have a tough time removing it. Use warm, clean water and a sponge to remove the old glue. Just be careful not to soak the drywall paper.

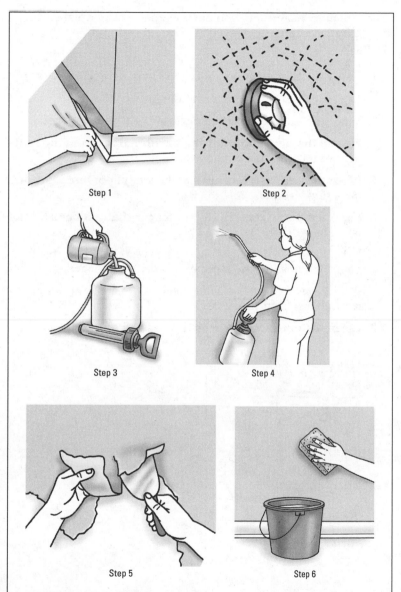

Step 1

Step 2

Step 3

Step 4

Step 5

Step 6

Figure 19-5:
The soak
and scrape
method of
wallpaper
removal.

Steam and strip method

For really tough wallpaper (such as vinyl) or multiple layers, applying
steam to the wallpaper is a surefire way to remove it as quickly as possible.
Wallpaper steamers can be rented for around $20 for half a day, or you can
buy one for around $50. The $50 units do a decent job; however, the rental

units are more heavy-duty and have a larger steamer plate, which means you can cover larger areas in less time. Here's how to turn up the heat on tough wallpaper:

1. **Cover the base molding and floors with drop cloths.**

   Tape the drop cloths to the molding.

2. **Score the wallpaper with a perforating wallpaper tool.**

3. **Fire up the steamer (following the directions from the rental store personnel) until it's hot enough to produce steam.**

4. **Place the steamer plate against the wallpaper and allow it to work for a few seconds.**

5. **Use a scraper to remove the wallpaper that has been steamed (see Figure 19-6).**

   If the steamer's doing its job, the scraper should be able to remove the paper. If not, allow the steamer to work a bit longer.

   Wear heavy work gloves when using a steamer. The water that drips is hot and can burn you.

6. **Clean off any excess glue on the wall while it's still wet.**

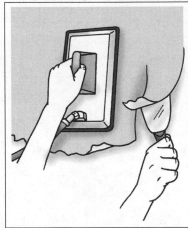

Figure 19-6:
Remove wallpaper with a steamer.

Prepping the surface for new wallpaper

The key to a good wallpapering job is the condition of the wall and how it was prepped before the new wallpaper goes on. Here are some things to keep in mind:

- ✔ **Before you do anything else, fix any damage to the wall surface.** Wallpaper accentuates even the smallest flaws and defects in the wall surface. See the "Repairing Drywall" section earlier in this chapter.

- ✔ **If you're wallpapering over new drywall, be sure to apply a coat of drywall primer.** If you don't prime the surface and then apply wallpaper, you'll never be able to remove the wallpaper without damaging the drywall's surface.

- ✔ **If you're going over existing or previously wallpapered drywall, simply apply sizing to the walls before hanging the wallpaper.** Sizing helps the wallpaper adhere to the wall surface and makes removing the wallpaper easier.

Adding trim can really make a difference!

Want to make a plain room look classier? Add trim along the ceiling or soffits or at doorways. Most kitchens have base trim along the floor and around doorways, but ceiling lines are another great place for trim. *Crown molding* is a popular choice; however, it's tricky to install. A simple *cove molding* will also dress up this area and is quite easy to put up. Cove moldings come in various dimensions/widths, so you can choose the size that works best in your kitchen.

Just remember to match the wood of your trim to your new cabinet wood.

An open doorway without a door is another place that often looks bare bones plain. Jazz up that opening as well by installing wood protective trim strips. They're about 3 feet long and are installed in the middle of the doorway corners, adding just enough color and texture to dress up an otherwise uninteresting doorway. They work like the plastic protective strips but look good!

Chapter 20

Floors: Stepping Out with Style

- -

In This Chapter

▶ Understanding what you want in a floor

▶ Looking over different flooring options

▶ Deciding whether to leave the old floor

- -

*T*he kitchen floor is probably the busiest floor in your house. The seemingly endless heavy-traffic flow puts the surface through a lot of wear-and-tear and abuse. Plus, the floor has to tolerate spills, dropped pots and pans, and even the occasional overflowing sink or dishwasher. Throw in the accumulation of dirt and grit from everyday foot traffic and you have to wonder how a kitchen floor lasts at all.

Choosing flooring that you like and that will also give you the best performance isn't an easy task. This chapter describes the various choices in flooring surfaces and explains the pros and cons of each one so that you can pick the flooring material that best suits your needs.

Keeping Your Needs in Mind

No matter what type of flooring you choose, you probably expect it to be beautiful and to last forever. Oh, and inexpensive, too. Now that I've stopped laughing, I'd like to continue.

You need to ask yourself these three questions when considering a specific type of flooring:

- ✔ Does it fit your kitchen's overall design?
- ✔ Is it durable enough?
- ✔ Does your choice fit within your budget?

Be honest with your answers, or you may be disappointed. The wrong flooring can be an expensive mistake if you have to replace it within a few years. Now, with these three questions firmly in mind, explore the pros and cons of the various types of flooring.

Perusing the Possibilities

Your choice in the types of flooring most widely used in kitchens usually comes down to one of three large categories: resilient, tile, and wood. Each has advantages and disadvantages. But, ultimately, your decision comes down to what you like in terms of style and designs, with the wear-factor or durability also playing a part in your decision. Take a look at each type of flooring so you can make the best choice to fit your kitchen floor needs.

Staying resilient: Sheet flooring versus vinyl squares

Sheet flooring and vinyl are the two most popular types of flooring in the category called *resilient flooring,* which is any thin, flexible flooring that's glued to the subfloor. Either sheet flooring or vinyl is a smart choice if you have young children in the house. Both are relatively flexible, water- and stain-resistant, and easy to clean and maintain. Both surfaces, but especially sheet flooring, are soft enough that a dropped glass stands a good chance of surviving the fall. The cost difference between vinyl squares and sheet flooring is not that large. Sheet flooring costs about 10 percent more than vinyl squares.

Sheet flooring

Sheet or rolled vinyl, made of varying grades of vinyl, is found in tens of thousands of kitchens around the country. The grade is based on the amount of vinyl used. Solid vinyl flooring uses vinyl pieces that are embedded into a vinyl base, and composite vinyl flooring fuses pieces of vinyl into non-vinyl fillers. Color and design choices are wide enough with either type that you should be able to find a style or two that you like.

Solid vinyl is the most durable, but also the most expensive. If you're going with sheet flooring, spend the extra money for better-quality vinyl. You can figure out which ones are better than others pretty easily: Check out the warranty. Inexpensive, low-end sheet flooring is only guaranteed for about five years. High-quality vinyl flooring usually has a ten-year guarantee. Sheet vinyl almost always requires using ¼-inch-thick underlayment over the subfloor before laying the vinyl, so you also need to add in the cost of the underlayment (usually around $8 to $10 for a 4-x-8-foot sheet).

All sheet flooring has a protective top layer called the wear layer. One type of wear layer is a clear, no-wax urethane surface. The other type is another layer of vinyl. The urethane wear layer stays glossier longer; however, it's much more slippery when it gets wet than vinyl-surface flooring. The vinyl-surface flooring is also more stain- and scuff-resistant.

Sheet flooring has an attached, cushioned back and is available in various thicknesses. A general guideline is: The thicker the flooring, the better the quality. The cushioned back helps in the kitchen where breakables, such as plates, cups, and glasses, are frequently dropped. On the downside, however, the softness of the cushioned backing means the flooring can be dented. And dents are almost impossible to remove. One other negative is that you secure the sheet flooring with adhesive that you need to spread. It can be messy, plus the smell of the adhesive can be strong and even overpowering to persons that are sensitive to this type of stuff. Make sure you do the installation when you can provide adequate ventilation.

Installation of sheet flooring is more involved than vinyl squares, and sheet flooring is not very forgiving if you make a mistake. Make a wrong cut in sheet flooring and you have to fix it (if you can) — or replace the entire sheet! If you miscut a vinyl square, the only thing you've ruined is that one tile. Because the installation can be tricky, especially if you have a lot of intricate cuts or angles, most folks have sheet flooring installed professionally.

Vinyl squares

Sure, they may remind you of your grandmother's kitchen, but vinyl squares are still a popular choice for kitchen floors. They're easier to install than sheet flooring, and if you screw up cutting, you're only out one tile.

Vinyl squares usually come with a self-adhesive backing; to lay the floor, merely peel and stick. After you stick a tile to the floor, you can't reposition it. And unfortunately, the seams between the tiles collect dirt and also allow moisture to get underneath the tile, which will eventually loosen the tiles from the subfloor. On the other hand, you won't have to mess around spreading adhesive on the subfloor, which you must do to secure sheet flooring.

A big plus with vinyl squares is in design options: Because you're using individual tiles, you can splash in a different color throughout the tile field for a neat-looking color accent. Accent tiles are also a great way to tie wall and floor colors together.

Tiles can be installed with seams that run parallel to the walls or they can be turned 45 degrees to give your floor angled seams. Another plus with vinyl squares is that you can lay out a few rows of tiles without having to secure them to the subfloor. The process is called *dry fitting* and allows you to see whether you like the look of the layout or pattern.

Choosing tile — Ceramic versus stone

Ceramic and stone tiles are used in many of today's upscale kitchens. They offer many design options in tile size, color, shape, texture, and pattern — all elements that factor into selecting a floor tile. You can pick tile that will give you a look ranging from traditional to modern. But ceramic and stone tiles differ in some ways that you should know about if you're considering a tile floor.

Ceramic

This category has several types of tiles, each with unique properties. Most are available in different sizes. Take a closer look at the various types of ceramic tile:

- **Glazed** tiles are machine-made clay tiles. They offer a variety of surfaces including uneven texture (to look like stone), a rough texture (for extra traction), a matte finish, or a protective glaze. Glazed clay tiles are either single- or double-fired: Single-fired tiles are stronger and recommended for use on floors; double-fired tiles are better suited for use on walls. Both methods impart tiles with rich color and a hard surface. Clay tiles range from low to high durability depending on how the glaze was applied; they have medium resistance to water (the glazed surface is water-resistant, but the unglazed edges are fairly porous); they're low maintenance (clean them with a damp sponge or cloth); and their cost can range from low to high. Tiles are priced from under $1 per tile to $5 or more per tile.

- **Porcelain** tiles use highly refined clay and are fired at very high temperature, which makes them very durable. They come either glazed or unglazed. Earth tones are the most common color family. These tiles are highly durable, very resistant to moisture, and low maintenance. They're also affordable, not costing much more than glazed floor tile.

- **Terracotta** tile is made of low-density natural clay and is fired at very low temperatures. What you get in old-world style and appearance is offset by a low durability rating and the need to regularly seal the tiles — at least once per year. If you don't seal them, cleaning is difficult. The tiles also become very porous as the sealer wears away. On the plus side, terracotta tiles are relatively inexpensive when compared to other tiles. Terracotta tiles are either hand- or machine-made and are imported from both Europe and Mexico. It costs around $3 to $4 a square foot (installed), compared to $4 to $6 a square foot for a high quality ceramic tile floor. However, the lower durability of the terracotta tile means they won't last as long and you'll be replacing them sooner than a ceramic floor.

✔ **Cement** tile is a fairly new type of tile. It can mimic the look of stone, glazed tile, or brick. These tiles are either *extruded* (shaped by forcing through a die or form) or cast in a mold and then cured. Cement tiles are very durable, have a high resistance to water, are low maintenance, and are low in cost. They cost about the same as terracotta tiles but are more durable, which makes them a better value.

Slate (And other stone tiles)

If you want to make your kitchen elegant, then go with something in the stone tile family. You may be surprised to find out that not all stone tiles are expensive. Different surface textures are available, ranging from shiny and polished (which is quite slippery when wet) to dull (not nearly as slippery but not as good looking, either). Prices for all these types of stone flooring vary widely depending on what part of the country you're in, so you'll need to check in your area to see how much you need to spend to buy such a floor. The biggest drawback with any stone floor is that its useful lifetime will outlast your decorating tastes. Additionally, they're higher maintenance than ceramic tile. Even so, here's a closer look at the types of stone tile that just may be the thing that trips your floor trigger.

✔ **Slate** comes in irregular shapes and is perfect when you want your floor to have a random pattern or rustic look. It comes in various colors including gray, blue, green, black, and even purple. Slate needs to be sealed and it will stain, so clean up spills as soon as possible. Slate costs about as much as ceramic tile, but is about the most durable flooring product you can find.

✔ **Granite** is one tough flooring material. It won't scratch or stain easily, but it is very slippery when wet. Select granite that has a honed or dull surface to reduce the chance of slipping. Granite does not need to be sealed.

✔ **Marble** gives you the widest variety of color and textures in the stone tile category. The colors vary greatly, even within a single slab, as do the veins that run through all marble. Marble is very porous and must be sealed to protect it from dirt, scratches, and stains. Even with sealing, marble scratches very easily.

Keeping it real with wood — Or going synthetic

If you're looking for added warmth, both actual and aesthetic, consider a real (*solid*) wood or wood look-alike (*synthetic*) floor. Besides adding beauty and elegance, a solid or synthetic wood floor does a marvelous job at creating a natural flow between rooms, especially in an open floor plan where there are no walls to define where, for example, the kitchen ends and the family room or dining room begins.

Don't expect to save money by buying synthetic wood flooring instead of solid wood. Material costs are about the same and the installation costs aren't much different, either.

So, how do know whether you want a solid wood or a synthetic wood floor? Take a look at the following information to help you decide.

Solid wood flooring

I've heard many people ask whether or not a solid wood floor can really handle the everyday wear-and-tear of kitchen traffic. The answer to that question is a firm YES! Apply the right finish, and a solid wood floor is very resistant to moisture and can last for years. However, solid wood flooring is recommended for above-grade installation only. This means you shouldn't install it in the basement!

Most solid wood strip flooring is either oak or maple. Most folks opt for the oak, which is very durable and much less expensive than maple. Oak has a more pronounced grain than maple, which may or may not appeal to you. Many feel that the grain adds character and richness.

Another species option is pine. However, pine is softwood, which means it's easily dented. Pine is also more porous than either oak or maple. But if you want your kitchen floor to have a more rustic look, pine would probably be your first choice. A drawback to pine boards is durability. It's a very soft wood so it may not stand up to everyday traffic that's common in most kitchens. Between the two, oak is your better choice.

Two other types of wood flooring products are parquet and engineered flooring. *Parquet flooring* consists of individual squares of smaller pieces of solid wood, held together with a web-type backing or small metal staples or splines. Parquet flooring comes in 9-x-9-, 11-x-11-, 12-x-12- and 19-x-19-inch squares.

Engineered flooring looks like solid wood flooring except that it's actually constructed in layers. This type of manufacturing lets you purchase an exotic wood (such as cherry or mahogany) at a fraction of what solid wood flooring of the same species would cost, because the exotic wood is only used on the top layer. Engineered wood comes in both strips and planks and in various widths.

Solid wood flooring boards come in various grades that affect both appearance and price. Oak and pine are available in three grade levels:

- ✔ **Clear** boards are the most expensive because each board must be free of defects. They are allowed only a few minor imperfections such as small knots.

- ✔ **Select** boards are next level down in board quality and appearance. These boards are, for the most part, still pretty much free of defects; however, they vary more in color and have larger knots.

- ✔ **Common** grade boards are the least expensive. They have the widest variation in color and usually have numerous and very large knots. Despite their rough appearance, many homeowners like this grade of flooring board because of the roughness and the character provided by the defects.

Maple boards have a similar grading system, but use numbers instead of names for the identifying the grades. The three grades for maple are

- ✔ **First:** The best appearance

- ✔ **Second:** Slightly less fine in appearance but still good

- ✔ **Third:** The most rustic look

Solid wood floors also offer an array of shades and grain patterns. The wide range of colors allows you to incorporate the floor into the room's décor and decorating scheme. For example, if your cabinets are a dark wood, such as cherry, a lighter shade of flooring provides an attractive contrast. Or if your cabinets are made of a light colored wood, such as maple or birch, a slightly darker floor provides a nice contrast. You can also create unique yet attractive patterns by using different colored pieces of wood in the floor's design and layout. Using a different colored strip around the outer edge of the floor is an attractive way to form a border.

Most solid wood flooring comes in strips ranging from between 2¼ to 3 inches wide. Plank flooring (also considered a solid wood flooring product) is another option with the plank widths starting at around 3 inches. And because the flooring is solid wood and not a veneer or synthetic, it can be sanded and refinish many times and come back to its original beauty.

The biggest drawback for any solid wood floor is a lack of stain-resistance, but only if you don't get spills wiped up immediately. If a spill is left for too long, you won't be able to stop a stain from forming. And once it's stained, you'll have to sand or strip and refinish the flooring to make it look even again. But, use the manufacturer's recommended finish and follow the schedule for cleaning and maintenance and you will get a long and satisfactory life from a wood floor.

Solid wood strip, plank, and parquet flooring is available either prefinished or unfinished. Engineered flooring is prefinished. The advantage of unfinished wood flooring is that you choose the stain color you like, limiting your color choice only by the number of stain colors that are available.

Speaking of finishes, most flooring manufacturers recommend clear water-based finishes. They're easy to recoat and touch up and, more importantly, they let the natural color of the wood show through. Finishes for floors are available in different sheens, ranging from a low-sheen satin to ultra high-gloss.

Synthetic flooring

You may hear people refer to synthetic wood flooring as Pergo, which is actually one brand-name that's commonly used as a term for the entire synthetic flooring category. Sort of like asking for a Kleenex when what you really want is a tissue.

Synthetic flooring is constructed much the same way as a laminated countertop; with different layers. The first layer is a melamine or paper base for stability, then a layer of fiberboard and a layer of resin are added for durability. The top or design layer has the pattern; the top layer is also protected by a wear layer of clear resins to resist scratches, scuffs, dents, and stains.

What makes synthetic flooring really super is its toughness and stain-resistance. The stuff is very durable and resists warping and scratches. And because it's a synthetic product, ultra-violet (UV) inhibitors can be added into the top surface formula during manufacturing to prevent the flooring from fading. Natural wood will fade if exposed to sunlight. Another difference is that the design layer is actually a printed pattern or photograph of real wood on the surface; synthetic wood has no actual texture.

Because of its toughness and durability, most synthetic flooring comes with a 15-year warranty. The tradeoff for this durability, however, is that you can't refinish it if it gets scratched, gouged, or damaged. The only real fix is to replace the damaged piece.

Installation of a synthetic floor is different from installing a solid wood floor. Synthetic flooring uses an *underlayment* (¼-inch-thick plywood) over the sub-floor before you install the flooring. You also need to include a plastic vapor barrier if you're installing synthetic flooring over a concrete slab. Synthetic flooring is the only recommended way to get the appearance of a wood floor where the floor is below grade or in the basement.

Staying away from carpet

One type of floor covering never recommended for the kitchen is carpet. It may provide a soft and warm surface, but it also absorbs odors, holds dirt, grease, and grime, and gets really dirty, really fast. And because it gets dirty and stays dirty, carpet is a perfect breeding ground for germs! I've lived in two homes where carpet was installed in the kitchen. In both cases, performance and especially appearance were less than satisfactory. Cleaning carpet regularly doesn't help, either. After the carpet is cleaned the first time, it actually gets dirtier faster. Traffic patterns are also quite pronounced after it's been cleaned. And using a tight-loop pile won't solve the problem. My parents put a tight-loop carpet in their kitchen. It looked good for about a year and a half but within two years they had to replace it with a new tile floor. I can't stress enough that carpet is not the way to go!

Choosing to Remove the Old Flooring — Or Not

You may not need to gut back to the subfloor when you take out the old flooring. In fact, old tiles, linoleum, and even sheet flooring can be difficult and sometimes impossible to remove without damaging the subfloor.

And depending on when the old floor was installed, the flooring and adhesive could contain asbestos. Flooring installed before 1986 probably contains some asbestos. If you decide to remove asbestos from your house, professionals trained in asbestos abatement must remove any material with asbestos in it.

Many people don't realize that just because a material contains asbestos that doesn't mean you have to remove it to make your home safe. Asbestos poses no health risks as long as it's left undisturbed. So, instead of ripping up the old flooring and removing the adhesive, just leave it and install the new floor right over it.

One potential problem you could face if you install a new floor over an old one is the added height of the new floor. Old floors usually add between ⅜ and ¾ of an inch, which means the new flooring will be higher on the base trim if you leave the base in place, and you'll also need to trim off the bottom of any interior doors that open over the new floor. Trimming doors isn't difficult, and I show you how to do it the right way in Chapter 21. Exterior doors, on the other hand, cannot be cut off. They'll have to be removed and reinstalled higher or replaced, and replacing a door adds to the total cost of the project.

If you do remove the old flooring, make sure to examine the existing subfloor and make any necessary repairs. Pay particular attention to the area under and around the sink. Leaking pipes or an overflowing sink may have soaked the wood (usually plywood), causing the wood to rot or the plywood layers to delaminate.

You can identify rot easily: The areas that got wet are severely discolored, and you may even see holes in the subflooring. Or the area may be spongy when you walk on it or push on it. Check for bubbled areas on the surface of plywood, too. Bubbles indicate delamination, which means you need to replace the damaged plywood. If you find any of theses problem, you must remove the damaged sections and install new subflooring.

After the old flooring is out, give the entire subfloor a thorough examination; look for nails, gouges, low spots, or other blemishes that will affect the look and performance of your new floor. If you fail to fix these problems and you do have a problem with the flooring, chances are good that the warranty will be voided because of improper subfloor preparation.

Chapter 21 shows you exactly what type of subfloor prep is required for the various types of flooring discussed in this chapter.

Chapter 21

Installing Your New Kitchen Floor

· ·

In This Chapter
▶ Getting your tools together
▶ Preparing for the big change
▶ Installing your dazzling new floor
▶ Anchoring in a kitchen island

· ·

*Y*our kitchen floor takes a lot of abuse and is visible all of the time. No matter what material you choose, your floor should add to the overall look of your kitchen and give you years of good service.

This chapter shows you what installing each type of flooring is like, and gives you some pointers on going from one type of flooring to another. Before I get into showing you how to install these different floors, however, I want you to know that this is one part of the remodel where you may want to seriously considering hiring a professional. Working around door openings, cabinets, and any other obstacles is tricky and doesn't give you much wiggle-room for errors. Besides, the installer will be in and out in about the same amount of time that you'll spend trying to get things laid out and ready to go.

Preparing to Be Floored

Before you can set foot on your gleaming new kitchen floor, you have some serious legwork to do, starting with getting an exact measurement of your floor and getting the floor below your new floor, the *subfloor,* ready. You'll know your kitchen floor inside and out — literally — before the first new tile even touches the subfloor.

Gathering the right tools

Here are the hand tools you need to prepare the subfloor:

- A pry bar (for removing old underlayment or subfloor)
- A cat's paw (used for getting under nail heads to start pulling them)
- A putty knife
- A V-notched trowel (for spreading adhesive)
- A square-notched trowel (also called a notched trowel)
- A smooth or square trowel (for patching)
- A flush-cut saw (for trimming door casings and jambs)
- A tape measure
- A carpenter's pencil
- Heavy-duty work gloves
- Eye protection
- A dust mask
- Plywood
- Drywall screws (1½ and 2 inches)
- Straight 2 x 4 (to check for low spots in subfloor)
- Latex underlayment
- Smooth trowel (for spreading the latex underlayment)
- Cardboard
- Masking tape
- A circular saw and/or a jigsaw (both is better, but either is okay, too)
- A belt sander (with coarse- and medium-grit sanding belts)
- A ⅜-inch drill (corded or cordless)
- Drill bits and screwdriver bits (for fastening the new subflooring)
- A chalk line
- A utility knife
- A hammer
- A framing square
- A compass (for scribing irregular shapes along the wall)
- Kneepads
- Rubber gloves (if working with mortar and adhesive)

Taking the measurements

Back in my home center management days, I helped a lot of customers purchase new flooring. And one of the most common problems I ran into was inaccurate room measurements. Too often, the customer measured the room from wall to wall, without taking into account the doorways and transition areas.

When measuring the kitchen, measure from the wall opposite each doorway and lay the tape rule into the doorway so that you include the extra inches of the doorway. A few inches doesn't sound like much, but a few doorways added together can make a difference in the size of a piece of material, for example sheet flooring, or in the quantity of tile or wood you will need. Also, remember to add or subtract material, depending on whether the flooring will run under the cabinets or just up to the toe-kick.

Prepping your subfloor

After you remove the old kitchen floor (as instructed in Chapter 6), the plywood or *subfloor* may need some repair before you install the new flooring. Or you may even need to replace the subfloor. A solid, smooth subfloor is critical for successful installation of your new flooring.

Depending on what type of flooring you put down, an underlayment may be required to meet the manufacturer's warranty requirements. And unless you have a sound subfloor, the underlayment won't be able to perform the way it should, which can ultimately void a warranty.

Some damage to the subfloor is to be expected, regardless of how easily the old flooring comes up. If you're removing a hardwood floor, you'll have nail heads to contend with. And if you're removing linoleum, tile squares, or sheet vinyl, you always end up with small pieces — and maybe even sections — of the old flooring that just won't come loose from the subfloor. At best, you'll have adhesive residue on the subfloor. But no matter what's left behind, it needs to be removed (I tell you how in Chapter 6) or covered before you install the new floor.

Replacing old subflooring

If you decided to tackle removing the old cabinets and countertops, then taking up any damaged sections of old subfloor is something that you can also handle. Depending on when the old subfloor was installed, the type of nail used dictates how difficult the removal will be. Cement-coated sinker nails are relatively easy to pull. Ring-shank flooring nails, on the other hand, are hard to remove, because the rings on the nail's shank are designed to hold the nail in place and not allow it to back out. You can get ring-shank flooring nails out, but only with effort. Figure 21-1 shows how to get the cat's paw under the nail head and loosen the nail.

Figure 21-1:
Use a
cat's paw
to loosen
floor nails.

To replace damaged subflooring

1. **Pull the nails from the subfloor.**

2. **Use the pry bar to get under the subfloor and raise it.**

   Remember, unless you find a lot of damage, you probably only need to replace small sections of subfloor. The most common type of damage to subflooring is when the plywood is soft or bouncy when it's walked on. This is caused by rot and the soft pieces need to be replaced.

3. **Cut plywood of the correct thickness to fit the area that you're replacing.**

   Most subfloor plywood is ¾ inch thick. If you're not sure what the thickness is, cut out a small section of the damaged area and measure the thickness of the plywood, or take the cutout piece with you when you go to purchase new plywood.

4. **Secure the plywood with 1½- or 2-inch-long drywall screws. Space the screws every three inches along the edges and every six inches across the face of the panel.**

   Make sure to drive the screws into the floor joints.

5. **If the joints of the new pieces of plywood don't fall on top of the floor joist, you need to provide a supported nailing surface below the joint.**

   You do this by installing blocking between the floor joists from below. If you're not familiar with this type of work, contact a professional to do it right. If you are familiar with it, you'll know what I'm talking about and how to do it correctly.

Leveling the subfloor

You also need to check the rest of the subfloor for low spots. If you have a low spot and don't level it, the underlayment (which I discuss in the "Laying down underlayment" section) will flex when the flooring is walked on. This can damage the flooring and void your warranty.

To check for and repair low spots

1. **Place a straight 2 x 4 on edge on the subfloor and look for any light shining under the 2 x 4.**

2. **Mark any low spots with a pencil.**

3. **To fill the low spots, spread latex underlayment (available at home centers and flooring stores) over the low spot with a trowel.**

4. **Smooth the edges thoroughly with the trowel.**

5. **After the latex underlayment has dried, use a belt sander with a medium-grit sanding belt to sand the area smooth.**

Laying down underlayment

Underlayment is the material that's required by the flooring manufacturers that's installed directly underneath the finished flooring material. The most commonly recommended thickness is ⅛ inch, but check your flooring installation instructions to be sure. Some may require ¼-inch thick underlayment.

If you're installing a ceramic tile floor, you need to put down a ½-inch thick cement backerboard as the underlayment. Cement backerboard is a drywall-like board that's made of cement. It's sturdier than plywood and is better suited for dealing with the weight of a ceramic tile floor.

The instructions for laying these underlayments are slightly different, but here are a few things to remember no matter what material you use:

✔ **Check for fit:** Make sure that any required underlayment will fit under the door casing. You may need to trim the door casing to accomplish this. To get the underlayment under the trim, place a piece of the underlayment against the trim and use a flush-cutting saw to remove the excess trim (see Figure 21-2).

✔ **Create a template:** You will run into areas where obstacles necessitate cutting the underlayment to fit a specific area, for example around cabinet corners. The easiest way to determine the size of these areas is to lay cardboard pieces down to form a template. You could also purchase a roll of red rosin paper (sold at any home center) and use it as a pattern. Trace the template onto the underlayment and cut it to fit. Tape each section of cardboard or rosin paper together to form the template (the shape) of your kitchen floor (see Figure 21-3). Save the template, too, because you can use it as the pattern for the flooring material and to cover the finished flooring after it's installed while you complete the final stages of the kitchen remodel.

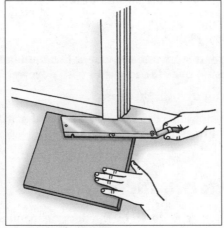

Figure 21-2:
Use a
flush-cutting
saw to
remove the
excess trim.

For vinyl flooring

Proper underlayment installation is critical for vinyl flooring. If it's done wrong, the new flooring will show every tiny imperfection in the old subfloor and new underlayment. Follow these steps to do the job right.

1. **Lay out your underlayment sheets on the subfloor.**

   Stagger the seams of the underlayment sheets. Leave a ¼-inch gap along the walls and a ⅛-inch gap between sheets to allow for expansion.

2. **Fasten the sheets to the subfloor with 1½-inch drywall screws.**

   Again, space the screws every three inches along the seams and every six inches across the face or field of the entire sheet.

3. **Fill the gaps at the seams.**

   Spread a cement-based floor patching compound at every seam. Use a smooth (unnotched) trowel to spread the filler the same way you filled in the low spots on the subfloor.

4. **Allow the filler to dry and then sand all seams smooth with a belt sander and medium-grit sanding belt.**

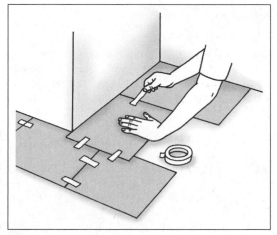

Figure 21-3:
Lay out
template
paper or
cardboard.

For tile floors

Proper underlayment prep is crucial here, too, for your new floor to perform as it should. The following steps tell you how to do it right:

1. **Cut the backerboard to fit.**

   The best way to cut the backerboard is to score it with a utility knife and snap it along the scored line. Smooth any rough edges with the knife blade.

2. **Lay out the sheets on the floor, staggering them and leaving a ¼-inch gap at the walls and a ⅛-inch gap between sheets.**

3. **Spread a layer of thinset mortar on the subfloor using a ¼-inch notched trowel.**

4. **Then, lay the backerboard sheet on the mortar. Work one sheet at a time so that the mortar doesn't setup before you're ready to lay the sheet in place.**

5. **Walk on the sheet to press it in place.**

6. **Secure the sheet with 1¼-inch backerboard screws.**

7. **Fill the gaps between sheets with a thin layer of the thinset mortar.**

   Feather the edges as you apply the mortar, because this stuff is really tough to sand smooth after it dries.

For wood flooring

Wood flooring typically does not require underlayment before installation. Most manufacturer's instructions say to install the flooring directly onto the subfloor. Consult your wood flooring installation instructions.

Installing Your Floor

How (and how fast) you install your particular kitchen floor depends on all kinds of things: the type of flooring you've chosen, the size and shape of your kitchen, and the quality and quantity of helpers you've managed to enlist. Remember what I mentioned earlier; this is one part of the remodel where hiring a pro makes sense.

Installing sheet flooring

Sheet vinyl flooring is a popular choice for kitchens. It's attractive, durable, and not too difficult to install.

 Sheet vinyl comes rolled into a tube shape. It needs to lay flat and sort of loosen up before you install it so that it's easier to use. When it's time to install the floor, get a helper to unroll the vinyl on a large flat surface with the pattern facing up. You'll do your template cutting with the flooring in this position.

Grabbing some special tools

Here's what you'll need to round up:

- A seam roller
- A rolling pin (for sheet flooring seams)
- A V-notched trowel (for spreading adhesive)
- A utility knife (for cutting vinyl flooring)
- Cement-based floor patching compound
- Straightedge
- Mastic
- Red rosin paper (for making template)
- A mixing blade (used in an electric drill for mixing mortar and adhesive)

Making a template

Most manufacturers sell a template kit for laying and cutting the vinyl that is inexpensive and provides really good instructions. You can also make your own sheets out of red rosin paper.

1. **Lay out the sheets of paper in the kit and tape them together with masking tape.**

The template will be the shape of the area of your kitchen floor. After the template is completed, carefully lift it off the kitchen floor and place it on the unrolled vinyl.

2. **Trace the outline of the template onto the flooring with a felt-tip pen.**

3. **Remove the template and cut the flooring with a utility knife with a new blade (see Figure 21-4).**

   Change the blade often, too, for smooth, even cuts.

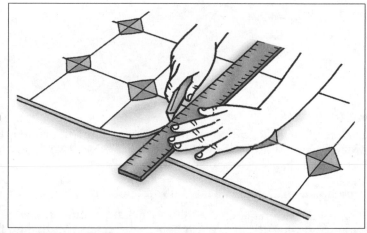

Figure 21-4:
Use a straight-edge as a guide when cutting vinyl.

4. **Place the cut vinyl in the kitchen.**

   Be careful when positioning the vinyl so that you don't nick or tear it. Slide the edges under the door casings that you've already trimmed to fit. Leave between a ⅛- and a ¼-inch gap along the walls.

Cutting a seam

Try to install your sheet flooring using one large piece. However, many kitchens are wider than the 12-foot-wide width that sheet vinyl comes in. If you do need to have a seam, plan to place it along a pattern line and not in a high-traffic area of the room.

1. **Overlap the sheets about two inches.**

2. **Match the pattern and tape the sheets together.**

   Masking tape works just fine.

3. **Hold a straightedge tightly and make several passes with a utility knife to cut through both layers of the flooring (see Figure 21-5).**

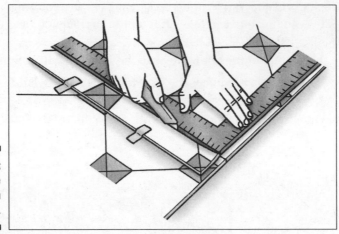

Figure 21-5:
Cut the seam pieces.

Gluing things down

You need to glue the flooring in an efficient, yet unhurried manner. The adhesive will begin to set up after a while, but you have plenty of time to do it right as long as you work in a logical order. Here's what to do:

1. **Pull up one half of the sheet and roll it loosely.**

2. **Spread the recommended adhesive (mastic) around the edge of the room and wherever there will be a seam, using a V-notched trowel (see Figure 21-6).**

3. **Let the adhesive set up for about 10 to 15 minutes until it gets tacky.**

4. **Unroll the flooring over the adhesive.**

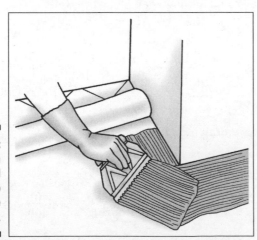

Figure 21-6:
Use a V-notched trowel to spread the adhesive.

5. **Press the flooring against the underlayment with a rolling pin.**

   You can also rent a floor roller. Work around the entire area, including the edges and the seams.

6. **The last step is to use a seam roller on each seam.**

   This ensures a solid bond of adhesive under both pieces of flooring. A seam roller is slightly smaller than a flooring roller, so it's better suited for rolling the seams. Just roll it slowly along each seam to ensure that the seam is completely flattened.

Installing vinyl tile squares

Vinyl tile squares are attractive and durable and even easier to install than sheet flooring. Most vinyl tiles have the adhesive already applied to the back — they're called peel-and-stick tiles. Simply remove the paper backing and you're ready to stick the tiles down in place. The advantage of a tile square floor versus a sheet vinyl floor is that you can easily replace a damaged tile down the road. If sheet vinyl gets damaged, it's difficult to repair and you can't replace just a small piece.

Grabbing some special tools

Here's what you'll need to round up:

- Chalk line
- Framing square
- Straight edge
- Utility knife (for cutting tiles to fit)
- Floor roller (for firmly setting tiles to underlayment)

Marking your guidelines

Here are the steps that determine whether a new vinyl tile floor looks good or bad after it's installed. You need two perpendicular guidelines so that you can dry lay a row of tiles in each direction to see where the tiles will end at the walls or cabinets. You don't want to have less than half a tile at any ending point, so be ready to adjust the guidelines. (Tiles cut to less than half their original size are more likely to develop cracks and generally don't wear as well.) Here's what you need to do:

1. **Start by finding and marking the center of two opposite walls.**

2. **Then, snap a chalk line across the floor using these two marks as your guide points.**

3. **Fasten a chalk line at the center point of one of the other (and adjacent) wall.**

4. **Next, have your helper pull the other end of the chalk line to form a perpendicular angle across the snapped line.**

5. **Use a framing square to make sure the angle formed by the two lines is 90 degrees (see Figure 21-7).**

6. **Snap the second line.**

   You'll end up with four "quartered" sections. You install the tiles working one quartered section at a time.

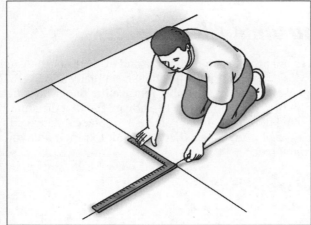

Figure 21-7:
Snap perpendicular chalk lines.

7. **Double-check the two lines again by using the 3-4-5 triangle method, which I discussed in Chapter 11.**

Installing the tiles

Now you finally get to see what the new floor will look like. Well, almost. Before you secure them to the floor, you must lay tiles in both directions along the guidelines to be sure the pattern and size works.

1. **Check the layout of the tiles by dry fitting (leave the paper backing in place for now) them on the floor.**

   Check to see how the tile meets the wall.

2. **If you end up with less than half of a tile at any of the walls, adjust the chalk lines so that at least a half a tile ends at the wall. After you've made these adjustments, dry fit the tiles again to be sure.**

3. **Starting at the center and working in one quartered area at a time, peel off the backing and start putting the tiles in place.**

4. **After the tiles have been laid, press them down with a rolling pin or tile/flooring roller.**

The space between: Transition strips

What do you do when you switch from one type of flooring material to another between rooms? In most cases, for example, with wood flooring or ceramic tile, there are thresholds and transitions strips of a similar material.

These strips are usually installed the same way the flooring is: wood strips are usually nailed down and ceramic (or similar man-made strips) are set in thinset mortar and grouted. For vinyl (both sheet and squares), the key is to get the edge securely glued down. Vinyl that butts against wood or ceramic needs to be straight for appearance and is simply glued down. If you're going from vinyl to carpet, a metal carpet strip should be used. Its curved lip holds the carpet in place and its straight edge forms the perfect line for the vinyl to butt against. Transition strips, thresholds, and carpet strips are sold wherever you purchase your flooring.

Installing ceramic tile

Ceramic tile in the kitchen is one of the most popular upgrades. Your choices in tile sizes, colors, and patterns are seemingly endless, and ceramic tile looks great, too. Installing a ceramic tile floor takes a lot of time, however, because you need to cut and fit the tile, plus you need to fill the gaps between the tiles with grout after the tile adhesive has set up (usually 24 hours). You also need to seal the grout.

Grabbing some special tools

Installing ceramic tile requires some tools that aren't used for any other type of flooring. In some cases, you'll rent what you need unless you plan do more than one floor. The choice is yours. Here's what you'll need to round up:

- A wet saw
- A manual tile cutter (in place of the wet saw)
- A rod saw (for cutting curves in ceramic tile)
- A notched trowel (for spreading mortar and adhesive)
- A rubber grout float
- A ½-inch-thick cement backerboard
- 1¼-inch backerboard screws
- Thinset mortar
- Grout
- A sponge (and bucket, too)

Layout and installation

The preliminary steps for installing ceramic tile are similar to those discussed in the vinyl tile section. You need perpendicular guidelines and you want to be sure that you have at least half a tile at all door openings and along the walls or cabinets. Small tile sections will crack and can break loose from the adhesive more easily than full or half tiles.

1. **Lay out chalk lines on the subfloor (cement backerboard) as described in Steps 1 through 4 of the "Installing vinyl tile squares" section.**

2. **Dry fit a row of tiles following the chalk lines.**

   Place plastic tile spacers between each tile to ensure even spacing. Don't rely on your eyes! See Figure 21-8.

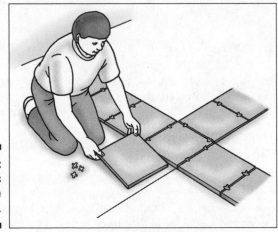

Figure 21-8: Dry fit tiles along the chalk lines.

3. **If you're left with less than half a tile at the wall, adjust your chalk lines and then dry fit the tile again to be sure.**

4. **After the pattern is established, start at the center and apply thinset mortar with a notched trowel to one of the sections (see Figure 21-9).**

   Don't cover up the chalk lines — you need them for reference when starting each of the other sections.

5. **Set the tiles onto the thinset and push down lightly (see Figure 21-10).**

   Place the plastic spacers between the tiles for even spacing. Occasionally, step back and look down the spaces (grout lines) to see if they're straight. Adjust tiles as necessary.

6. **Continue to spread thinset and install tiles one section at a time. Remove the spacers after about an hour (before the thinset has completely dried).**

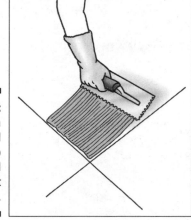

Figure 21-9:
Use a
notched
trowel to
spread
thinset
mortar.

Cutting border tiles

Cutting tiles to fit along the walls or at the cabinet toe kick isn't difficult if you follow these steps.

1. **Start by placing a ¼-inch spacer against the wall before measuring the tile to be cut.**

   The space is needed to allow for expansion and contraction of the subfloor.

2. **Place a full tile directly over the last full tile that was laid (see tile A in Figure 21-11).**

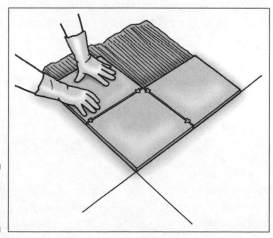

Figure 21-10:
Set tiles in
the thinset.

3. **To determine the size of the border tile, place a second (or marker) tile (see tile B in Figure 21-11) against the ¼-inch spacer and over the full tile.**

4. **Trace the edge of the second tile onto the first tile.**

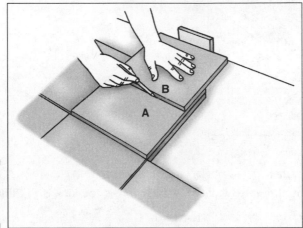

Figure 21-11:
Cut border
tiles.

5. **Cut the border tile with either a manual tile cutter or a wet saw, depending on what you have available.**

   The manual cutter takes longer but it's cleaner. Simply set the cutting guide to the correct width and draw the cutting wheel blade over the tile face to score the tile. The tile will snap on the score line. A wet saw is fast because it's electrically powered, but it's messy because you use water to keep the tile and the blade cool while cutting. For that reason, you need to make all of your tile cuts in an area that can get really messy. Outside works best.

The same techniques are needed when cutting tiles to fit around corners. However, if you have to make a right-angle cut, use a rod saw and not a wet saw. The rod saw is a little slower, but much more accurate.

After all the tiles are installed, allow the thinset to dry for 24 hours. Stay off the tiles during this time or you'll probably loosen or shift a couple of them.

Grouting and sealing

To finish the tile job, you need to fill the spaces between the tiles with grout. And after the grout has dried, you need to seal it to keep it clean.

1. **Mix the grout according to the instructions.**

2. **Spread the grout diagonally across the tiles using a rubber grout float.**

   Hold the float at about a 45-degree angle to the floor to force the grout into the gaps.

3. **Wait 15 to 20 minutes (but no longer!) and wipe off the excess grout with a damp sponge and clean water.**

4. **Now wait about two hours and then sponge off the tiles again.**

   This will remove the thin haze that you'll see on the tiles.

5. **Let the grout cure according to the manufacturer's directions and then brush on a coat of silicone grout sealer over each grout line using a foam brush.**

Installing a wood floor

Ah, the beauty of wood! And sometimes that beauty isn't even real wood. You have many choices in wood flooring, ranging from planks and strips of real wood to wood-look laminate to wood parquet squares. The different kinds of wood flooring (strips, planks, and parquet) are very popular because of their richness and beauty. But the constant wear-and-tear and the presence of moisture in the kitchen can cause problems with wood floors. Laminate wood-look flooring is gaining popularity, plus it's easy to install. Here's a quick look at the differences in installing the three types of flooring including the tools you need.

Grabbing some special tools

Once again, you may have most of tools you'll need but you may want to rent some, too. Here's what to pull together:

- Flooring nailer and mallet/hammer (rent this!)
- A tapping block (for setting flooring pieces tightly together)
- A 12-inch small pry/pull bar (often called a mini-pry bar)
- A combination square

Strips and planks

Both strips and planks come cut to varying lengths so that the seams between rows are staggered. Both types are secured to each adjacent row with nails. The first row of strips is nailed to the subfloor. The length of nail you need to use to secure the strips to each other depends on the thickness of the flooring. You can nail by hand; however, you'll need to drill pilot holes for each nail to avoid splitting the strip or plank — WHEW! A faster and better way to nail is with a flooring nailer. The nailer is designed to drive the nail at the correct angle for maximum holding power. You drive the nails by striking the nailer's plunger with the weighted mallet (see Figure 21-12).

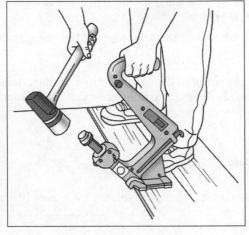

Figure 21-12:
Drive nails with a flooring nailer.

Laminate

Why is this type of flooring so popular? Well, laminate is tough as nails, attractive, and affordable. Laminate flooring is also easy to install, because you don't nail it to the floor. These floors float on an underlayment pad that you simply lay down over the subfloor. The strips use a tongue-and-groove attaching system and glue to ensure that joints stay together. Many of the manufacturers offer systems that click and lock in place and some actually make a clicking noise when the tongue-and-groove is properly fitted together.

Now, I may have made this seem like you can install your kitchen floor in a couple of hours. You won't finish up quite that fast, but installing laminate is easy and manageable by anyone with moderate DIY skills. Allow at least a full day or probably two.

Parquet

Parquet flooring squares are similar in installation to vinyl tile squares or ceramic tile. You need to layout chalk lines and dry fit the squares to make sure you have at least a half a square at the wall. These wood squares are also secured with adhesive. Check your flooring manufacturer for the type of adhesive to use. After the parquet pieces are in place, use the roller to set them into the adhesive.

Some parquet manufacturers do not recommend rolling their tiles. Instead, use a rubber mallet and lightly tap each square to set it into the adhesive.

Dealing with not-so-perfect edges

Even the professionals have a hard time making perfectly straight cuts along walls, under the cabinet toe kicks, and around islands. Installing base-shoe trim over the edge cuts covers up those rough spots and adds some class to the flooring job. Base-shoe is a ¾ x ¾ inch piece of trim that has a rounded face. The flat ¾-inch sides go against the floor and wall, cabinet, or island and the rounded face faces out. Check out just about any hard flooring surface and you're likely to see base-shoe.

Securing an Island Unit

After your new floors are in place, you may need to reattach an island (or attach a new one). Fortunately, this process is not too difficult.

Base cabinets have one side attached to the wall. But an island is sitting out there all by itself with nothing to attach itself to and it must be secured. So, how do you do it? By keeping things out of sight.

1. **Position the island where it is to be located. Draw lines around the entire base, marking its ends and sides.**

2. **Tip the island back and measure the thickness of the cabinet panels. They could be ¼, ½, or ¾ inch thick.**

   You need to know the thickness of the panels so that you will install the four mounting blocks back off of the lines enough to allow the unit to fit down over the blocks. Remember, the lines you drew in Step 1 are for the outside footprint of the island. The mounting blocks are usually 6-inch-long pieces of 2 x 4.

3. **Measure the appropriate distance back from each line and screw the wood blocks to the floor (see Figure 21-13).**

   Three-inch drywall screws work just fine.

4. **Place the island over the blocks and secure it to the blocks with screws or 6d finish nails.**

   The advantage of finish nails is that the small head is nearly invisible. The advantage of screws is that they're easier to remove if you ever need to get under the island cabinet.

Figure 21-13: Install mounting blocks to help secure the island to the floor.

Keep the screws no more than ¾ inch from the floor so they can be concealed by base-shoe later.

Finally, if your island has a sink or cooktop, you may need the help of professional to get these extras up and running.

Part VI
The Part of Tens

The 5th Wave   By Rich Tennant

"I just don't know where the money's going."

In this part . . .

*I*n this part, you find ten of the hottest trends in kitchen design today, ten ways to upgrade your kitchen that won't break the bank, and much more!

Chapter 22

Ten Critical Design Issues

In This Chapter
▶ Work areas
▶ Countertop issues
▶ Safer appliances
▶ Free floor space

Your kitchen may be the most popular room in your home, so you want it to work right. And if your kitchen is designed properly, it will become an area where family and guests will naturally gravitate. This chapter offers you ten (okay, eleven) ways to make sure your kitchen space functions well.

The Work Triangle Formula

Creating a smooth workflow should be a primary objective in a kitchen redesign. And the best way to have a smooth flow is to create a work triangle between the sink, stove, and refrigerator that makes a kitchen either usable or a room to avoid. No leg of the triangle should be shorter than 4 feet or longer than 9 feet and the total of the triangle's three legs should be no greater than 26 feet. Chapter 2 discusses the work triangle in greater detail.

Making Sure Your Workspace Is Separate

Being interrupted when working in the kitchen because you're standing in the normal flow of traffic is a real headache. To avoid this frustration, make sure the work triangle is out of the flow of the main traffic. You need to have an alternate way to move through the kitchen without interfering with the cook.

Your walkway doesn't have to be a large space, but you do need enough room to avoid bumping into other people in the kitchen.

Installing Adequate Doors

It's the scene that creates a lot of laughter in the movies: Two people coming from opposite directions and headed through a too-narrow doorway. You know what's coming, but it's not funny if it happens to you. To avoid a potentially messy and dangerous collision, make sure the doorways are wide enough. All doorways should be at least 32 inches wide. Anything narrower and you'll feel like you're walking through a cramped tunnel. Besides, narrow doorways create the real possibility of collisions and spilled food!

Avoid Knocking Knuckles When Opening Doors

Smashing your knuckles between two doors is a painful experience and one that I'm sure most of us have experienced. To avoid knocking knuckles, follow some simple, yet logical design concepts. Be sure that no entry doors, appliance doors, or cabinet doors interfere with each other when opening. Check this stuff out early on in the design process. You'll be glad you did.

Easy Dish Loading

Don't make moving dishes from the sink into the dishwasher seem like a long-distance excursion. The edge of the dishwasher should be within 36 inches of the sink. Any greater distance and you have to take a short stroll just to load the dishwasher. Not a big deal, but it can get frustrating after a while.

Situating One Sink

Most people have only one sink, so remember that its position is crucial. The sink should be located between or across from the cooking surface, preparation area, or refrigerator. That way, you can quickly and safely move items to and from the sink with little worry about having a food-transferring accident. Remember, convenience leads to safety.

Considering Countertops at Different Heights

A 6-foot, 2-inch volleyball-playing sister doesn't have the same viewpoint on a countertop as her 7-year-old brother, yet both enjoy working in the kitchen. Or maybe you have an elderly parent living with you who needs to sit while cooking. Because of examples like this, the National Kitchen and Bath Association (NKBA) recommends two work-counter heights in a kitchen to make the kitchen more accessible for people of all ages. One counter should be between 28 and 36 inches above the finished floor and the other between 36 and 45 inches above the floor.

Storing Those Dirty Dishes

No one likes dirty dishes piled high and left for days. But you do need enough space to temporarily stack the dishes while you're cleaning up after meals. To do this efficiently, you'll want at least 24 inches of countertop space on one side of the sink and 18 inches on the other. Anything less and you can expect to lose a dish or two if you try to stack them to clean them.

Grocery Resting Area

Just as having enough space for stacking dishes is important, you also need adequate space for placing items that you're moving from the grocery bags into the refrigerator. You need at least 15 inches of clear counterspace on either side of the refrigerator so that you can safely set a bag of groceries down while loading the refrigerator.

Microwave Oven Safety

Kids love the speed and convenience of a microwave oven. But if they're young children or not very tall, removing hot food or liquid from the microwave oven could be a problem. For safe use, especially for younger or shorter people, all microwave ovens should be placed so that the bottom of the oven is 24 to 48 inches above the finished floor.

Plenty of Floor Space

You want to be able to move easily and smoothly around and in front of the appliances in your kitchen and not have to worry about becoming a contortionist! There should be a clear floor space of 30 x 48 inches in front of the sink, dishwasher, cooktop, oven, and refrigerator. These spaces can overlap — if they couldn't, we'd all have kitchens the size of most garages!

Chapter 23

Ten Hot Trends in Kitchen Design

In This Chapter

▶ Accommodating two cooks

▶ Bringing the family together

▶ Cabinets, colors, and style

If you're remodeling your kitchen, you probably want your new kitchen to look fresh and new. This chapter overviews ten plus hot trends in kitchen design that you just might want to work into your kitchen.

Adding an Extra Sink

The more we cook, the more we clean. An extra sink can work as either a food preparation station or as a cleanup area.

Spreading Out the Work: Multiple Workstations

Just as two sinks are becoming more popular, so are multiple work areas. When a family has more cooks, then several people are working in the kitchen at one time. Giving each person her own workstation makes kitchen tasks flow more smoothly.

Visiting the Islands — Mon!

As kitchen square footage gets bigger, the possibilities for a center island grow, too. An island can be a food preparation area if a sink is installed, a cooking area if a cooktop is installed, or a serving area.

Entertaining in the Kitchen

Today, more people use the kitchen for a gathering place, so more time is being spent in the kitchen. That's why computer stations and TVs are becoming part of the equipment found in today's kitchens.

Eating-In Areas: Casual Style

Just grabbing a quick snack? Want to just stand while you eat and chat with friends? Well, you don't need to pull out a chair and sit at the table anymore. Breakfast bars or casual eating areas are being included in today's kitchen designs. Stools and booths are also popular, instead of the traditional table and chairs.

Gathering the Family

According to NKBA surveys, families are spending more time in the kitchen, so the overall design of many kitchens is to make them more open and inviting for the family to be together. Creating areas, even small ones, such as a workstation or computer work area makes your kitchen feel more like home. The fact that more of the family's activities go on in the kitchen makes it feel more like the place to meet.

Creating Kid Friendly Kitchens

Most kids love to cook and be part of the action. Multiple-level workstations (varying countertop heights, in particular) are making it easier for children to become part of the food preparation and cooking aspect of family life. Making the kitchen kid friendly is also a great way for you to spend time with your kids!

Merging Kitchens with the Rest of the House

There used to be a distinct separation between the kitchen and other rooms — well, not anymore. Today's designers are merging the kitchen with adjoining rooms, such as a den or dining room, to create an open and inviting floor plan and traffic flow.

Adding Decorative Touches

Little additions can make a huge difference in the look of your kitchen. Adding moldings, pot racks, trim on countertops, and even fancy drawer and door hardware can change an ordinary kitchen into one that seems ready for a home tour.

Visiting Europe without Leaving Home

European kitchen styling is very popular. The open work areas and the large serving areas make the European-style kitchen design a popular choice for many homeowners.

Toning for Elegance

Dark wood tones are back, especially cherry and maple. The richness of the wood creates both elegance and warmth and makes a kitchen a most inviting room to spend time in.

Chapter 24

Ten Easy Kitchen Upgrades

In This Chapter

▶ Freshening up the walls

▶ Handling new handles

▶ Save the sink but out with the faucet

▶ Just hanging things around

You don't have to replace everything in your kitchen to jazz things up. This chapter shows you how even simple, rather inexpensive changes can make others think you redid your kitchen.

Brightening Up the Room with a Fresh Coat of Paint

Unfortunately, your kitchen walls are prone to getting dull and dirty. The daily accumulation of grease and grime can make a kitchen appear dull and lifeless in a hurry. A fresh coat of paint on the walls and ceiling brightens up any kitchen.

Working with Wallpaper That Wows

Yes, wallpaper works in the kitchen, as long as you can wash it. And you don't need to do all the walls or even an entire wall. Adding wallpaper to all or part of one wall brings color and texture to otherwise plain surfaces.

Venturing Beyond the Border

If you don't want to wallpaper, then consider adding a border strip near the ceiling or even in the middle of the wall as a visual break. These 8- or 9-inch wide wonders add color and life without being overbearing.

Treating Your Windows to a New Dress

Adding a valance or even a single set of curtains over a sink window, spruces up plain areas. Once again, the introduction of color and texture to one small area can change the appearance and feel of the entire kitchen.

Replacing Handles and Knobs

Cabinets look okay? Then leave them be. But you can upgrade their appearance by purchasing new knobs or pulls. Believe me, replacing old black, wrought-iron style hardware with shiny brass stuff makes it look like you spent a ton of money, without breaking the bank!

Giving Your Faucet a Facelift

Replacing your old kitchen sink faucet with one that has today's features and color combinations is a nice and affordable upgrade. And replacing faucets is a project most people can handle on their own.

Lightening Up

Just as a new faucet can brighten up your kitchen sink, new overhead light fixtures can help shed new light in the kitchen and make it look better, too. You can go fancy or conservative, but either way, the change will make your kitchen look different. And isn't that what you're after?

Trimmin' Time

Adding cove molding along the ceiling or where your cabinets meet the soffit really makes a plain kitchen classy. Even a small-sized style of trim will add texture and dimension to otherwise dull, lifeless spots.

Racking Up Your Pots and Pan

Want to gain some cabinet storage space and create an attractive wall feature? Installing a pot rack does both. The rack lets you hang pans and pots (freeing up storage space) and gives your kitchen a real close-at-hand feel with the cooking utensils right at your fingertips.

Throwing In the Towel

This may be the easiest upgrade around. Go buy some new towels and linens! They'll not only look better — without all those frayed edges we're all used to seeing — but new towels are also a great way to add color to your kitchen.

Index

• A •

accent lighting, 222, 224
adhesives, 151
adjustable wrench, 73
AIA (American Institute of Architects), 47
air compressor, 76
air mask, 61
ambient lighting, 222–223
American Institute of Architects (AIA), 47
appliance garage, 119
appliances
  brands, 189
  choosing, 20
  colors, 189, 191–192
  commercial, 191
  configurations, 189
  connecting, 17
  cooktops, 197
  costs, 34, 189
  dishwashers, 200–201
  disposing of, 83
  door openings, 312
  ductwork, 93–94
  electric, 190
  faceplates, 192
  floor space, 314
  fuel source, 190, 204–208
  garbage disposers, 201–202
  gas, 190
  hook up, 17
  installing, 16
  matching to cabinets, 192
  microwave ovens, 200
  ovens, 198–200
  range hoods, 199
  ranges, 196–197
  refrigerators, 192–195
  residential, 191
  reviews (Consumer Reports), 189
  sizes, 189
  stainless steel, 192
  throwing away, 83
  trash compactors, 202
  using during the remodel, 37
  voltage requirements, 96
  warranties, 202
architect
  finding, 47
  hiring, 46–47
asbestos in flooring materials, 287
auger, 78

• B •

backsplash
  countertops, 139, 157
  painting, 255–256
  wallpaper, 261
base cabinets
  countertop installation, 150–152
  flooring, 124
  heights, 124–125
  installing, 132–135
  removing, 81–82
  sizes, 112–113
basin wrench, 73
bids, 50–51
blades (saws), 67–68
booth, 28
boxing paint, 258
breakfast bar, 28
budget
  cost-saving tips, 38
  creating, 33–38
  delivery charges, 42
  major remodel project, 12
  makeover project, 12
  meals out during the remodel, 37–38
  minor remodel project, 12
  sales, 41
  timetable, 42–43
  tracking expenses, 41
  unexpected costs, 34
  upgrade project, 12
building codes, 12–14

• C •

cabinetmakers, 109–110
cabinets
  appliance garage, 119
  base, 81–82, 112–113, 124–125, 132, 134–135
  blind corner, 128
  choosing, 19
  corners, 119–120, 128
  costs, 19, 34, 103
  custom made, 108–109
  disposing of, 83
  door catches, 117
  door openings, 312
  doors, 115–116, 119
  drawer glides, 117–118
  drawers, 115–116
  finishes, 116
  flooring, 124
  framed, 110–111
  frameless, 111–112
  handles, 104, 117–118, 320
  hardware, 104, 117–118
  heights, 124–125
  hinges, 104–105, 118
  home centers, 19, 110
  installing, 16, 121–135
  kitchen design centers, 109
  knobs, 104, 117–118, 320
  laminate, 114
  Lazy Susan, 119–120
  lighting, 227–229, 246–249
  matching appliances to, 192
  medium-density fiberboard (MDF), 114
  melamine, 114
  painting, 105–106
  particleboard, 114
  plywood, 114
  positioning, 127–128
  pulls, 104, 117–118
  refacing, 107
  removing, 81–82
  replacing, 107–109
  rollout baskets and bins, 119
  shelves, 118–119
  side substrate, 113–114
  sizes, 112–113
  spice racks, 119
  staining, 106
  stock, 108–109
  storage options, 118–120
  surface materials, 114–115
  throwing away, 83
  tilt-out drawer fronts, 119
  trim molding, 132
  upgrades, 320
  utility, 113
  valance, 132
  veneers, 107, 114–115
  vinyl films, 115
  wall, 81, 113, 124–132
  wood, 113–115
callbacks (general contractor), 55
canned lights, 245
carpentry work, 17
carpet, 286–287
casual eating-in areas, 316
cat's paw tool, 63
caulk, 151–152
C-clamp, 71
ceiling
  lighting fixtures, 226, 238–241
  painting, 254
ceiling fans
  installing, 241–243
  lighting, 227
  sizes, 228
ceramic tile
  bull-nose, 157
  cement, 283
  costs, 282–283
  countertops, 140, 156–160
  field, 157
  flooring, 282–283, 301–305
  glazed, 282
  porcelain, 282
  snap cutter, 76
  terracotta, 282–283
chair rail molding, 261
chalk line/reel, 70
changing fuel source, 204–208
checking
  floor for level, 123
  walls for plumb, 127
child-friendly kitchen design, 316

circular saw, 66
city inspectors, 12–14
clamps, 71
cleaning
  before painting a surface, 272–273
  during the remodel, 16
coil-spring tubing bender, 73–74
comfort level, determining, 18
commercial appliances, 191
compass, 70
compass saw, 66
computer stations, 316
conditioned water, 173
connecting appliances, 17
construction adhesive, 151
Consumer Reports magazine, 19, 36, 189
contractor
  bids, 50–51
  callbacks, 55
  final sign-offs, 55–56
  finding, 48
  hiring, 47–48
  interviewing, 48–50
  liens, 56
  punch list, 55
  working with, 54–55
contractor's wheelbarrow, 63
contracts, 52–54
convection ovens, 198
cooktops
  dual-fuel combinations, 197
  electric, 197
  fuel source, 204–208
  gas, 197
  installing, 209
  island, 28–29, 197
  options, 197
  ventilation, 29, 196–197
coping saw, 66
corridor kitchen, 25
costs
  appliances, 34, 189
  cabinets, 19, 34, 103
  ceramic tile, 282–283
  chalk line/reel, 70
  circular saws, 66
  clamps, 71

contractor's wheelbarrow, 62–63
countertops, 19, 137, 145
drills, 72
drywall lift, 77
dumpster rental, 64
dust mask, 61
faucets, 172–174
filtering mask, 61
finish nailer, 76
fish tape, 78
flooring, 20, 34–35
flooring nailer, 78
framing nailer, 75
hammers, 64
handles (cabinets), 117
hinges (cabinets), 118
knobs (cabinets), 117
levels, 70
lighting, 34
paint, 35, 257
portable table saw, 75
power drills, 72
reciprocating saw, 75
saber saw, 75
safety glasses, 60
safety goggles, 60
sawhorses, 72
sinks, 34, 164–166
sledgehammers, 62
soap dispensers, 175
tape measure, 70
wallpaper, 35
window treatments, 35
wine refrigerator, 195
wire cutters/strippers, 73
work gloves, 60–61
counter space, 27, 313
countertops
  adhesives, 151
  backsplash, 139, 157
  butcher-block, 141
  ceramic tile, 140, 156–160
  choosing, 19
  concrete, 144
  costs, 19, 137, 145
  cutting, 153–155
  disposing of, 83

countertops *(continued)*
  edge styles, 139–140
  end caps, 155–156
  fitting, 147–149
  Formica, 138–140
  granite, 143
  heights, 313
  home centers, 144
  installing, 16, 135, 138, 141, 145–156
  kitchen design studios, 144
  laminate, 138–140, 147–156
  marble, 143
  mitered corners, 149–150
  pre-formed, 147
  removing, 82
  replacing, 137
  reusing, 138
  securing to base cabinets, 150–152
  sink cut-out, 152–153
  solid surface, 142–143
  throwing away, 83
  wood, 141
cove molding, 277
cracks in drywall, 268–270
crosscut saw, 65
crowbar, 62–63
crown molding, 277
custom-made cabinets, 108–109
cutting countertops, 153–155

• D •

decorative touches, 262, 317
decorative valance (cabinets), 132
deglossers, 272
delivery charges, 42
demolition
  cabinet removal, 81–82
  countertop removal, 82
  debris removal, 61, 63–64, 83
  doing it yourself, 15, 51
  drywall, 84
  faucet removal, 82–83
  flooring, 83
  labor costs, 51
  process, 15
  sink removal, 82–83

tools, 62–64
  walls, 84
  what to expect, 15
design considerations
  checking appliance and cabinet door
    openings, 312
  counter space, 313
  countertop heights, 313
  dishwasher placement, 312
  doorways, 312
  floor space, 314
  microwave oven placement, 313
  sink placement, 312
  space around sink, 313
  work triangle, 25–26, 311
  workspace, 311–312
design trends
  decorative touches, 317
  eating-in areas, 316
  European-style kitchens, 317
  extra sink, 315
  family areas, 316
  islands, 315
  kid-friendly design, 316
  merging kitchen with the rest of the
    house, 316–317
  multiple workstations, 315
  wood, 317
designer
  finding, 30, 46
  hiring, 27, 46
dimmer switches (for lights), 229, 245–246
dining space, 27–28
dishwasher
  features, 200–201
  installing, 212–215
  placement of, 312
disposal options
  for appliances, 83
  for cabinets, 83
  for countertops, 83
doorways
  design considerations, 312
  measuring, 31–32
  trim strips, 277
downdraft cooktops, 29, 196
drain height (sinks), 178–179

drain kits, 185–187
drills, 72
drywall
  cracks, 268–270
  hanging, 16, 77
  holes, 264–266
  nail pops, 267–268
  priming, 16
  repairing, 264–271
  tape joints, 270–271
  taping, 16
  tearing out, 84
  wallpaper, 277
drywall lift, 77
drywall saw, 66
ductwork
  fitting to new appliances, 93–94
  installing, 93–94
  locating, 93
dumpster
  dos and don'ts, 61
  rental costs, 64
  renting, 61, 63–64
  sizes of, 64
dust mask, 61

● *E* ●

eating space, 27–28
eating-in areas, 316
electric appliances, 190
electric power stripper, 76
electric wire numbers, 204
electrical tools
  fish tape, 78
  insulated screwdrivers, 69
  multi-tester, 74
  needle-nose pliers, 73
  wire cutter/stripper, 73
electrical wiring
  blown fuses, 95
  changing, 17
  circuit breakers, 95, 97
  circuits, 96–97
  doing it yourself, 97
  Ground Fault Circuit Interrupter (GFCI)
    protection, 95–96

inspection, 14
National Electric Code (NEC), 95–96
numbering, 204
outlets, 97
running cable, 95, 98–99
smoke detectors, 99
end caps (countertops), 155–156
entertaining, 28, 316
equipment
  air compressors, 76
  auger, 78
  cabinet installation, 122
  cat's paw, 63
  ceramic tile installation, 156
  ceramic tile snap cutter, 76
  clamps, 71
  coil-spring tubing bender, 73–74
  compass, 70
  countertop installation, 145–147
  crowbar, 62–63
  electric power stripper, 76
  electrical tools, 73–74, 78
  faucet installation, 177–178
  fish tape, 78
  flooring installation, 290
  flooring nailer, 78
  hammers, 64–65
  levels, 70
  light fixture installation, 237–238
  maul, 62
  multi-tester, 74
  needle-nose pliers, 73
  painting tools, 271
  pliers, 69
  plumbing tools, 73, 78
  power drills, 72
  power nailers, 75–76
  pry bar, 63
  sawhorses, 72
  saws, 65–68, 74–75, 77
  screwdrivers, 68–69
  sink installation, 177–178
  slammer bar, 76
  sledgehammer, 62
  snake, 78
  tape measure, 69–70
  tile nippers, 76
  tile tools, 76

equipment *(continued)*
  tubing cutter, 73
  wet saw, 77
  wheelbarrow, 63
  wire cutter/stripper, 73
  wrenches, 73
estimates
  labor costs, 36
  materials, 35–36
  obtaining, 35
European-style kitchen design, 317
evaluating your kitchen, 10–11
exhaust boots, 93
exhaust hood, 93
eye protection, 60

• *F* •

family areas, 316
faucet
  attaching to sink, 179–181
  attaching to water supply line, 181–183
  braided steel supply tubes, 182–183
  choosing, 19–20
  colors, 171
  connecting supply line, 185
  copper supply tubes, 181–182
  costs, 172–174
  drain kits, 185–187
  drinking water, 172–173
  filters, 172–173
  finishes, 171
  handle designs, 170–171
  installing, 16, 177–183
  leaks, 187–188
  positioning, 169–170
  removing, 82–83
  spouts, 174
  sprayers, 169–170, 174
  tailpiece, 181
  upgrade, 320
  warranties, 176
feather dusting (painting technique), 259
filtered water
  from faucet, 172–173
  from refrigerator, 217
filtering mask, 61

financing the remodel
  with cash, 40
  with a credit card, 40
  with a home improvement loan, 40
  with a refinanced mortgage, 39
finding
  architect, 47
  general contractor, 48
  kitchen designer, 30, 46
finish nailer, 76
finish work, 17
finished inspection, 14, 17
fish tape, 78
fitting
  countertops, 147–149
  ductwork to appliances, 93–94
floor space, 314
flooring
  asbestos, 287
  cabinets, 124
  carpet, 286–287
  ceramic tile, 282–283, 301–305
  choosing, 20
  costs, 20, 34–35
  granite, 283
  height, 287
  installing, 13, 16, 124, 290–307
  marble, 283
  needs assessment, 279–280
  removing, 83, 287–288
  resilient, 280–281
  rot, 287–288
  sheet flooring, 280–281, 296–299
  slate, 283
  stone, 283
  subfloor, 291–293
  synthetic, 286
  tile tools, 76
  transition strips, 301
  underlayment, 293–295
  vinyl squares, 281–282, 299–300
  wear and tear, 289
  wood, 283–286, 305–307
framed cabinets, 110–111
frameless cabinets, 111–112
framing, 17
framing nailer, 75

fridges
adjustable door bins, 195
beepers, 195
built-in, 194
free-standing, 194
ice dispensers, 195
icemakers, 217
in-line water filters, 217
installing, 210–212
lock-out systems, 195
over-under, 193
refreshment centers, 195
second refrigerator, 195
side-by-side, 193–194
sliding shelves, 195
spill-proof shelves, 195
temperature controls, 195
under-over, 193
water dispensers, 195
water supply line, 210–212
wine, 195
fuel source
changing, 204–208
options, 190

• G •

galley kitchen, 25
garbage disposer
features, 175
installing, 215–217
sizes, 201–202
gas appliances, 190
gas line, 207–208
general contractor
bids, 50–51
callbacks, 55
final sign-offs, 55–56
finding, 48
hiring, 47–48
interviewing, 48–50
liens, 56
punch list, 55
working with, 54–55
getting started, 14–15
glazed ceramic tile, 282
gloves, 60–61

granite
countertops, 143
flooring, 283
G-shaped kitchen, 24

• H •

hairline cracks in drywall, 268–270
hammers, 64–65
handsaws, 65–68
hanging drywall, 16, 77
hanging rack for pots, 321
hiring professionals
architect, 46–47
contracts, 52–54
general contractor, 47–48
kitchen designer, 27, 46
home centers
appliances, 20
cabinets, 19, 110
countertops, 144
faucets, 19
flooring, 20
sinks, 19
home improvement loan, 40
hoods, 199
hot-water dispenser, 175

• I •

icemakers, 217
inspections, 12–15, 17
installing. *See also* installing cabinets;
installing countertops; installing
flooring
appliances, 16
ceiling fans, 241–243
cooktops, 209
dimmer switches, 245–246
dishwashers, 212–215
doors, 16
ductwork, 93–94
faucet, 16, 177–183
flooring, 13, 16, 124
garbage disposer, 215–217
gas line, 207–208
handles (cabinets), 117
island, 307–308
lighting fixtures, 16, 237–241

installing *(continued)*
  ovens, 209–210
  ranges, 208–209
  refrigerators, 210–212
  shut-off valves, 88–90
  sink, 16, 177–181, 183–184
  sink baskets, 184
  skylight, 231
  smoke detectors, 99
  soap dispensers, 175
  track lighting, 243–244
  trash compactor, 217
  under-cabinet lighting, 246–249
  window film, 234
  windows, 16, 230–231, 250–251
installing cabinets
  base cabinets, 132–135
  cabinet positions, 127–128
  checking floor for level, 123
  checking walls for plumb, 127
  decorative valance, 132
  flooring installation, 124
  ledger board, 126–127
  measuring cabinet heights, 124–125
  reference lines, 123
  skills required, 121
  time required, 121
  tools, 122
  trim molding, 132
  wall cabinets, 128–132
  wall studs, 125–126
  when to do it, 16
installing countertops
  adhesives, 151
  attaching pieces, 150–152
  backerboard, 157
  cabinet doors, 135
  ceramic tile countertops, 156–160
  cutting the sink hole, 152–153
  end caps, 155–156
  fitting to walls, 147–149
  level, 148
  mitered corners, 149–150
  pre-formed countertops, 147–156
  professional installation, 141
  sizing, 154–155
  skills required, 138, 141, 145
  tools, 145–147, 156
  when to do it, 16

installing flooring
  cabinet installation, 124
  ceramic tile, 301–305
  island, 307–308
  measurements, 291
  sheet flooring, 296–299
  subfloor preparation, 291–293
  tools, 290
  transition strips, 301
  underlayment, 293–295
  vinyl tile squares, 299–300
  when to do it, 13, 16
  wood, 305–307
insulated screwdrivers, 69
insulation inspection, 14
interviewing general contractor
      candidates, 48–50
I-shaped kitchen, 24–25
island
  cooktops, 28–29, 197
  entertaining, 28
  installing, 307–308
  L-shaped kitchens, 22–23
  sink, 28, 188
  space required, 29
  uses, 315
  work triangle, 28

• *J* •

jigsaw, 75

• *K* •

keyhole saw, 66
kid-friendly kitchen design, 316
Kitchen and Bath Workbook (publication
      from the National Kitchen and Bath
      Association), 10
kitchen design
  checking appliance and cabinet door
      openings, 312
  counter space, 313
  countertop heights, 313
  dishwasher placement, 312
  doorways, 312
  floor space, 314

merging kitchen with the rest of the
  house, 316–317
microwave oven placement, 313
sink placement, 312
space around sink, 313
work triangle, 25–26, 311
workspace, 311–312
kitchen design centers
cabinets, 109
countertops, 144
lighting, 223
kitchen designer
finding, 30, 46
hiring, 27, 46
kitchen office, 30
kitchen shape
galley, 25
G-shape, 24
I-shape, 24–25
L-shape, 22–23
U-shape, 23–24

● **L** ●

labor costs
cost-saving tips, 51
estimates, 36
Lazy Susan, 119–120
leaks, 187–188
level, 70
liens, 56
lighting
accent, 222, 224
ambient, 222–223
kitchen design center, 223
natural light, 222, 229–230, 234, 251
needs assessment, 221–222, 228–229
paint, 229
skylight, 231
task, 222, 224
work stations, 222
lighting fixtures
canned lights, 245
ceiling fans, 227–228, 241–243
ceiling-mounted, 226, 238–241
choosing, 20
costs, 34
dimmer switches, 229, 245–246

fluorescent bulbs, 225
incandescent bulbs, 225
installing, 16, 237–241
recessed lights, 245
removing, 238–240
returning, 226
suspended-ceiling, 226
track lighting, 226, 243–244
under-cabinet lighting, 227–229, 246–249
upgrade, 320
linens, 321
loans, 40
locating ductwork, 93
L-shaped kitchen, 22–23

● **M** ●

major remodel (defined), 12
makeover (defined), 12
marble
countertops, 143
flooring, 283
masks, 61
maul, 62
MDF (medium-density fiberboard), 114
measurements
cabinet heights, 124–125
countertops, 147–149
doorways, 31–32
floors, 291
walls, 31
windows, 249–250
measuring tools, 69–70
mechanical codes, 12–14
mechanic's liens, 56
microwave oven
features, 200
positioning, 200, 313
safety, 313
minor remodel (defined), 12
molding
chair rail molding, 261
cove molding, 277
crown molding, 277
trim molding, 132
upgrade, 321
multi-tester, 74

• N •

NAHB (National Association of Home
    Builders), 49
nail pops, 267–268
nail sizes, 65
NARI (National Association of the
    Remodeling Industry), 49
National Association of Home
    Builders (NAHB), 49
National Association of the Remodeling
    Industry (NARI), 49
National Electric Code (NEC), 95–96
National Fire Protection Agency (NFPA), 99
National Kitchen and Bath
    Association (NKBA)
    Kitchen and Bath Workbook, 10
    product and service locator, 30
    telephone number, 10
    Web site address, 10
natural light
    availability of, 222
    skylight, 231
    windows, 229–236
    without windows, 251
NEC (National Electric Code), 95–96
needle-nose pliers, 73
NFPA (National Fire Protection Agency), 99
NKBA. *See* National Kitchen and Bath
    Association

• O •

obtaining estimates
    for labor costs, 36, 50
    for materials, 35–36
office, 30
opening up walls, 84
outfitting yourself
    dust mask, 61
    safety glasses, 60
    safety goggles, 60
    work gloves, 60
ovens
    combination units, 198
    convection, 198
    conventional, 198
    dimensions, 198
    fuel source, 204–208
    installing, 209–210
    self-cleaning, 200
    wall, 198–199, 209–210

• P •

packing, 15, 79–80
paint
    boxing, 258
    calculating how much you need, 257–258
    ceiling paint, 254
    colors, 254–255
    costs, 35, 257
    eggshell, 256
    flat finish, 256
    high-gloss, 255–256
    latex, 255
    lighting, 229
    oil-based, 255
    quality, 256–257
    satin finish, 256
    semi-gloss, 256
    water-based, 255
painting
    cabinets, 105–106
    caulk, 152
    ceiling, 254
    cleaning surfaces, 272–273
    deglossers, 272
    preparing for, 271–273
    priming drywall, 16
    rough spots, 272
    timing of, 13
    tools, 271
    upgrade, 319
    walls, 253–259, 271–272
    windows, 233–234
painting techniques
    feather dusting, 259
    rag painting, 259
    sponge painting, 258–259
    stenciling, 259
paperwork space, 30
parallel wall kitchen, 25
permits, 12–14

Phillips screwdrivers, 68–69
phone numbers
    National Kitchen and Bath
        Association (NKBA), 10
    Quality Door Company, 107
plan
    budget, 12
    building and mechanical codes, 12–13
    defined, 21
    evaluation of current kitchen, 10–11
    importance of, 9–10
    inspection, 12–14
    marking openings, 32
    measurements, 31–32
    sketching, 32
    time of year, 13
pliers, 69
plumb, 127
plumbing
    cast-iron pipes, 86
    changing, 17
    code regulations, 86
    copper pipes, 87, 89–92
    couplings, 92
    CPVC pipes, 91
    drain lines, 86
    drain, vent, and waste (DVW) side, 85
    fittings, 92
    galvanized pipes, 90–91
    inspection, 14
    joining pipes, 92
    main shut-off, 87–88
    moving drain lines, 86
    moving water lines, 87–90
    PB pipes, 92
    PEX pipes, 91
    PVC/ABS plastic pipes, 86
    shut-off valves, 88–90
    supply side, 85
    tools, 73, 78
    water lines, 87–91
porcelain tile, 282
portable table saw, 75
positioning
    cabinets, 127–128
    dishwasher, 312

faucets, 169–170
microwave oven, 200, 313
sink, 312
windows, 32
pot racks, 321
power tools
    auger, 78
    drills, 72
    nailers, 75–76
    stripper, 76
pre-formed countertops, 147
prices
    appliances, 34, 189
    cabinets, 19, 34, 103
    ceramic tile, 282–283
    chalk line/reel, 70
    circular saws, 66
    clamps, 71
    contractor's wheelbarrow, 62–63
    countertops, 19, 137, 145
    drills, 72
    drywall lift, 77
    dumpster rental, 64
    dust mask, 61
    faucets, 172–174
    filtering mask, 61
    finish nailer, 76
    fish tape, 78
    flooring, 20, 34–35
    flooring nailer, 78
    framing nailer, 75
    hammers, 64
    handles (cabinets), 117
    hinges (cabinets), 118
    knobs (cabinets), 117
    levels, 70
    lighting, 34
    paint, 35, 257
    portable table saw, 75
    power drills, 72
    reciprocating saw, 75
    saber saw, 75
    safety glasses, 60
    safety goggles, 60
    sawhorses, 72
    sinks, 34, 164–166

prices *(continued)*
  sledgehammers, 62
  soap dispensers, 175
  tape measure, 70
  wallpaper, 35
  window treatments, 35
  wine refrigerator, 195
  wire cutters/strippers, 73
  work gloves, 60–61
priming drywall, 16
protective gear
  for eyes, 60
  for hands, 60–61
  for lungs (breathing), 61
pry bar, 63
punch list, 55

• Q •

Quality Door Company, 107

• R •

racks for hanging pots, 321
rag painting, 259
range hoods, 199
ranges
  drop-in, 196–197
  electric, 197
  free-standing, 196–197
  fuel source, 204–208
  gas, 197
  installing, 208–209
  sizes, 197
  slide-in, 196–197
recessed lights, 245
reciprocating saw, 74–75
record keeping, 36
recycling center, 30
refacing cabinets, 107
refrigerators
  adjustable door bins, 195
  beepers, 195
  built-in, 194
  free-standing, 194
  ice dispensers, 195
  icemakers, 217
  in-line water filters, 217
  installing, 210–212

lock-out systems, 195
  over-under, 193
  refreshment centers, 195
  second refrigerator, 195
  side-by-side, 193–194
  sliding shelves, 195
  spill-proof shelves, 195
  temperature controls, 195
  under-over, 193
  water dispensers, 195
  water supply line, 210–212
  wine, 195
removing
  cabinets, 81–82
  countertops, 82
  faucets, 82–83
  flooring, 83, 287–288
  light fixtures, 238–240
  sinks, 82–83
  wallpaper, 273–276
renting
  auger, 78
  drywall lift, 77
  dumpster, 61, 63–64
  fish tape, 78
  flooring nailer, 78
repairing
  drywall, 264–271
  subfloor, 291
replacing
  cabinets, 107–109
  countertops, 137
  subfloor, 291–292
  windows, 232–233
residential appliances, 191
resilient flooring
  sheet flooring, 280–281
  vinyl squares, 280–282
reusing countertops, 138
ripsaw, 65–66
rolled vinyl flooring, 280–281
rough-in inspection, 14–15

• S •

saber saw, 75
safety glasses, 60
safety goggles, 60

sales, 41
salespeople, 36
sanding window interiors, 233–234
sawhorses, 72
saws
  blades, 67–68
  circular saw, 66
  handsaws, 65–66
  portable table saw, 75
  reciprocating saw, 74–75
  saber saw, 75
  wet saw, 77
screwdrivers, 68–69
self-cleaning ovens, 200
shapes of kitchens
  galley, 25
  G-shape, 24
  I-shape, 24–25
  L-shape, 22–23
  U-shape, 23–24
sheet flooring
  features, 280–281
  installing, 296–299
shopping tips, 19–20, 41–42
shut-off valves, 88–90, 179
silicone caulk, 151–152
sink
  attaching faucet, 179–181
  basket, 181, 184
  bowls, 166–169
  choosing, 19–20
  colors, 164–165
  composite, 165–166
  connecting supply line, 185
  costs, 34, 164–166
  countertop cut-out, 152–153
  decorative valance, 132
  dishwasher placement, 312
  drain height, 178–179
  drain kits, 185–187
  enameled, 164–165
  extra sink, 315
  faux marble, 165–166
  garbage disposer, 175
  hand (right or left), 168–169
  holes (factory-drilled), 179
  hot-water dispenser, 175
  installing, 16, 177–181, 183–184
  island, 28, 188
  leaks, 187–188
  metal, 164
  positioning, 312
  removing, 82–83
  shut-off valve height, 179
  soap dispenser, 175
  solid surface, 165
  space around, 313
skill level, determining, 18
skylight, 231
slammer bar, 76
slate flooring, 283
sledgehammer, 62
slotted screwdrivers, 68–69
Small Home Council of the University of
    Illinois, 25
smoke detectors, 99
snap cutter, 76
soap dispensers, 175
soffit, 31, 125
soldering copper pipe, 92
sponge painting, 258–259
sprayers, 169–170, 174
spring-action clamp, 71
spud wrench, 73
squeeze-style bar clamp, 71
staining
  cabinets, 106
  windows, 233–234
stenciling, 259
stock cabinets, 108–109
stone flooring, 283
structural cracks in drywall, 268–270
subfloor
  level, 293
  repairing, 291
  replacing, 291–292
synthetic flooring, 286

● *T* ●

table saw, 75
take-off, 35
tape joints (drywall), 270–271
tape measure, 69–70
taping drywall, 16
task lighting, 222, 224

tearing out drywall, 84
telephone numbers
    National Kitchen and Bath
        Association (NKBA), 10
    Quality Door Company, 107
terracotta tile, 282–283
thresholds (floors), 301
tile
    bull-nose, 157
    cement, 283
    costs, 282–283
    countertops, 140, 156–160
    field, 157
    flooring, 282–283, 301–305
    glazed, 282
    nippers, 76
    porcelain, 282
    terracotta, 282–283
    tools, 76
timetable, 42–43
timing, 13
toolbox, 72
tools
    air compressors, 76
    auger, 78
    cabinet installation, 122
    cat's paw, 63
    ceramic tile installation, 156
    ceramic tile snap cutter, 76
    clamps, 71
    coil-spring tubing bender, 73–74
    compass, 70
    countertop installation, 145–147
    crowbar, 62–63
    electric power stripper, 76
    electrical tools, 73–74, 78
    faucet installation, 177–178
    fish tape, 78
    flooring installation, 290
    flooring nailer, 78
    hammers, 64–65
    levels, 70
    light fixture installation, 237–238
    maul, 62
    multi-tester, 74
    needle-nose pliers, 73

painting tools, 271
pliers, 69
plumbing tools, 73, 78
power drills, 72
power nailers, 75–76
pry bar, 63
sawhorses, 72
saws, 65–68, 74–75, 77
screwdrivers, 68–69
sink installation, 177–178
slammer bar, 76
sledgehammer, 62
snake, 78
tape measure, 69–70
tile nippers, 76
tile tools, 76
tubing cutter, 73
wet saw, 77
wheelbarrow, 63
wire cutter/stripper, 73
wrenches, 73
towels, 321
track lighting
    installing, 243–244
    kits, 243
    light fixtures, 226
transition strips (floors), 301
trash compactor
    features, 202
    installing, 217
trash removal, 61, 83
treatments for walls
    chair rail molding, 261
    choosing, 20
    coordinating with window treatments, 20
    cove molding, 277
    crown molding, 277
    decorations, 262
    paint, 253–259, 271–272, 319
    preparing for, 263–271
    wallpaper, 260–262, 273–277, 319
    wallpaper border, 261, 320
treatments for windows
    blinds, 235
    choosing, 20, 234
    coordinating with wall treatments, 20

costs, 35
drapes, 235
natural light, 234
shades, 235
shutters, 235
upgrade, 320
valances, 235
trends
decorative touches, 317
eating-in areas, 316
entertaining, 316
European-style kitchens, 317
extra sink, 315
family areas, 316
islands, 315
kid-friendly design, 316
merging kitchen with the rest of the
house, 316–317
multiple workstations, 315
wood, 317
tubing cutter, 73
TV, 316

• U •

under-cabinet lighting
ambient light, 229
fluorescent bulbs, 227
halogen bulbs, 227
hard-wired, 227, 246–249
installing, 246–249
plug-in units, 227, 246
strip-wired, 227, 246
task lighting, 229
xenon bulbs, 228
underlayment (for flooring), 293–295
unexpected costs, 34
University of Illinois Small Home
Council, 25
upgrades
budget, 12
cabinet knobs or handles, 320
faucet, 320
lighting fixtures, 320
linens, 321
molding, 321

paint, 319
pot racks, 321
towels, 321
wallpaper, 319
wallpaper border, 320
window treatments, 320
U-shaped kitchen, 23–24
utility cabinets, 113

• V •

valance (cabinets), 132
valves, 88–90
veneers (cabinets), 107, 114–115
ventilation system
cooktops, 29, 196–197
ductwork, 93–94
exhaust boot, 93
exhaust hood, 93
moisture, 92
odors, 92
range hoods, 199
vinyl flooring
features, 280–282
installing, 299–300

• W •

wall cabinets
heights, 124–125
installing, 124–132
removing, 81
sizes, 113
wall ovens, 198–199, 209–210
wall treatments
chair rail molding, 261
choosing, 20
coordinating with window treatments, 20
cove molding, 277
crown molding, 277
decorations, 262
paint, 253–259, 271–272, 319
preparing for, 263–271
wallpaper, 260–262, 273–277, 319
wallpaper border, 261, 320

walls
  measuring, 31
  opening up, 84
  partition wall, 84
  plumb, 127
  supporting wall, 84
warranties
  appliances, 202
  faucets, 176
water conditioning, 173
water filtering
  faucet, 172–173
  refrigerator, 217
water supply line
  faucet, 181–183
  refrigerator, 210–212
Web sites
  Consumer Reports, 19, 36, 189
  National Association of Home
    Builders (NAHB), 49
  National Association of the Remodeling
    Industry (NARI), 49
  National Kitchen and Bath
    Association (NKBA), 10
wet saw, 77
wheelbarrow, 63
window film, 234, 236
window treatments
  blinds, 235
  choosing, 20, 234
  coordinating with wall treatments, 20
  costs, 35
  drapes, 235
  natural light, 234
  shades, 235
  shutters, 235

upgrade, 320
valances, 235
windows
  custom-built, 231
  double-pane, 233
  fenestration rating, 233
  installing, 16, 230–231, 250–251
  low-E coating, 233, 236
  measuring for, 249–250
  painting, 233–234
  positioning, 32
  replacing, 232–233
  sanding, 233–234
  shapes, 230–232
  sizes, 230–232
  skylight, 231
  staining, 233–234
  timing installation of, 13
  triple-pane, 233
  UV-reflective coating, 233
wine refrigerator, 195
wire cutter/stripper, 73
wiring. *See* electrical wiring
wood
  countertops, 141
  flooring, 283–286, 305–307
  popularity of, 317
work gloves, 60–61
work triangle, 25–26, 311
workstations
  cleanup, 29
  cooking, 29
  design considerations, 311–312
  food preparation, 29
  lighting, 222
  multiple, 315
wrenches, 73

FOR DUMMIES®

The easy way to get more done and have more fun

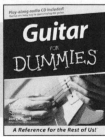

FOR DUMMIES®

A world of resources to help you grow

TRAVEL

0-7645-5453-0

0-7645-5438-7

0-7645-5444-1

Also available:

America's National Parks For Dummies
(0-7645-6204-5)
Caribbean For Dummies
(0-7645-5445-X)
Cruise Vacations For Dummies 2003
(0-7645-5459-X)
Europe For Dummies
(0-7645-5456-5)
Ireland For Dummies
(0-7645-6199-5)

France For Dummies
(0-7645-6292-4)
Las Vegas For Dummies
(0-7645-5448-4)
London For Dummies
(0-7645-5416-6)
Mexico's Beach Resorts For Dummies
(0-7645-6262-2)
Paris For Dummies
(0-7645-5494-8)
RV Vacations For Dummies
(0-7645-5443-3)

EDUCATION & TEST PREPARATION

0-7645-5194-9

0-7645-5325-9

0-7645-5249-X

Also available:

The ACT For Dummies
(0-7645-5210-4)
Chemistry For Dummies
(0-7645-5430-1)
English Grammar For Dummies
(0-7645-5322-4)
French For Dummies
(0-7645-5193-0)
GMAT For Dummies
(0-7645-5251-1)
Inglés Para Dummies
(0-7645-5427-1)

Italian For Dummies
(0-7645-5196-5)
Research Papers For Dummies
(0-7645-5426-3)
SAT I For Dummies
(0-7645-5472-7)
U.S. History For Dummies
(0-7645-5249-X)
World History For Dummies
(0-7645-5242-2)

HEALTH, SELF-HELP & SPIRITUALITY

0-7645-5154-X

0-7645-5302-X

0-7645-5418-2

Also available:

The Bible For Dummies
(0-7645-5296-1)
Controlling Cholesterol For Dummies
(0-7645-5440-9)
Dating For Dummies
(0-7645-5072-1)
Dieting For Dummies
(0-7645-5126-4)
High Blood Pressure For Dummies
(0-7645-5424-7)
Judaism For Dummies
(0-7645-5299-6)

Menopause For Dummies
(0-7645-5458-1)
Nutrition For Dummies
(0-7645-5180-9)
Potty Training For Dummies
(0-7645-5417-4)
Pregnancy For Dummies
(0-7645-5074-8)
Rekindling Romance For Dummies
(0-7645-5303-8)
Religion For Dummies
(0-7645-5264-3)

Available wherever books are sold. Go to www.dummies.com or call 1-877-762-2974 to order direct

FOR DUMMIES®

Plain-English solutions for everyday challenges

HOME & BUSINESS COMPUTER BASICS

0-7645-0838-5

0-7645-1663-9

0-7645-1548-9

Also available:

Excel 2002 All-in-One Desk Reference For Dummies (0-7645-1794-5)

Office XP 9-in-1 Desk Reference For Dummies (0-7645-0819-9)

PCs All-in-One Desk Reference For Dummies (0-7645-0791-5)

Troubleshooting Your PC For Dummies (0-7645-1669-8)

Upgrading & Fixing PCs For Dummies (0-7645-1665-5)

Windows XP For Dummies (0-7645-0893-8)

Windows XP For Dummies Quick Reference (0-7645-0897-0)

Word 2002 For Dummies (0-7645-0839-3)

INTERNET & DIGITAL MEDIA

0-7645-0894-6

0-7645-1642-6

0-7645-1664-7

Also available:

CD and DVD Recording For Dummies (0-7645-1627-2)

Digital Photography All-in-One Desk Reference For Dummies (0-7645-1800-3)

eBay For Dummies (0-7645-1642-6)

Genealogy Online For Dummies (0-7645-0807-5)

Internet All-in-One Desk Reference For Dummies (0-7645-1659-0)

Internet For Dummies Quick Reference (0-7645-1645-0)

Internet Privacy For Dummies (0-7645-0846-6)

Paint Shop Pro For Dummies (0-7645-2440-2)

Photo Retouching & Restoration For Dummies (0-7645-1662-0)

Photoshop Elements For Dummies (0-7645-1675-2)

Scanners For Dummies (0-7645-0783-4)

Get smart! Visit www.dummies.com

- **Find listings of even more Dummies titles**
- **Browse online articles, excerpts, and how-to's**
- **Sign up for daily or weekly e-mail tips**
- **Check out Dummies fitness videos and other products**
- **Order from our online bookstore**

Available wherever books are sold. Go to www.dummies.com or call 1-877-762-2974 to order direct